C000050946

John Martinkus is an acclaimed Australian journalist and author of *A Dirty Little War* and *Paradise Betrayed: West Papua's Struggle for Independence* (Quarterly Essay 7).

Praise for *A Dirty Little War*

'This is a vivid, searing account of "one of the great crimes of the century" that left the witness–author sometimes "too inarticulate with rage to say anything". What he has told is extraordinary – shocking, inspiring, and rich in insights and lessons. It's an impressive achievement, in the finest tradition of the best journalism.'

Noam Chomsky

'Of all the works published so far on East Timor's brutal passage to independence, and there have been many, *A Dirty Little War* is the most useful for anyone wanting to understand what went on.'

Jon Greenaway, *Sydney Morning Herald*

'*A Dirty Little War* is a major contribution . . . an intensely and movingly personal chronicle of the dreadful suffering of brave people . . . It should be widely read and contemplated.'

Merle Ricklefs, *Age*

'Martinkus's book simmers with controlled emotion . . . *A Dirty Little War* is a riveting eyewitness account by an Australian freelance journalist of East Timor's 1997–2000 agony.'

Tony Kevin, *Australian Financial Review*

'*A Dirty Little War* is the best book in English about East Timor since James Dunn published his revised history, *Timor: A People Betrayed* in 1996 . . . the narrative is sustained at thriller-like pace from the first page to last.'

Brian Woodley, *Weekend Australian*

'For anyone with more than a passing interest in East Timor, Martinkus's book is essential. It will tell you more about what really happened in East Timor in the lead-up to the 1999 ballot, and afterwards, and why, than any other book I know.'

Damien Kingsbury, *Australian Book Review*

John Martinkus

INDONESIA'S SECRET WAR IN ACEH

RANDOM HOUSE AUSTRALIA

Every effort has been made to acknowledge and contact the owners of copyright for permission to reproduce material which falls under the 1968 Copyright Act. Any copyright owners who have inadvertently been omitted from acknowledgements and credits should contact the publisher and omission will be rectified in subsequent editions.

Random House Australia Pty Ltd
20 Alfred Street, Milsons Point, NSW 2061
http://www.randomhouse.com.au

Sydney   New York   Toronto
London   Auckland   Johannesburg

First published by Random House Australia 2004

Copyright © John Martinkus 2004

All rights reserved. No part of this publication may be reproduced, stored in a retrieval system, or transmitted in any form or by any means, electronic, mechanical, photocopying, recording or otherwise, without the prior written permission of the publisher.

National Library of Australia
Cataloguing-in-Publication Entry
Martinkus, John.
 Indonesia's secret war in Aceh.

ISBN 1 74051 209 X.

1. Political persecution - Indonesia - Aceh. 2. Political atrocities - Indonesia - Aceh. 3. Human rights - Indonesia - Aceh. 4. Aceh (Indonesia) - History - Autonomy and independence movements. 5. Aceh (Indonesia) - Politics and government. I. Title.

323.15986

Cover photograph by Jason South
Cover design by Greendot Design
Typeset in Adobe Garamond by Midland Typesetters, Maryborough, Victoria
Printed and bound by Griffin Press, Netley, South Australia

10 9 8 7 6 5 4 3 2 1

This book is dedicated to East Timor campaigner Dr Andrew McNaughton and documentary maker Mark Worth whose work on West Papua was an inspiration. Both were good friends who encouraged me to complete this book before Andrew died in Sydney in December 2003 and Mark in West Papua in January 2004.

Contents

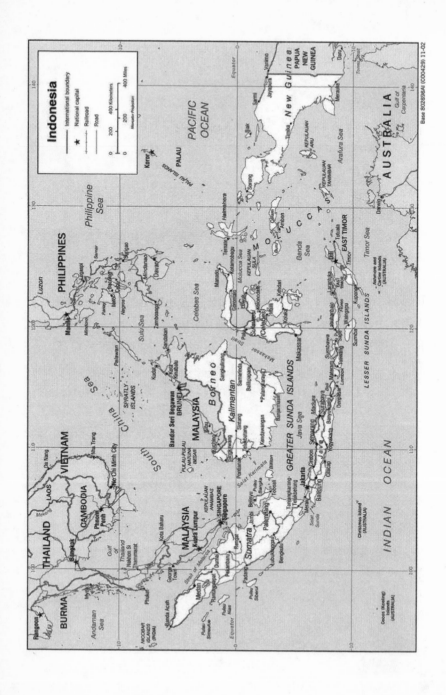

Glossary

ANSLF	Aceh North Sumatra Liberation Front
Brimob	*Brigada Mobil* – Indonesian riot police
DOM	*Daerah Operasi Militer* – area of military operations
ELSHAM	Institute for Human Rights Study and Advocacy West Papua
Falintil	*Forcas Armadas de Libertacao de Timor Leste* (Armed forces for an independent East Timor)
Front Pulyamat Aceh	Safe Aceh
GAM	*Gerakan Aceh Merdeka* – Free Aceh Movement
ICRC	International Committee of the Red Cross
INTEL	Indonesian state intelligence, military, police or civilian
JSC	Joint Security Commission
Kodim	Local Indonesian military command
Kontras	Commission for Missing Persons and Victims of Violence
Kopassus	Indonesian special forces

Kopkamtib	Intelligence unit
Kostrad	Indonesian army's strategic reserve
LBH	*Lembaga Bantuan Hukum* – Legal Aid Foundation
MPR	*Majelis Permusyawaratan Rakyat* – People's Consultative Assembly (Indonesia's highest legislative body)
NII	*Negara Islam Indonesia* – the Islamic State of Indonesia
NU	*Nahdlatul Ulama* – Muslim Scholar Organisation
OPM	*Organisasi Papua Merdeka* – Free Papua Movement
PBHAM	*Pas Bantuan Hukum dan Hak Asasi Manusia Aceh* – Human Rights and Legal Aid Office
PHIA	*Pemberdayaan Hareukat Inong Aceh* – Empowerment for Acehnese Women
PKF	United Nations Peacekeeping Force
PMI	Indonesian Red Cross
Polri	Republic of Indonesia Police – Indonesian police
PUSA	Persatuan Ulama Seluruh Aceh – All Aceh Religious Scholars' Association
RATA	Rehabilitation Action for Victims of Torture in Aceh
SGI	*Satuan Gabungan Intelijen* – Indonesian Combat Intelligence Unit

SIRA	Aceh Referendum Information Centre
SMUR	*Solidaritas Mahasiswa Untuk Rakyat* – Student Solidarity for the People Movement
TAPOL	Indonesian human rights NGO
TNA	*Tentara Nasional Aceh* – National Army of Aceh
TNI	*Tentara Nasional Indonesia* – Indonesian Regular Army
UNAMET	United Nations Assistance Mission in East Timor
UNHCR	United Nations High Commission for Refugees – the UN Refugee Agency
UNTAET	United Nations Transitional Administration in East Timor

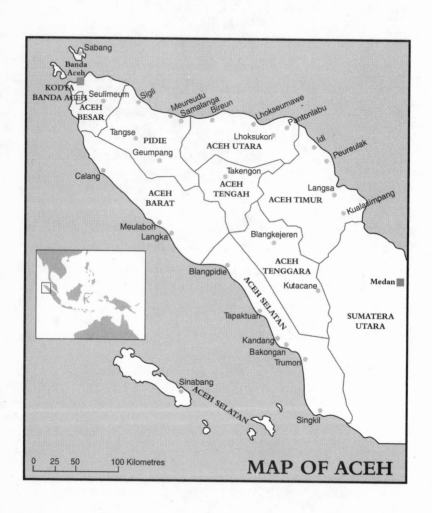

Sabang
Banda Aceh
KODYA BANDA ACEH
Seulimeum
Sigli
ACEH BESAR
Tangse
Meureudu
Samalanga
Bireun
Lhokseumawe
Pantonlabu
PIDIE
Lhoksukon
ACEH UTARA
Idi
Peureulak
Geumpang
Calang
Takengon
ACEH TENGAH
Langsa
ACEH BARAT
ACEH TIMUR
Kualasimpang
Meulaboh
Langka
Blangkejeren
Blangpidie
ACEH TENGGARA
Medan
ACEH SELATAN
Kutacane
Tapaktuan
SUMATERA UTARA
Kandang
Bakongan
Trumon
Sinabang
ACEH SELATAN
Singkil

0 25 50 100 Kilometres

MAP OF ACEH

PART I

A Festering Wound: The Acehnese Fight for Independence

At the north-western tip of the Indonesian archipelago, on top of a cliff above the sea, there is a monument. It is a circular tower, three storeys high, made of white marble. A small plaque says it was opened in 1997 by the then Indonesian vice president, Try Sutrisno. Standing there, it doesn't take much to imagine the opening ceremony. There are pagodas in the wide, overgrown gardens that would have sheltered the crowds of Suharto-era officials and soldiers who attended. There are painted-in parking spaces for the buses that would have travelled on the then brand-new double-lane asphalt road to this point on the island of Sabang that marks the north-westernmost end of Indonesian territory as it protrudes into the Indian Ocean and the Malacca Straits. The then minister for technology and future president of Indonesia, Dr B.J. Habibie, was there as well, unveiling a monument with the exact latitude and longitude of the extremity of the country, calculated – as the placard proudly proclaims – by using the latest satellite positioning technology, the global positioning system (GPS).The souvenir shops and restaurants, now empty and boarded up, would have been open and, no doubt, red and white Indonesian flags would have hung in abundance as the national anthem was played and speeches were made declaring the achievements of the nation of Indonesia, all the way from here at the tip of Sabang to far away Merauke, on the south coast of Papua.

But that was 1997. The Asian financial crisis that led to the downfall of Indonesia's second president, Suharto, was only just beginning, and the people were yet to turn on the dictator who had made himself and his family one of the richest in Asia at the expense of a country whose economy was about to crash. Foreign governments still supported Suharto then and colluded in playing down the consequences of his rule in places like Aceh, West Papua and East Timor.

At the end of the year 2002, the monument at kilometre zero, the starting point of Indonesia, is deserted and derelict. The blue translucent roof is broken and the floor is covered with mud, dotted with pools of water and strewn with leaves. The white marble walls are ruined by green algae and the war on the nearby Sumatran mainland in Aceh has left its mark in the form of graffiti on this symbol of Indonesian unity.

Out past the abandoned gate posts, the two-lane asphalt road is already being reclaimed by the jungle. Roots from 30-metre high trees are pushing ridges into and breaking through the surface of the smooth road. Overgrown branches and ferns from the dense tropical jungle hang low and dirt and rocks from sodden landslides cover parts of the winding road. The first sign of human life in the jungle is a derelict air-force base. The signs warn in English and Indonesian: 'We born to kill. Peace or death', above a grinning skull with a knife dripping blood clenched between its teeth. The skull wears the orange beret of the Indonesian air-force ground troops. Another sign indicates that they are ready to die on command. It is an eerie place – deserted, overgrown, and full of the abandoned symbols of Indonesia as it represented itself to its own people under Suharto. Strong, united, indivisible and proud, all the way from Sabang to Merauke. But then, unsettling this wholesome image, is another sign which threatens passers-by not to enter the side road to the air-force base on pain of death.

The only way to get to Sabang is via ferry from Banda Aceh on the island of Sumatra. Since 1976, the Free Aceh Movement (GAM – *Gerakan Aceh Merdeka*) has been fighting to secede from Indonesia, and the province of 4.5 million people has suffered almost continuous military operations by the Indonesians. At least 12,000 deaths have resulted. This kept the tourist resorts on the island isolated and cheap, and a steady trickle of backpackers and divers passed through. To get to the secluded beaches and four-dollar-a-night bungalows, the mostly young European travellers had to first pass through Banda Aceh to get a ferry, then had to go by bus across the island to the town of Sabang. Despite the Brimob troops – the Indonesian riot police – with their brown fatigues and automatic weapons, checking the identification of all who disembark on the island, and the armed Indonesian military troops in camouflage in the main street of the town, most of the foreigners who passed through never really knew nor cared what was going on. As the soldiers stared into the buses as if they were watching a show, the young travellers talked of the cheap food, the cheap accommodation, the beaches and the dope (the best in Indonesia).

Since Indonesia's first president, Sukarno, used the slogan 'from Sabang to Merauke' in the late fifties to rally support for his campaign to oust the Dutch from what was then called West New Guinea at the other end of the archipelago, Sabang has been a heavily subsidised town with a large military base and a high percentage of transmigrants from Java. The war in Aceh, a two-hour ferry ride away, has been kept at bay. Sabang is a part of the ideal of Indonesian unity, and what that meant in December 2000, when I first went there, was that the main street was full of swaggering armed soldiers releasing tension from combat duty in nearby Aceh. After dark the town was full of men, in and out of uniform, carrying guns; the military still didn't feel confident enough to be without them, and they drank and yelled and roared up and down the main street in the backs of trucks and utilities. Later there would be a few gunshots into the air accompanied by yells and laughter. The local businesses shuttered their shops early and people watched the troops anxiously.

It seemed strange that so many tourists were still going to the place. Admittedly, the beaches were good and it was very cheap, but that year more than 960 people had died in the conflict in Aceh. The foreign visitors seemed not to – or not to want to – notice; if you caught an early flight to Banda Aceh and transferred straight to the ferry, you could be at the beach resort in Sabang in time for dinner. If you didn't ask questions, the people, wary anyway or bored by the disinterest of foreigners, left you alone. You might just see something strange along the road to the port – soldiers leaping out of a truck and running up a hill – or you might notice the silence on the bus when it was stopped by men in civilian clothes with military haircuts who boarded briefly to scrutinise all the passengers. But if you didn't want to know, Sabang could feel like a quiet hideaway at the end of the world, with just a few too many soldiers.

⊷•◦•⊶

THE GAM office is a room on the third floor of the Kuala Tripa, which passes as the only luxury hotel in Banda Aceh. Three Acehnese men sit on the two single beds. They introduce themselves as Amni Marzuki, Zulfani bin Abdul Rani and Teuku Kamaruzzaman, who is older than the other two. They are the GAM representatives for the security committee that is supposed to be monitoring the halt in hostilities between the fighters of GAM and the Indonesian military under the first cease-fire agreement in Aceh. The 'humanitarian pause', as it is called, was negotiated by the Swiss-based Henry Dunant Centre for Humanitarian Dialogue (the HDC) in June 2000. This agreement was meant to be a cooling-off period in the conflict in Aceh to allow humanitarian assistance to reach the population and a negotiated settlement to be put in place. But by now, December 2000, it has already fallen apart and the death toll for the year is higher than it has ever been. Zulfani gives me the figures for the month of November. According to GAM, at least 72 people were killed, 109 wounded and 562 detained and beaten or tortured in an attempt by the military to prevent the

7

Acehnese attending a rally for independence in the capital, Banda Aceh. I ask if he has any evidence for these figures and Zulfani responds aggressively, telling the slightly built Amni to get the photos.

The folder is overflowing with pictures of people – civilians – shot in the head, shot in the chest, lying in pools of blood on the ground, sometimes on the black asphalt of the road at a roadblock. One after the other, Zulfani hands the photos to me, mentioning dates and places. There are gruesome close-ups of shattered skulls, intestines spilling out of ruptured stomachs; bowels; others of people lying on their backs with just one small hole in the head. The photos seem to have been taken with small, cheap cameras with built-in flashes and autofocus. They are stark, flat and graphic.

One after the other, Zulfani runs through the details. Most had been taken at roadblocks where the Indonesian military had attempted to stop people from attending the pro-referendum rally in Banda Aceh on November 11, 2000. The previous year, on November 8, more than 1 million people had attended such a rally, roughly one out of every four people in the entire province of Aceh, and the Indonesian authorities were terrified of a repeat occurrence.

The Indonesian authorities in Aceh had declared that all means available would be used to prevent people travelling to the capital. Brimob units, armed as infantry, set up roadblocks on all major routes. The Indonesian military was also called out and all that week deaths were reported in every region of Aceh as people trying to get to the capital were shot at by the authorities; firstly above their heads as a warning, then at their vehicles and then directly. By Friday, November 10, the day before the planned rally, reports from all over Aceh showed a total of 178 civilians dead.

The rally had gone ahead on November 11 despite the attempt to forestall it and was addressed by the leader of the Aceh Referendum Information Centre (SIRA), Muhammed Nazar; a female activist, Masyita; and a local female journalist, Cut Nur Asikin. Some reports put the crowd in front of the Baiturrahman mosque in the centre of the capital at nearly 500,000. The speeches reported in the press were emotional condemnations of the violence. According to local reports of the rally, Masyita interrupted her speech with shouts of 'Freedom!' and the crowd roared their approval. 'The Acehnese struggle for independence because the central government oppresses the people,' she said.

Cut Nur Asikin condemned the police actions: 'Susilo Bambang Yudhoyono [Co-ordinating Minister for Political, Social and Security Affairs] actually allowed people to attend, but why is the Aceh police chief opposed?' This expression of what everybody was angry about would come back to haunt her later.

The photos Zulfani was showing me were over a month old and I think he sensed my impatience. The killings at the time of the rally had been reasonably well covered and there was nothing new in these photos, no matter how gruesome they were. In a way it made me sick to be flicking through them, trying to find something new that I could use in a report, and I could tell it was making him angry. He started going through them quickly, pulled out three and placed them on the bed.

'They are the RATA people. You know about them,' he said. They were three Acehnese humanitarian workers who were shot dead on December 6, 2000. Working for RATA, the Rehabilitation Action for Victims of Torture in Aceh, a Danish-funded nongovernment organisation (NGO) that aims to assist victims of torture, they were killed near the town of Lhokseumahwe. A fourth worker escaped and was protected by the Danish embassy in Jakarta, from where he identified those responsible for the killings as military personnel.

The protests that came from international human rights organisations over the killing of the RATA personnel were largely ignored by the military, as had been the calls for an investigation into the recent death of well-known Acehnese activist Jaffar Siddiq Hamzah, who had been found dead near the North Sumatran capital of Medan. Hamzah had been staying there with relatives following a visit to Aceh from New York, where he had been living. A lawyer well-known for raising the issue of Acehnese human rights abuses at the hands of the military abroad, he had fled Indonesia in 1996 and established two Aceh support NGOs in New York, as well as studying there. He had returned to Aceh to help the Acehnese NGOs that had begun operating since the fall of Suharto in 1998. In Aceh he had been warned his life was in danger so he had gone to Medan. The military kidnapped him there on August 5, 2000 and his mutilated body was found four weeks later in an area used previously by the TNI (the Indonesian Regular Army) to dump bodies from Aceh, roughly 80 kilometres from Medan.

In retrospect, the muted international response to Hamzah's death, the RATA killings and the deaths of those who had tried to march for a referendum in November 2000 should have sent a warning signal to the Acehnese that the world did not support their push for independence from Indonesia. But too much had happened in the last two years for the people of Aceh to stop.

As soon as Suharto fell, nine years of military rule came to an end. The Acehnese could travel without restrictions, foreigners could visit and some basic rights were restored. It was no longer a designated area of military operations – *Daerah Operasi Militer*, known as DOM – which had kept the province under virtual martial law and sealed off from the rest of the country since 1990. The accepted figure among Acehnese and human rights organisations is 10,000 people killed by the military during the DOM period, and when it was finally over, the people of Aceh wanted justice. Mass graves were exhumed and, with the help of Indonesian NGOs empowered by the collapse of Suharto, the crimes of the military in Aceh began to be exposed.

In June 1998, two Acehnese widows visited the Indonesian parliament to tell of the atrocities that had taken place during the DOM era. A parliamentary fact-finding mission was sent to the province the following month and the testimonies given, telling of rape, abduction, torture and killings by the military – in particular by the Indonesian special forces, Kopassus – became national news in a press intoxicated with its new-found freedom after Suharto's fall. At least ten mass graves were identified at this time, containing anywhere from 1000 to 1500 bodies.

But no-one knew the real extent of the atrocities and exhumations were never properly carried out. Those who spoke out to the press or worked with NGOs were soon receiving visits by 'unidentified people' who told them to be quiet. Armed forces chief General Wiranto declared in August 1998 that Kopassus would be withdrawn from the province along with other 'nonorganic' troops (those not based in Aceh). But the disappearances and the violence continued, particularly near the town of Lhokseumahwe, home to the PT Arun Liquefied natural gas plant established by American company ExxonMobil (the second-largest foreign tax-payer to the central government in Jakarta). The abductions and killing by the security forces began again in that area almost as soon as General Wiranto announced the military withdrawal in August 1998.

The Acehnese, encouraged by the entry of the UN into East Timor for the holding of a referendum in mid-1999, continued to demonstrate for their own referendum to give them a chance to vote for independence from Indonesia. It was one such rally in Lhokseumahwe on May 3, 1999 that turned bloody. Forty-five people were killed and more than 100 wounded when the military opened fire on a demonstration in the town. Video footage shows a military truck spraying the crowd with gunfire as they flee around a corner. The sound of the shots on the footage gets louder as the truck with troops hanging off its sides firing into the crowd moves slowly into the frame, leaving no doubt as to who is responsible.

Gunfire woke me at about two in the morning on Tuesday, December 19, 2000, the day President Wahid made a brief visit to Banda Aceh. I was staying on the third floor of a cheap hotel in the middle of town. It had balconies in the front of all the rooms facing inwards and the building backed onto the river. Standing on the balcony, I could hear the shots ringing out across the river and over towards the military barracks. The terrified face of a man in the opposite room peered out across the river and he mouthed the word 'GAM' before disappearing back behind the curtain. Downstairs, the young reception clerk kept watching the football and chain-smoking, ignoring the gunfire before finally admitting, 'It happens all the time. It could be GAM scaring the military, or the military trying to scare the people, or the military pretending to be GAM trying to scare the people, or GAM pretending to be the military trying to scare the people, or just the military feeling nervous, or the military trying to make sure there is no problem tomorrow when the president comes,' he said.

I joined him and we went back to watching the football. It was cool in the evening and, because it was Ramadan, we could neither smoke outside nor drink coffee during the daylight hours, so we did both. Outside, the square was deserted and the gunfire spat occasionally into the night, but the whole city seemed as unconcerned as the desk clerk about who was firing and for what reason.

By December 2000, even in Banda Aceh it was apparent the military had only a temporary hold on large parts of the country; basically for as long as it took their convoys to pass through or their patrols to move on. As I travelled with my partner Meredyth up from Medan on the near-empty express bus, the first sign of the conflict were groups of armed men in the town of Peureulak in East Aceh. These men wore civilian clothes and had beards and Muslim skullcaps. They sat on small stools in the middle of the busy market with their Chinese-made light machine guns propped on wooden boxes and watched the street that was clogged with traffic and people going to and from the market. Nobody gave them a second glance.

Back on the highway heading north to Lhokseumahwe, we passed back into government control with the more familiar brown and black uniformed Brimob troops manning a machine-gun post that was heavily sandbagged and covered in cyclone wire as protection against grenades. It wasn't hard to see that the police were more concerned about attack at their lonely posts along the highway than were the GAM fighters, lounging in the marketplace with their weapons resting on the ground. Brimob had taken on the role of the troops withdrawn in 1998 but that hadn't stopped the violence against the population that was the reason for their withdrawal – it had only ensured it was carried out by less well-trained personnel.

Who was in control of the main northern highway to Banda Aceh from Medan was an indicator of the status of the conflict. When Indonesia was facing international pressure and its military was afraid to act, it was in the hands of the rebels; when the government reasserted its power, the highway became lined with convoys, checkpoints and armoured vehicles. It was like a pendulum. You could work out which side was in control of the section you were travelling through by whoever collected the taxes that all buses and trucks had to pay to travel the road to Banda Aceh. Generally, Brimob and the military were both very efficient at taxing vehicles; occasionally GAM would take over that role.

Lhokseumahwe was deserted at night except for a small knot of Brimob personnel relaxing at the outdoor restaurants across the road from their headquarters. They whistled and yelled obscenities and invitations at Meredyth. There were hardly any civilians in the street, even though it was not much past nine in the evening. The first hotel the taxi took us to was across the road from the military barracks and full of police. The next displayed the wealth of the gas-rich town and had a wide circular driveway and a concierge who came out to meet us. Indonesian military officers were the only occupants.

Driving through the streets of Lhokseumahwe was eerie. Large new banks lined the main road and outside of town a grey concrete shell that had been planned as a shopping mall and never finished sat in a vacant block of land full of weeds and rubbish. The Indonesian government buildings were new and imposing and the black and white verges on the roads meticulously maintained. But there were hardly any people or traffic and those who ventured out stood furtively in shadows as vehicles moved past. Thanks to ExxonMobil, this was one of the richest towns in Indonesia. But the people were too afraid to be outdoors after dark.

The large gas deposits discovered by Mobil Oil were announced in 1971. Mobil Oil, which merged with Exxon in 1999 to become ExxonMobil, operates the plant in partnership with the Indonesian state oil company, Pertamina. The PT Liquified natural gas fields near Lhokseumahwe are Indonesia's fourth largest contributor of export earnings. Jakarta receives US$1 billion a year from the gas fields. It is such an important revenue stream for the central government that when GAM activity halted production at the Arun gas facility near Lhokseumahwe for four months early in 2001, the government was reported to be losing US$100 million a month. On that occasion an extra 2128 troops were deployed to protect the plant and President Wahid changed Indonesian law by issuing Presidential Decree Number Four to authorise military action to get the plant up and running again. According to the *Wall Street Journal*, in the early 1990s the Aceh operation produced nearly a quarter of Mobil's earnings worldwide. And ExxonMobil reported around US$210 billion in profits for the year 2000 – the world's largest corporate profits of the year.

A lawsuit was launched against ExxonMobil in June 2001, filed by the Washington-based International Labor Rights Fund. The action was taken on behalf of 11 villagers from Aceh who alleged the company had contributed to the rape, imprisonment at company facilities and torture of themselves and the murder of their relatives by paying and aiding the security forces who had carried out the abuses. The abuses took place in the years 2000 and 2001 in the area around the gas facility where the Indonesian military at that time had maintained an average of 5000 troops to protect the plant. Later, as the security situation in that area deteriorated, the number of troops increased dramatically.

In 2002, the Columbia District Court, USA, which was hearing the claim, responded to a request from ExxonMobil to seek advice from the US State Department regarding the case. The reply, in a letter dated July 29, 2002, from the State Department's legal adviser, stated that the lawsuit could stop Indonesia co-operating in the 'war on terror' and prejudice the Indonesians to discriminate against US firms. As a result, the court dropped the lawsuit.

The decision by the State Department to intervene in the case and to cite the 'war on terror' as an excuse not to proceed in a court case related to the corporate responsibility of an American company employing a security force that committed human rights abuses in its name, says a lot about the basis of US-Indonesian relations and what drives them. The willingness of the State Department to throw its weight behind ExxonMobil could easily be explained by pointing out, as the lawyers representing the 11 Acehnese did, that ExxonMobil was the second-largest campaign contributor to George W. Bush after Enron, and that US$100,000 alone was given to the George W. Bush inauguration by the Washington representative of ExxonMobil.

Evidence of ExxonMobil's bankrolling of the security forces assigned to protect their operations has been common knowledge in the NGO community since the fall of Suharto, when such organisations began to operate. In 2000, Kontras, an Indonesian human rights group, said it had conducted an investigation that had determined at least 17 military and police stations in Aceh with a personnel of 1000 were subsidised by ExxonMobil. In January 2001, GAM spokesman Sofyan Dawood put the figure paid by the company at 3 million rupiah per month per soldier. In 2003, respected Indonesian news magazine *Tempo* published the figure of those directly on the ExxonMobil payroll as around 5000 troops based in the immediate area of the plant.

The allegations of involvement in human rights abuses by troops on the ExxonMobil payroll go back throughout the Suharto period of martial law, and in 1998 it was alleged in detailed testimonies presented by the International Labor Rights Fund that ExxonMobil earth-moving equipment had been used in the construction of mass graves, and its buildings had been used as torture centres and places of detention. The abuses against the local population are said to continue on a daily basis; they were still being reported throughout 2004.

⊱─✦─◦─✦─⊰

DESPITE THE killings and roadblocks and warnings from the authorities for people not to attend the rally in November 2000, as estimated 500,000 people did. For two days crowds rallied outside the grand mosque in the centre of Banda Aceh and at the university. Press reports talked of how people carried United Nations flags and banners emblazoned with the word 'Referendum'. The event had been called 'The Aceh mass gathering for peace' and had been organised by SIRA, the Aceh Referendum Information Centre. This organisation, led by Muhammed Nazar, had held their own referendum in Aceh the previous year. The results of the polling conducted all over Aceh then were overwhelmingly in favour of independence. The organisation had emerged as a rallying point for the Acehnese, especially those in the larger cities, who wanted an end to the military violence but did not identify with the militants of GAM. Nazar was arrested for the first time on November 20, 2000. The charge was disturbing order and peace and spreading hateful stories. He was still under detention when I arrived in Aceh in December 2000.

In a small house in a side street in the centre of Banda Aceh, the young SIRA activists were still collating the information on the violence in November. They had lists of names and details of one violent incident after another directed at those who had tried to attend the rally. Because the violence had escalated in the past year, they had expected more than the 1 million incidents of the previous year. They knew the military and police would try to prevent the rally, but they wanted to send their signal clearly to the outside world: 'We want a democracy like in your country. GAM sometimes says they want to restore the sultanate but we want the people to be given the chance to decide for themselves on how an independent Aceh will be run.'

It was a difficult point and several of the students sitting on the floor began discussing the issue amongst themselves. SIRA was always at great pains to distinguish itself from GAM. The members of SIRA were avowedly nonviolent and were attempting to bring about change through legal means and protest. Their self-conducted referendum had been one example of this. However, now they were in a similar position to GAM, but without the weapons to protect themselves; like GAM, their activists were subject to arrest and, in some cases, summary execution by the security forces. But, at this stage, they still functioned as a legitimate, above-ground organisation exercising their right to free speech.

The Indonesian response to their rallies and calls for independence had increasingly come in the forms of violence and attempts at intimidation. Now the discussion between the students reflected the pressure on the organisation as to how they would respond to this and how they could continue their activities. The attempt by the authorities to stop people from travelling to the rally by violent means had at one stage led Nazar to try to call off the event. Despite this attempt to stop the bloodshed, the people still kept trying to come. It was a question as old as protest itself: at what stage does the cost of nonviolent action become too much to bear if confronted with a state that uses only violence and seems immune to criticism of its methods? They discussed this, but in the very real context of what they could attempt to do next.

As I left the small house, a man approached me and asked if I was a journalist. Two men had just been killed in another suburb that afternoon by the military and he just wanted to let me know. The casual way he told me suggested this happened all the time.

The next day I spent about three hours talking to Feisal Hamdi, the coordinator for the Aceh Coalition for Human Rights, an NGO. He told me that these acts of violence were an almost daily occurence in Aceh and described how police in South Aceh had responded to a grenade attack on their post the previous Tuesday: 'They called for back-up and then surrounded a house. They started shooting and they arrested a man and beat him after dragging him out. They grabbed the other two in the house and beat them. The men denied they were members of GAM. After half an hour of beating, they didn't confess and the police shot them dead.'

Hamdi said the perpetrators of such violence cannot be identified because they don't wear uniforms and often wear face masks. 'But the villagers note their dialects, from Java or north Sumatra. The people know no GAM activists are Javanese.'

This was something new. The threat of being held responsible for their actions meant that the police and military at many roadblocks in Aceh were now wearing civilian clothing. Sometimes they would claim to be GAM, but mostly the plain clothes were worn simply to deny the victims the chance to identify the soldiers through the unit numbers on their uniforms. Previously they hadn't felt the need to hide their identity.

Hamdi said the culture of impunity in the Indonesian military and police was behind the rising levels of violence. 'That is one of the main reasons for the continuation of this conflict. The people are angry,' he said. According to him, the only case when action was taken against military personnel for abuses in Aceh was after the massacre of 53 civilians in the village of Beutang Ateuh in July 1999. In that case the Indonesian commanding officer of the operation, Lieutenant Colonel Sujono, simply disappeared, leaving 31 of his subordinates to be tried and sentenced to an average of two to three years' imprisonment for the killings.

At the Kontras office it was the same story. The organisation had been formed in Jakarta by a well-known lawyer called Munir to investigate those who had 'disappeared' in politically motivated cases during the Suharto era. One of the first high-profile cases for Kontra involved the discovery of the mass graves in Aceh in 1998. Their report on the latest violence described a similar pattern of death squad-style killings.

On the Monday before our meeting in East Aceh, Bari Bin Bahkri answered the door of his home to two men wearing plain clothes; they shot him in the face and he died immediately. In north Aceh two days earlier, Iskander Hamden was grabbed by four men and taken away; the next day his body was found nearby, with gunshot wounds to the head.

Kontras records at the time stated that since the start of the 'humanitarian pause' in June 2000 until December of the same year 524 people were killed, 140 disappeared and 549 were arrested and tortured. The figures for the whole of 2000 were 840 dead; more people had died in Aceh since the agreement had been signed in May than in the previous five months. Almost all of these incidents had been traced back to the military but no prosecutions had resulted.

Kontras coordinator in Banda Aceh, Aguswand, described the killings they were documenting. 'For the GAM the target is very clear; the military or the police or the informers. Sometimes the *camat* [village head] or the *bupati* [district head], if they do not have good relations with the people,' he said, referring to the local-Indonesian appointed officials; it was no secret in Aceh that GAM sometimes targeted the civilian representatives of Indonesian power in the countryside, and they freely admitted to most of these cases. GAM saw these people as extensions of Indonesian military rule and therefore legitimate targets. Often, the regional chiefs were former military men from outside Aceh, or else they were closely linked to the authorities. They would not have held the positions otherwise.

'For the military, the targets are not so clear,' said Aguswand. 'The majority of the civilian killings are by the police and the military. If we look at every report, we can see the civilians are killed after the arrest. We believe the police and the military are responsible. The bodies are found almost every day now. We publish the reports but the aides of the president always accuse GAM of the violence. But we know it is the Indonesian security forces,' said Aguswand.

The killing of the three RATA workers had shaken the NGOs in Banda Aceh. It was a realisation that the thin legal space that had allowed their establishment in post-Suharto Indonesia was now coming under pressure. In December 2000 Kontras told how they still had people in the field and were collecting data on each incident with a view to carrying out eventual prosecutions of those responsible. Feisal Hamdi's work mainly dealt with locating the missing relatives of the people who came to his office. It usually involved establishing whether the military or the police had them, and then trying to work out a way to appeal or establish why they were being held. In very few cases was there any crime involved other than being Acehnese.

In the office of Kontras in Banda Aceh hung a printout of a front page of the *Sydney Morning Herald*. It was from the previous year and carried the headline: 'Jakarta's Assassins', and a colour photo of some militias from East Timor that had been taken before the UN-sponsored ballot. The militia wore civilian clothes and carried M-16s and SKS rifles, and were followed closely by some Indonesian military in uniform. After the ballot, the military and the militia had systematically destroyed East Timor, and here in Aceh the same military were in control and carrying out the same kind of program. I was therefore amazed to see the newspaper article displayed so prominently. But in actual fact it made sense. These human rights workers knew they were a target and they also knew that despite the razing of East Timor by the Indonesian military, the East Timorese had won in the end – just a little over a year earlier, at that time. They looked to the East Timorese victory as an inspiration, and if the newspaper on the wall offended the military, so be it. If the military were going to be in the office, they would be raiding it anyway, remarked Aguswand.

Similarly, in the office of the Aceh Coalition for Human Rights, the tally of arrests, killings, armed clashes, disappearances and rapes was displayed on a large white board in the waiting room. Stickers and pamphlets printed on glossy paper sat in piles on a coffee table with titles like 'Free DOM. Stop the killing in Aceh'. The very existence of these offices and the work they carried out was a slap in the face to the military and their neverending attempts to blame the entire conflict on GAM. They were allowed to stay open, under surveillance and occasionally raided, but still functioning, nevertheless.

The existence of these NGOs in Banda Aceh had nothing to do with a newfound tolerance by the TNI. It just reflected the weakness of the Indonesian state in the face of international pressure. Of course, the fact that these groups were working in Aceh was pointed to by the Indonesian government and their foreign backers as evidence of good faith on behalf of the military and the government. Nowhere was this more evident than in the only hotel in Banda Aceh that had pretensions to a star rating, the Kuala Tripa. In this five-storey circular structure in the centre of town, near the historic Baiturrahman mosque, lived the representatives of the HDC, the GAM negotiating team and representatives of the police and the military.

━━◆━○━◆━━

THE HENRY Dunant Centre for Humanitarian Dialogue – the HDC – is a Swiss-based NGO that sees itself as a mediator in international disputes and is attempting to carve itself a niche in the international community as a kind of low-key alternative to the UN. In late 1999, at the invitation of President Wahid, it sent a team to assist in negotiations between GAM and the security forces. In early 2000 it established a small, permanent presence in Aceh to create and monitor the 'humanitarian pause'. The aim was to create a peaceful environment for the delivery of humanitarian aid to the conflict zones in the province. Central to this arrangement was the formation of a security committee with representatives from GAM, the security forces and the HDC, who were supposed to – in a civil way – discuss any breaches in the accord and determine who was responsible.

The HDC office was downstairs at the Kuala Tripa, and the GAM and police representatives were based in rooms on the third floor. They all ate in the same dining room, met in the same foyer and used the same tiny elevator. The place was rife with spies for both sides and the atmosphere was overbearing. Everybody knew who everybody else was, and what their business was, and in the end the place became a kind of gilded prison for both the GAM representatives and the foreign peace negotiators, with only the representatives of the Indonesian military and government able to speak freely and come and go at will.

The senior Indonesian security official on the committee was Colonel Ridwhan Karim of the police. When I spoke to him at the Kuala Tripa Hotel he was very blunt about the chances of the humanitarian pause being extended: 'The dialogue is important because it can solve the political issues. But they just want independence and it is impossible.' He blamed the violence on GAM and claimed they were using the pause to re-arm themselves. The major founding principle of the entire GAM movement – the independence of Aceh – was the one point that was simply not negotiable. For the Indonesian authorities, independence for Aceh was simply not part of the equation. And the relatively junior rank that Karim held in the command structure of the province reflected the low priority the authorities placed on the negotiating process. His answers were brief and not open to question. It was clear he had neither the authority nor the inclination to do anything but deliver a very short, sharp, scripted version of the conflict to visiting journalists. Like his superiors, he viewed the negotiations as a futile but necessary charade for the sake of the visiting foreign representatives and certain members of the government in Jakarta. To him, the real solution to the problem lay here with the local military and police commands. When I asked what would happen if the pause was not extended when it was due to expire on January 15, 2001, he said simply, 'We will disarm GAM by force.'

A few doors down in the GAM negotiators room, Zulfani said it was the Indonesians who were preventing any progress in the dialogue because they were continuing operations against GAM. He spoke about the ongoing attempts by Brimob to hunt down GAM operatives, the extortion of the local population by patrols, the labelling of civilians – often killed in disputes with troops over demands for money – as GAM members and the recruitment of non-Acehnese settlers in Aceh into self-defence units or militia. His comments were echoed by the older, grey-haired lawyer, Kamaruzzaman, and the slightly built Amni. The three of them sat in their room on the beds in mobile phone contact with those in the field, but there wasn't a lot they could do. At the Kuala Tripa they were heavily monitored. Their room was bugged and the movements of anybody who went in and out of their room were logged by the intelligence operatives in the hotel. Of the three, only Kamaruzzaman seemed calm. Zulfani nervously paced the small room and Amni constantly checked documents and his laptop. The powerlessness of their position was obvious.

The information about the militia groups given to me by the GAM negotiators wasn't new. Kontras had told me how a defector from one of the groups had come to them in October 2000 with information regarding the activities of a group in West Aceh called *Front Pulyumat Aceh* (Safe Aceh). This group was led by a man called Syaifruddin Latief, a local leader who had links to the military. The group was trained by the local Indonesian military command (Kodim) in East Aceh and sent on operations with the army and police in West Aceh. During such operations, the defector said, they were simply told that a certain house was the target and they were to kill the people they found there. The men were paid and the weapons were collected by the military after the operation was complete. They were told not to be afraid of the police and the military. The three GAM representatives had the same information.

They added a few more details and said they had forwarded the information to the HDC.

The formation of militia in this way allowed the authorities to claim they were upholding their part of the humanitarian pause agreement without actually halting operations; they just got someone else to do the killing for them.

The figures for deaths from unknown gunmen in this period increased. The authorities, represented by Colonel Ridwhan Karim in the negotiations, just blamed the increased activity on GAM.

At that time, the HDC representatives in Banda Aceh had a very strict policy of not talking to the press. It was part of their 'softly, softly' approach to humanitarian dialogue, aimed at being able to carry out their work away from the pressures of accountability to the press and without causing embarrassment to their hosts, the Indonesians. They were trying to achieve an outcome in Aceh that halted the bloodshed whilst allowing the Indonesian military to save face. At the time, much was made of the anger and frustration of the Indonesian military over their 'humiliating' defeat in East Timor, and the discretion of the HDC attempts to broker peace in Aceh were a salve to that perception. But perhaps they held their silence too long, or perhaps it was interpreted by the Indonesians as acquiescence, because the first humanitarian pause collapsed under the weight of the ongoing deaths in 2000.

When President Wahid visited Banda Aceh on December 19, 2000, the indications were that the military was pushing him to authorise a full-scale crackdown on GAM. His visit was cut short to little over three hours and he flew out before schedule.

SIRA had earlier warned that the military would try to use the occasion to assassinate the president and then blame it on the Acehnese. According to SIRA, the military had planted specialist snipers among the 2000 extra troops flown in to guarantee security during the president's visit. An assassination would, the logic ran, remove a president who was trying to curtail the military's power and provide a pretext for a massive operation to wipe out GAM.

Wahid's earlier offer to conduct a referendum had been taken seriously in Aceh but the president himself and some of the journalists who had reported the so-called offer knew that his comment, made at a press conference, had been taken out of context.

Wahid had been the first Indonesian president to initiate contact with GAM. Shortly after he came to power in October 1999, Wahid assigned his state secretary, Bondan Gunawan, to meet the commander of the GAM armed forces, Tengku Abdullah Syafei. The meeting had gone ahead without the involvement of the security forces. There was much goodwill generated as a result, and the negotiations involving the HDC followed. But tensions within the government, particularly with Vice President Megawati Sukarnoputri and her military supporters, forced Wahid's hand on the issues of Aceh and Papua away from his conciliatory stance and he began to revert his position to the solutions favoured by the military.

The tensions within Wahid's government and between the government and the military had reached such a high point by December 2000, that when two bombs exploded in government offices in the capital two days before President Wahid's visit, nobody really knew who was behind the explosions. The following day, when shooting forced a plane chartered by Mobil Oil to abort its landing at Lhokseumahwe, reports that the military were responsible raised few eyebrows. And the discovery of 13 dead bodies over the weekend before his visit was interpreted by most observers as the military sending a message to Wahid, warning him not to make concessions to the Acehnese during his visit.

SECURITY WAS tight around the Baiturrahman mosque as Wahid arrived to speak to the 300 or so officials – mostly Indonesian civil servants and religious leaders – gathered inside. Troops with automatic weapons stood within two metres of each other around the entire perimeter as armoured trucks and cars loaded with troops cut laps around the mosque. Inside, Wahid made a contradictory speech. Referring to GAM, whose leaders had refused to attend, he said, 'They are brothers, protesting past injustices in their own way, which have left a bitter after-taste in their mouth. Future steps to improve and create an independent Aceh within the environs of the Indonesian Republic can be made together.'

He was pleasing no-one by acknowledging all sides. By admitting GAM had a case based on the TNI's brutal past but recognising the military would never accept independence for Aceh, he was revealing the contradictions inherent in his policy. He left immediately after the meeting, cancelling a prayer session at the mosque and refusing to meet local leaders.

FOR THE fourth time in less than 100 kilometres, Brimob troops with automatic weapons ordered everybody off the bus. It was

31

December 24, 2000, and the imminent end of the Muslim fasting month of Ramadan meant the bus to Medan, through the conflict area out of Aceh, was full of people trying to get home for the Lebaran holidays. Ramadan is observed more strictly in Aceh than anywhere else in Indonesia. It is impossible to find anywhere to eat during daylight hours, and smoking or even drinking water outdoors is frowned upon and liable to see you surrounded by an angry mob. The strictness of the fasting is one of the differences between the Muslims of Aceh and those of the rest of Indonesia. In Aceh, where Islam was introduced for the first time in the 12th century by Arab traders from the Middle East, the more permissive Islam of Indonesia is looked down upon. The Acehnese see the Muslims of Java as following a hybrid version of their religion.

The physical realities of having nothing to drink nor eat from before dawn until dusk in the hot and humid December weather of Aceh means that by the end of the day, tempers are frayed and exhaustion has set in. Thirst and hunger only exacerbate the tension of travelling through an area where every roadblock holds the potential for identity checks, demands for money and impromptu arrest by soldiers well-known for murder and torture.

On this occasion, the men were ordered to one side and told to raise their shirts as the Brimob troops checked them for weapons. Then they searched the women and the luggage as other troops stood behind them with weapons held at the ready. When everybody was allowed back onto the bus, the Brimob troops did one final walk down the aisle with weapons trained, checking the faces of the passengers for any signs of guilt or suspicion. Two young men were ordered off again and nobody said a word as they were questioned just outside the door. Finally, they were allowed back on and the bus was permitted to continue.

The driver was crunching up through the gears, accelerating heavily. It was a combination of wanting to get away from the Brimob soldiers and a more basic need. It was almost 6.30 pm and everybody was starving; it was almost time to break the fast for the day but because of all the roadblocks, the bus was running late. A massive red, white and black GAM flag hung from a power pylon within sight of the highway, marking who was in control of this section of the road, but there was no other sign of them. At exactly 6.30 everyone in the bus began smoking. The fast was over and the tension relaxed as the small town of Juenib came into sight.

In Acehnese villages during Ramadan, the daily breaking of the fast is the major event of the day. The food is prepared and juice, tea and coffee are lined up to be ready for the exact time when people are permitted to eat. Most men smoke, so the moment the fast is over, people are simultaneously eating, drinking and smoking. For the first few minutes there is no talking as everybody concentrates on what is going into their mouths. Then things start to relax and the relief on people's faces is obvious. They start to talk and laugh. It doesn't take much food to satisfy someone who has not eaten all day and within a very quick space of time the eating is completed, the plates cleared away and the people sit down to smoke and drink the thick black coffee the Acehnese prefer. Such was the situation in the town of Juenib when we arrived.

After we'd eaten, it became obvious that the bus wasn't going any further for a while. There was fighting a few kilometres down the road. The GAM fighters were attacking the next Brimob post on the highway. The traffic was banked up in the main street and shopkeepers were reopening their stores to take advantage of the unexpected trade. People sat around outside on chairs in front of restaurants, enjoying the cooler evening air and chatting.

Over coffee at a small table, Abdul, a young man of 24, told us he was going to Lhokseumahwe to see if his parents had returned to their house after being forced to flee by an Indonesian military operation a month before. 'Eighty, no, 90 per cent of the people here support GAM,' he said, then quickly lowered his voice as the mostly Indonesian bus passengers glared at him.

He went on to say that his situation was quite normal. The fact that his family lived in an area where there was a lot of GAM activity didn't mean they were directly involved, but it didn't mean they don't support GAM, either. 'We all support them here. Independence is the only way to stop this,' he said. But he shouldn't talk any more because there were many spies and, he added dramatically, the next day he could be dead.

After a few hours the bus finally got going. A few kilometres out of town at the next roadblock the police were young and nervous, pointing their weapons further along the road in the direction the bus was headed. They were wearing bandanas and T-shirts, and they had the wide-eyed adrenaline-charged look of those in recent fear for their lives. They gave the bus a cursory search and soon we were roaring along the stretch of road where the fighting had only just subsided. Probably two-thirds of the people on the bus were from outside Aceh and their faces were tense. They were afraid of GAM. The rest, the Acehnese, were silent. Only a few minutes earlier, the hyped-up young Brimob soldiers could have pulled them off the bus and shot them for no other reason than because they were Acehnese and one of their own had just been killed by GAM.

It was one of the usual results of deaths in firefights between GAM and the Indonesians – if there were any casualties among the security forces, the same number of Acehnese would quickly meet the same fate. More often than not they were just individuals unlucky enough to be in the area. The GAM fighters were usually long gone or too well armed to approach, but the unfortunate civilians were almost always referred to as GAM after their deaths, if they were acknowledged at all by the authorities. Fighting a war amongst a largely unsympathetic population, the Indonesian police and military never had any shortage of victims to avenge the deaths of their own men.

It was a long all-night bus trip down to the relative normality of the North Sumatran capital of Medan, with the bus stopping frequently at checkpoints in the dark. Often it was hard to tell who controlled the checkpoints, the government or GAM. At most of them the bus driver handed over a small amount of money. Sometime before dawn the checkpoints stopped and we were back in North Sumatra.

⊢•⊦⊳•◦•⊲•⊣•

IN 2000, year, the end of Idul Fitri (a religious holiday that follows the fasting month of Ramadan) fell on Christmas Eve, and between 8.30 and 10 pm, 38 bombs were delivered to

38 churches and priests in 11 cities across Indonesia. The bombs were placed as widely as Jakarta and five other cities on the island of Java, as well as Sumatra, Lombok, Pulau Batam (an island near Singapore) and Medan. Nineteen people were killed and 120 wounded in the well-coordinated wave of bombings. In Medan itself, 14 packages were sent to churches and one to the home of a priest. Only one exploded.

In the Indonesia of late 2000, there were many groups to blame for the attack. But most reports at the time mentioned the Indonesian military or members of the disgraced dictator Suharto's family, or both.

President Wahid almost immediately laid the blame on members of the military still loyal to Suharto who were at that time actively trying to destabilise his presidency and saw his attempts to reform the military as a threat. Predictably, the military itself blamed GAM, as they had done for bombing incidents at the Jakarta Stock Exchange in September and the Malaysian embassy in August of that year. GAM vigorously denied this.

Commander Darwis Juenib of GAM, who controlled the area around the town of the same name, told the Indonesian press: 'We deeply regret the incident. But we were not involved in it. Our business is only in Aceh, to free Aceh so that it may be independent. So we don't have any business outside of that, let alone carrying out bombings at places of worship belonging to another religion.' Sofyan Dawood, commander and spokesman for the Passe region of Aceh, agreed. 'GAM has no business in Jakarta,' he said.

Media sources in Indonesia close to the military and the former Suharto regime, such as the state news agency, Antara, continued to blame GAM despite the denials and lack of evidence. To some extent, the impression of GAM as a shadowy terrorist organisation began to take hold in the minds of the Indonesian public and foreign observers. But evidence of military involvement in the bombings continued to dribble out. A man suspected to be an intelligence officer from Kopassus was detained by the police for infiltrating the Karmat Franciscan community in Central Java. He was living in the Franciscans' house and had given them a false name. The police told Father Sumardi, a Franciscan monk, that the man was an intelligence officer and that an identity card under a different name to the one he had used had been found in his room. The police later released the man on the grounds that he was insane.

In the case of the Jakarta Stock Exchange bomb, three serving noncommissioned officers from the army's elite Kostrad (strategic reserve) and Kopassus were eventually convicted of the bombing, in which the military explosive RDX was used. Corporal Ibrahim Hasan from Kostrad and Sergeant Irwan Ibrahim from Kopassus were given life sentences, but Sergeant Ibrahim Abdul Manaf Wahab escaped from prison in February 2001 and was never recaptured.

It was when the police arrested three suspects over the construction and placement of the bombs on Christmas Eve in Medan that the links between the military and the bombings started to become clear. A check of the prisoners' phone records by reporters from the Indonesian news magazine *Tempo* showed calls had been made to Kopassus intelligence officer Lieutenant Colonel Iwan Prilianto, and to another number belonging to the intelligence unit of the Medan-based Bukit Barisan military command, which at that time had responsibility for troops in Aceh and North Sumatra. Prilianto had just taken over as chief intelligence assistant to the Bukit Barisan command shortly before the bombings.

According to the *Tempo* investigation, when police raided a house on January 11, 2001, they arrested the three suspects and also found detonators, alarm clocks, batteries and roughly AU$30,000 worth of Indonesian currency. They also found documents that stated that Fauzi Hasbi was an informant of the Bukit Barisan military command intelligence assistant, and an earlier document that identified him as having received an assignment from Kopkamtib (the intelligence unit) in 1979.

Fauzi Hasbi was a well-known Acehnese who had previously supported GAM. His father, Teungku Fauzi Hasbi Geudong, was a leader in the Darul Islam (House of Islam) rebellion in Aceh that lasted from 1953 until 1962. The movement, led by Daud Beureueh, was the Acehnese branch of an Indonesia-wide movement that fought against the central authority of Jakarta for an Islamic-based state. In Aceh, the movement had a distinctly nationalist edge. GAM sees the Darul Islam movement as the forerunner to their struggle for independence, but those loyal to the Darul Islam idea, such as Teungku Fauzi Hasbi Geudong, see the struggle in terms of establishing an Islamic Indonesian state, not just a separate state of Aceh. This was why Teungku Fauzi Hasbi Geudong later fell out with the exiled GAM leader, Hasan Di Tiro, when he himself went into exile. But his son, Fauzi Hasbi, had had a long history of involvement with Indonesian intelligence since his detention by the military in 1979 when he surrendered to then Lieutenant Syaffrie Samsuddin, who later became a TNI spokesman and a major general.

In a later interview with *Tempo*, Fauzi admitted he had helped convince his father and his brother to surrender to the Indonesian authorities in Aceh when they still supported GAM. His father was imprisoned for three years in 1979 and eventually went into exile in 1984.

Hasbi emerged as the link between the three men charged over the bombing and the local Indonesian military intelligence command. One of the men, half Javanese-Acehnese Edi Sugianto, a radio repair worker associated with both Kopassus and GAM through his business in Aceh, admitted making the bombs, and the other two admitted to providing the explosive that had been stolen from an ExxonMobil warehouse in Aceh. The investigation in Medan revealed the involvement of the Indonesian military in the bombings at the same time as they were blaming GAM and trying to use the events as a pretext to end the humanitarian pause.

ASIDE FROM the two *Tempo* articles in early 2001, the revelation of Indonesian military intelligence involvement passed relatively unnoticed. Such allegations were common during the presidency of Abdurrahman Wahid. It was not until after the Bali nightclub bombing in October 2002 that the link between the Indonesian military intelligence and the Christmas 2000 bombings came under more scrutiny. A report by the Brussels-based International Crisis Group (ICG), released in December 2002, which examined the Jemaah Islamiah network in relation to the Bali bombing, also probed the relationship between Fauzi Hasbi and Indonesian intelligence on the one hand, and Fauzi

Hasbi and Jemaah Islamiah on the other. The report stated that the links between Fauzi Hasbi and Kopassus went back as far as 1980, when Muchtar Hasbi – Fauzi Hasbi's brother and the GAM vice president at that time – was killed in a Kopassus operation. The death of his vice president sent GAM's founding leader, Hasan Di Tiro, into exile; first to Singapore, then to Mozambique, and eventually to Sweden where the GAM leadership is still based today.

According to the ICG, GAM still believes Fauzi Hasbi was responsible for the operation that killed his brother. At the same time, Dr Huseini Hasan, GAM's chief of staff, fled to Penang and then Kuala Lumpur in Malaysia, and eventually settled in Sweden. Hasbi's father also eventually joined the leadership in Sweden, but differences between the three leaders eventually led to the formation of a new group – MP-GAM – in 1999 under Dr Huseini Hasan, which has been courted by the Indonesian government to attract Acehnese away from the original GAM under Hasan Di Tiro. The ICG report talks of funds being diverted to the MP-GAM group in Malaysia from Acehnese Golkar party (the party of former dictator Suharto) sources close to the military.

Both Fauzi Hasbi and his father had strong links with Jemaah Islamiah members going back to the 1970s. Several of the Jemaah Islamiah leaders who were to attain notoriety following the Bali bombing were also exiled in Malaysia in the 1980s, and it was there the relationships between the two groups were developed.

Even though Fauzi Hasbi had a longstanding connection with Indonesian military intelligence, he was still invited to meetings with Jemaah Islamiah leader Abu Bakar Bashir in late 1999 in

Malaysia and, according to the ICG, 'he treats Hambali like a son'. Hambali is one of the masterminds behind the Bali bombings and was arrested in Thailand by the CIA in August 2003.

The connection between Indonesian military intelligence, Fauzi Hasbi and Jemaah Islamiah – identified through the Medan Christmas bombings by *Tempo* and the ICG – is intriguing, as it shows how, in the murky world of Indonesian counter-insurgency, second and third party figures like Fauzi Hasbi are used to create the appearances of responsibility for violent acts against those who are opposing the Indonesian military. In this case they were trying to set up GAM as the church bombers. That didn't really work, so the focus was returned to Jemaah Islamiah as the source of terrorism in Indonesia; Jemaah Islamiah being an organisation that, through the ICG report and the *Tempo* investigation, we now know was infiltrated at a high level by someone like Fauzi Hasbi who had been involved for a long time with Indonesian military intelligence.

The implication here is that if the military were directing the bombing in Medan through Hasbi, they must have known of or been involved with the nationwide bombings of Christmas Eve 2000; bombings that have since been blamed on Jemaah Islamiah leader Abu Bakar Bashir, who received a 15-year jail term in August 2003 for organising these attacks as well as an alleged plot to assassinate President Megawati Sukarnoputri.

⊱⋅•⋅⊰

AN INTERESTING postscript to this story is that on February 22, 2003, Fauzi Hasbi and two colleagues were abducted from a hotel in Ambon city on the island of Ambon, capital of the

Malukus, and murdered. His son later made the allegation that a police detective was involved in the kidnap and murder. The police denied involvement and arrested seven men who they claim had used the deceased Hasbi's ATM card to withdraw money. The so-called leader of the group, Yanto, was a local Muslim with a history of violence against the police.

If Hasbi was a link between military intelligence and Jemaah Islamiah, he was probably killed so that he could never reveal such a sensational connection. In the current environment of renewed cooperation between the Indonesian military and the United States and Australia over the war on international terrorism, such a revelation would be disastrous for the Indonesian military, and would directly implicate them in the deaths of the 88 Australians in the October 12, 2002 bombing in Bali.

I t's the kind of thing you'd hear as a journalist that would make
you roll your eyes and glance around quickly for someone else
to talk to: in order to understand the current war in Aceh, you
have to first be familiar with the Darul Islam rebellion of the
1950s. In order to understand that, you have to look at Aceh's
role in the war of Indonesian liberation against the Dutch. Of
course to understand that, you have to understand Aceh's
40-year war against the Dutch and, in turn, to really know why
the Acehnese held out so long against the Dutch, you have to
understand the wars of the Acehnese empire going back as far as
the 15th century.

But in Aceh, this historical context is very relevant. The
history and the conflict are being relived every day in various
ways: the social organisation of the villages that had evolved to
alert the Acehnese guerrillas in their fight against the Indonesian

military in the Darul Islam rebellion; the suicide tactics of the Acehnese *muslimin* fighters against the occupying Dutch in the 1920s and '30s; the crippling of transport and communications in the war against the Dutch attempts to retake Aceh after World War II – all are still daily occurences in GAM's fight against the Indonesian military in the 21st century.

The spacing of the conflicts over the last 150 years is almost an indicator of the time it takes for one generation to be defeated and for their stories of rebellion, fighting and revenge to be passed on to the next. Veterans and survivors of Aceh's 40-year war against the Dutch between 1873 and 1913 inspired and taught the next generation about continued resistance against the Dutch throughout the 1920s and '30s. The guerrilla tactics originally used against the Dutch were retaught and reimplemented when the Dutch and British troops tried to return after the Japanese surrendered. It was the veterans of that struggle who led classes in warfare under the guise of an Islamic boy scout organisation prior to the Darul Islam rebellion in 1953 – a rebellion that was to leave Indonesia in control of only a few of the major towns in Aceh for the next four years. When Hasan Di Tiro and only 24 leaders declared Aceh's independence in the wilderness in the Pidie district on December 4, 1976, it was the Darul Islam veterans who joined in and began training again for an armed struggle that continues until now.

By violently resisting the first colonial incursions into the area by the Portuguese, and then by coming to a deal with the British that culminated in the London treaty of 1824 that guaranteed Acehnese sovereignty, the sultanate of Aceh had managed to avoid becoming a part of the Dutch East Indies. But by the

1870s, the Dutch had had enough of this irritant at the tip of Sumatra and started accusing Aceh of being a base for pirates who were operating against the lucrative pepper trade in the Malacca Straits. The real reason was, of course, economic. The Dutch wanted the trade to themselves and they invaded the capital, Banda Aceh, in 1873. They were defeated and forced to withdraw but returned with a larger force in 1874 and this time defeated the armies of the sultan, forcing him to flee to the countryside. This carried the fight into the districts where the regional chiefs, known as Ulebalang, resisted the Dutch. When they were defeated, the resistance was led by the village religious chiefs, the Ulama. The Dutch tried, and succeeded, over the next 40 years to separate the two leaderships, creating a rift in Acehnese society that is still relevant today. The defeat and subordination of the Ulebalang by the Dutch left the Ulama leadership more radical and committed to defeating the Dutch *kafirs*, the non-believers. It was from the ranks of the Ulama that the Acehnese leader Tengku Cik Di Tiro emerged. As the war against the Dutch became a guerrilla conflict, it was under Cik Di Tiro that the Acehnese began to identify as Muslims fighting a holy war against the invaders – not as subjects loyal to individual leaders and regions. Such tactics as collecting taxes from the people, building rural bases and hit-and-run attacks against the Dutch were started by the Ulama-led resistance. In the iconography of modern-day GAM, this was the real start of Acehnese national resistance to outside control.

The war dragged on and became a strain on the Dutch East Indies administration. By some accounts, it almost bankrupted the colony and about 8000 Dutch and 30,000 native soldiers were killed. Acehnese deaths were put at 39,000, but the real statistic was probably higher as the Dutch were the only ones keeping records; the Acehnese themselves now put the figure at around 100,000. Despite the surrender of most of the Acehnese leaders, including the royal family, in 1903, the Ulama in the countryside kept fighting. The Dutch admitted to killing a further 14,000 of these fighters over the next ten years, and it wasn't until the followers of the Tiro clan were defeated in the Pidie region in 1913 that the Dutch could safely declare Aceh defeated.

But that wasn't the end of it for the Dutch. By the 1920s they were dealing with small bands of suicidal Acehnese fighters called *muslimin*, who would take an oath together after reading the *Hikayat*, a forbidden collection of stories from the Koran and Arabic literature that extolled the privileges of martyrdom. They would then attack a Dutch outpost or target, and usually die in the attempt. These small-scale attacks and individual killings reached a peak between 1925 and 1927, and arrests and reprisals by the Dutch led to the organised attacks by groups of Ulama-led *muslimin* ceasing altogether in the early 1930s. Individual attacks, which the Dutch called *Atjeh-moord* (Acehnese murder), continued right up until the Dutch were displaced by the Japanese; an Acehnese would decide upon martyrdom and, after putting his affairs in order and saying the appropriate prayers, he would go looking for a Dutchman upon whom he would set with his dagger. There were 35 such attacks recorded between 1930 and 1938. It was only in the few years before the Japanese arrived that things finally quietened down for the Dutch in Aceh.

It was the Ulama organisation, the All-Aceh Religious Scholars' Association (PUSA), that organised a revolt against the Dutch administration as the Japanese approached Sumatra in February 1942. By the time the Japanese arrived, the Dutch administration had already surrendered and the province was free of their control. But the Japanese were in no mood to make concessions to the Acehnese, and it was their attempts to impose Japanese customs – such as bowing towards Tokyo and not towards Mecca – that angered the local people. The Japanese also tended to replicate the Dutch administration by employing the Ulebalang as their regional administrators, which angered the Ulama and led them to take up arms against the new regime.

In November 1942, the Japanese found themselves putting down a local rebellion against their rule carried out by the same Acehnese who had removed the Dutch to make way for their arrival. One leader of a religious school in Cot Plieng, in Bayu, defied the Japanese. Tengku Abdul Djalil, a young Ulama, preached to his students that the Acehnese PUSA leadership had, 'driven out the dogs and brought in the pigs' and that they must now fight the Japanese occupation. He continued to encourage his students to resist the Japanese and prepared both himself and them for martyrdom. Pro-Japanese Acehnese leaders implored him to desist and stop preaching resistance, to which he was recorded as replying, 'It is not resistance which is futile; it is the attack which is futile. The aggressors are not certain of martyrdom, but there is no doubt that those who resist die as martyrs.'

The Japanese eventually attacked the mosque and the school, destroying it. Over 100 Acehnese were massacred with mortars and machine guns but not before killing 18 Japanese. Many Acehnese saw Abdul Djalil and his students as martyrs and followed their example. It was the first of many clashes between the Acehnese and the Japanese that continued until 1945.

After the Japanese capitulation to the Allies, the Japanese units based in Aceh were ordered to maintain stability in Aceh by the British troops who had landed in Medan in North Sumatra. Aside from the occupation of the island of Sabang by the British navy in September 1945, the only attempt to impose Allied rule on Aceh was the dispatch of a Dutch major to the capital to liaise with the surrendering Japanese. Before any attempts to re-impose Dutch rule could take place, the Acehnese were already attacking the Japanese troops in order to get their weapons from them.

Many of the Japanese units were disarmed by the Acehnese in the PUSA organisation. Some of these attacks were phony battles in which the Japanese agreed to be attacked by the Acehnese to escape punishment from their own command for not handing their weapons over to the British. Many Japanese troops, now defeated but not disarmed, sympathised with the Acehnese and some even defected to the Acehnese cause to keep fighting against the Allies. But not all of the disarming was amicable. Trains carrying Japanese troops were attacked and they were forced to hand over their weapons. The main Japanese garrison of Lokhnga was surrounded and attacked and only through negotiation with the Acehnese were they allowed to leave after handing over weapons. They were allowed to leave to join the other Japanese at Blang Bintang where they had to launch a large operation to clear their way to the coast to be evacuated by the British.

Over 100 Japanese soldiers stayed behind to fight with the Acehnese. A major confrontation happened in Langsa in East Aceh in late December 1945 after the Japanese had left the rest of Aceh. Against the orders of the British command in Medan, the Japanese negotiated a withdrawal of their forces in exchange for most of their weapons to the attacking Acehnese.

The Acehnese embraced the struggle against the Dutch returning, and for Indonesian independence, but in the context of their own society. The Ulama-led PUSA became stronger and led attacks on the Ulebalang, who had benefited under the Dutch. Many Ulebalang were killed and their property seized and later auctioned off. One Ulebalang in the Pidie district led his supporters against independence but he was quickly defeated. It was the Ulama who finally won the old struggle between the two forces in Acehnese society and the bloody seizure of Ulebalang property had all the trappings of a brief civil war but led the way to a turbulent period of democratisation. The Dutch, for their part, soon gave up on attempts to regain control of Aceh after several bloody noses from the well-organised and armed Acehnese, and for a period after the declaration of Indonesian independence on August 17, 1945, Aceh was the only truly independent part of the new nation, free as it was from foreign troops trying to regain control.

Acehnese nowadays will tell you how they paid for Indonesian independence. There are the famous planes bought by the Acehnese and donated to the Indonesian government, one of which became the flagship of Indonesia's national carrier, Garuda. They talk of the financial support given by the Acehnese to the new republican government. There is truth in this. In the chaotic years of the struggle for Indonesian independence between 1945 and 1948, Aceh was relatively stable and Acehnese businessmen carried out lucrative trading, at a time of great shortages, across the Malacca Straits, circumventing any government controls. Support for the Republic of Indonesia was widespread and the Acehnese believed they would have their own state, and autonomous rule within the Indonesian state, and that their long struggle against foreign domination would be over.

In 1949, the leader of the PUSA, Daud Beureueh, was declared governor of the State of Aceh in the sovereign Federal Republic of Indonesia. The following year, the Federal Republic of Indonesia reverted to the Republic of Indonesia and divided into ten provinces, with Aceh to be merged with North Sumatra. The promises to the Acehnese by Indonesia's founding president, Sukarno, were already forgotten and Aceh was formally dissolved as an administrative entity in 1951. Daud Beureueh was removed as governor and assigned to the Ministry of Home Affairs in Jakarta.

It didn't take long for the Acehnese to find expression for their grievances against the central government in Jakarta. On the evening of September 19, 1953, groups of men armed with spears, knives, swords and rifles began gathering on major roads. All communication lines between Aceh and the outside world were cut and the armed men attacked police stations and Indonesian military barracks throughout North and East Aceh. A plan to take over the capital Kuturaja (now called Banda Aceh) was foiled by the military. Lhokseumahwe was subject to a four-hour battle on the first day of the rebellion as thousands tried to take over the town. These battles went on for a week. The provincial towns of Takengon, Meureudu and Blangkejeren in Central Aceh and Pidie all fell to the rebels in the first week, and in Bireuen and Sigli, the Indonesian air force was deployed to bomb and strafe rebels who were fighting government forces. On the west coast of Aceh, Meulaboh and Tapaktuan fell to the rebels. In most towns not overrun by the rebels, the military were simply defending their barracks, and virtually the whole countryside was in rebel hands.

Daud Beureueh led the Acehnese to insurrection under the banner of the Darul Islam movement, which had been rebelling against the central government in West Java since 1948. The movement's aim was the establishment of an Indonesian Islamic state, and it had already been joined by disenchanted elements of the Indonesian military in South Sulawesi. The Acehnese saw an opportunity to regain control of their province through joining the Darul Islam movement, and their views on the corrupting influence of the secular Indonesian state coincided with those of Darul Islam. It was a fight for political independence within a new form of Indonesian state, the *Negara Islam Indonesia* (NII, the Islamic State of Indonesia) and the enemy was the existing Indonesian government and institutions. The Acehnese fought under the banner of *Tentara Islam Indonesia*, the Islamic Army of Indonesia.

Contact between the Darul Islam leader in West Java, Kartosuwirjo, and the leaders in Aceh grouped around Beureueh, had begun in 1952 when it was clear to them the central government had no intention of honouring any of its promises for autonomy for the province. Training began and Ulamas in Aceh began preaching about the alien values being imported by Indonesia and the necessity for rebellion. A youth organisation was established to facilitate military training in the villages and veterans of the independence war were given refresher training and in turn became instructors. When the campaign eventually started, the population was behind the soldiers of the Darul Islam and supported them in the way they would later support GAM. As Anthony Reid notes in his book *The Blood of the People: Revolution and the End of Traditional Rule in Northern Sumatra* (Oxford University Press, Kuala Lumpur, 1979), when government soldiers would approach a village on patrol,

> . . . the soldiers normally asked about the activities of the rebels in the area. Such a question always met with the stereotypical answer: *Tidak tahu, Tuan.* (I don't know, sir.) The soldiers' reaction to that answer varied according to their mood. If they had just been ambushed by the rebels near the village, the non-cooperative attitude of the villagers would certainly result in scolding, beating, and even killing and house-burning. As soon as the soldiers had left the village, the Keuchik [village chief] would haul down the [Indonesian] flag and put it away for next time. The drum would again be sounded to signal to the villagers and the rebels that the soldiers had gone.

The military knew the villagers supported the rebellion and responded accordingly. The government had arrested 4046 people between September 19, 1953, the start of the rebellion, and January 1954. In February 1954, newspapers reported that almost 100 villagers had been killed by soldiers in two incidents.

On February 26, a platoon of West Sumatran soldiers killed 25 villagers in cold blood after being ambushed two days earlier and losing 15 of their own men. The same unit killed a further 64 fishermen between the ages of 11 and 100 two days later. It was reported widely that in both cases the unit entered the villages, rounded up all the males they could find and killed them without questioning. Soldiers blocked all roads into the villages while the killings were carried out. That incident became known as the Pulot-Cot Jeumpa affair, after the villages where the killings took place.

The rebellion dragged on and the majority of the countryside remained in rebel hands. The Indonesian military was forced to land troops from the sea, as the roads were cut off, and most of its activity was confined to supplying its own garrisons throughout the province. Rebel territory usually began within two to three kilometres of a major town and was governed by the Darul Islam movement. All transport, bar heavily guarded military convoys, was unable to use the roads and even the military were subject to constant ambushes, which then caused the troops to conduct reprisal operations.

Jakarta's response was to vow to crush the rebels with military force. But with rebellions to cope with in West Java and South Sulawesi, the military was unable to spare as many troops as they needed to deal with Aceh. Another side-effect was the increase in smuggling activities by the military as it struggled to pay for the ongoing operation. Previously, the military had only been involved in these kinds of activities in eastern Indonesia, but North Sumatra quickly became a base for these operations and contraband deals remain a core military revenue raiser in the province.

The confused response to the rebellion by the government also saw the appointment of a separate governor for Aceh less than a month after the insurrection broke out. Although the Darul Islam leaders initially welcomed the idea, it soon became apparent that the new governor was trying to strengthen Acehnese opposition to the rebellion by appointing the old rivals of the Ulama, the Ulebalang, to positions in the local administration. The rebels responded by destroying the regional offices of the appointee, and in some cases, kidnapping and assassinating the officials themselves, a tactic that GAM later embraced in dealing with local Indonesian-appointed officials.

Jakarta also tried to throw money at the problem. Shortly after the rebellion broke out, a budget of 20 million rupiah was allocated for immediate development of the province and road construction, and scholarship programs were announced. But many of the projects never got underway and the following year the central government even asked for the return of some of the funds that had not been spent. The ineffectual nature of these concessions only increased support for the Darul Islam movement until finally it was the military itself that pushed for the opening of negotiations with the rebels in 1956.

Aceh was restored as a full province in 1957, and the restoration of the 1945 constitution in 1959 contributed to a growing sense of confidence in the central government. A form of special autonomy for Aceh was granted in 1959. A peace deal was signed in 1961, some of the TII (Tentara Islam Indonesia) soldiers were allowed to enter the regular Indonesian military, and agreement was reached on religious freedoms for Aceh. In many ways, Daud Beureueh had achieved what he set out to do

– reversing the absorption of Aceh into North Sumatra, with its large proportion of Christian Bataks and a lifestyle and history alien to the Acehnese. It was the areas of Pidie, North Aceh and East Aceh that held out the longest, and it was to be precisely those areas that would comprise the strongest support for GAM in the years to come.

The rebellion finally collapsed in late 1962 following the capture and execution of Darul Islam leader Kartosuwirjo in West Java.

ACCORDING TO his autobiography, Hasan Di Tiro arrived in the fishing village of Pasi Lhok in a small boat on the morning of October 30, 1976. It was the first time he had set foot in Aceh for 25 years, and he had come with the express intention of declaring Aceh independent from Indonesia and fomenting a movement that would make this possible.

Born in the Pidie district in 1930 Teungku Hasan Muhammad Di Tiro is the grandson of Teuku Tjik Di Tiro Muhammad Saman, who received the approval of the last Sultan of Aceh, Muhammed Daud; to succeed him as sultan. Muhammed Daud then surrendered to the Dutch in 1903, and was exiled in Ambon before dying in the Dutch capital of Batavia without ever returning to Aceh.

Coming from a family of legendary anti-Dutch Ulama, Hasan Di Tiro grew up surrounded by the history of the sacrifices his people had made in the war against the Dutch. But like most Acehnese, after World War II he was a supporter of the Indonesian nation. According to one academic, Nurdin Abdul Rahman, the young Hasan Di Tiro wrote the first history of the Aceh war against the Dutch in Indonesian when he was studying in Yogyakarta, saying that it was a contribution to 'one history for one Indonesian nation'. After studying in Yogyakarta in Java in the late 1940s, he returned briefly to Aceh before taking a scholarship in the US. He settled in New York, working part time at the Indonesian mission at the UN until the 1953 Darul Islam rebellion caused him to become openly critical of Indonesia. He accused the Indonesians of genocide and threatened to open a representative office of the Islamic Republic of Indonesia at the UN. Indonesia responded by withdrawing his diplomatic passport and expected the US to expel him. But Hasan Di Tiro managed to get US citizenship and remained in the US until he returned to Aceh in 1976.

Di Tiro had written and self-published several books on Acehnese history by the time he returned. His views had become more stridently anti-Indonesian and specifically critical of what he called the 'Javanese empire'. His writings revealed a rejection of the Indonesian state that struck a chord in Aceh. He wrote:

If the concept of 'decolonisation à la Indonesia' would have been applied to all other colonial territories in the world, there would have been only seven – instead of 51 – new states established in Africa after World War II, namely, one for each of the foreign colonies of Britain, France, Portugal, Belgium, Italy, Spain and Germany . . .

DECOLONISATION REQUIRES liquidation of all colonial empires with specific steps and procedures, but Indonesia exists on the principle of total territorial integrity of the colonial empire; and an empire is not liquidated if its territorial integrity is preserved. Thus Indonesia is still an un-liquidated and un-decolonised colonial empire with Java-men replacing Dutchmen as colonialists.

The above is from Hasan Di Tiro's *Unfinished Diary* which he later published. The message is simple: Aceh had always been a separate entity to Indonesia and it was only by a historical trick after World War II that the Acehnese now had to accept Indonesian domination.

Because of his background, Hasan Di Tiro would have enjoyed loyalty in Aceh regardless of what he was saying, but it helped that his message to reject the Indonesian state was married to a hefty dose of the historical glories and reasons for legitimacy of the Acehnese state. The Acehnese people's attention may also have been roused by the not unconnected activity of the ExxonMobil plant in Arun, near Lhokseumahwe, which was entering full production. Seeing their natural resources being exploited by a foreign company for the benefit of Suharto's elite in Jakarta would have helped make the Acehnese even more receptive to Hasan Di Tiro's ideas.

But it was a small, almost unnoticed start. The declaration of Acehnese independence on December 4, 1976, involved only 24 people. Hasan Di Tiro formally established the Aceh North Sumatra Liberation Front (ANSLF) as the armed wing of the Free Aceh Movement (GAM), which was charged with campaigning amongst the people to make them aware of their history. One of the first tasks carried out by this group was to produce pamphlets outlining their aims. The distribution of these pamphlets was what first alerted the Indonesian authorities that something was going on. One former university lecturer in Aceh, Nurdin Abdul Rahman, later received four years in jail for possessing one of these pamphlets.

By 1981, ten of the original 24 signatories to the independence declaration had been hunted down and killed by the Indonesian military, who tried to wipe out the organisation before their ideas could take hold. There was no fighting; GAM was as yet barely organised and possessed no weapons. Those who were not killed escaped abroad in the early 1980s, including Hasan Di Tiro and Abdullah Zaini who both eventually went to Sweden, along with the current prime minister of the exiled GAM leadership in Sweden, Malik Mahmood, where they still constitute the leadership of GAM.

In those first five years, the military also arrested and killed the family members of those involved in the nascent movement. Throughout Aceh, and even in the North Sumatran capital of Medan – where many Acehnese lived – and in Jakarta, Acehnese with very little knowledge of or sympathy with the new movement were rounded up by the Indonesian military. In the mid-1980s those whose family members who had been killed or arrested began to collect money amongst themselves and organised to send people abroad. Because of Aceh's proximity to Malaysia across the Malacca Straits, many of them went there, and from there many of them travelled on and worked in Thailand, the Philippines, Hong Kong and the Netherlands. Military training was organised by Hasan Di Tiro in Gaddafi's

Libya; the first groups went there in the mid-1980s but there was also clandestine training available in the large Acehnese communities in Malaysia.

By 1987 and 1988, those who had gone abroad began to return. With guns mainly bought from the Indonesians themselves and later with captured weaponry, GAM began a military campaign. It was small at first. Targeting isolated police and military posts and military transport, the main aim of the attacks was to acquire weapons. Australian volunteer worker Leon Jones, who was living in the Pidie district at the time, later wrote that the violence began in that area in late May 1989 with the killing of two police officers in the Tiro sub-district (Hasan Di Tiro's ancestral home) and the seizure of their weapons. As he wrote at the time, the reasons behind the killings were debated amongst officials as being related to the marijuana trade or some indiscretions with local women on the part of the police. He also noted, however, that many of the younger men at the university where he worked regarded the incident as the start of another rebellion.

As the frequency of attacks increased, the military continued to publicly maintain that the problems were due to criminal activities. But, virtually unheard of outside military circles in Indonesia due to Suharto's censorship of the press, a very well-coordinated armed movement had begun.

It was not until February 1990 that the military commander of the North Sumatra region that included Aceh, Major General Djoko Pramono, finally admitted to the press that the attacks, by then occurring regularly in Aceh, carried out by GAM against the Indonesian military 'do not aim to harm the common people.

Their target is the armed forces.' In April 1990 the news agency Reuters in Jakarta quoted human rights sources in Indonesia as saying that the military had suffered 72 casualties in clashes with well-armed guerrillas and that the probable toll was in the hundreds. By June the military had publicly identified *Aceh Merdeka* – GAM – as the source of the attacks and operations officially began in earnest. A further 6000 troops from Kopassus, the marines and the police Mobile Brigade, as they were then known, were dispatched to Aceh, doubling the military presence to 12,000. The territorial troops already based in Aceh had been conducting an officially unacknowledged counterinsurgency operation since the attacks had begun the previous year. Their tactics of setting up roadblocks and interrogating and arresting civilians in areas of rebel activity had already led to casualties in late 1989, but it was with the deployment of the new troops in mid-1990 that the atrocities became widespread and carefully planned. President Suharto announced that Aceh had become an area of military operations – *Daerah Operasi Militer*, or DOM.

Unidentified corpses began appearing along major roads and in towns. Often bodies were mutilated, their hands bound, and there were gunshot wounds to the head. In November 1990 villagers discovered about 200 decomposing bodies in a pit near the village of Alue Mira. In late 1990 Indonesian journalists from *Tempo* wrote of bodies in groups of three or four left in sacks; bodies bludgeoned to death; bodies with mutilated genitals, ears cut off; with blindfolded heads, hands tied behind backs, bullet wounds to the head. Literally scores of bodies were found along the Banda Aceh to Medan highway in the second half of 1990. Other reports from North Aceh spoke of civilians being executed along the edge of a deep ravine, their bodies left to fall into the pit where a bulldozer would cover them with dirt and rubble. Soldiers conducted public executions in the town of Sigli. Bodies turned up on a daily basis or were sometimes buried with a leg or an arm showing above ground to ensure discovery. The deaths became so common that, as one human rights lawyer told Reuters in November 1990, 'It's got to the point where villagers say they are bored of having to bury the bodies they fish out of the river. It happens every day in some areas.'

But there were several layers to the campaign to destroy the rebels. The 'mysterious killings' and the public intimidation of leaving the corpses for all to see was accompanied by widespread arrests of Acehnese people in the countryside. In December 1990, the ANSLF issued a press release, quoted by the Indonesian human rights NGO, TAPOL, which stated that internment camps had been established by the military in 13 different locations from Banda Aceh through to Medan in North Sumatra. The military were holding up to 1000 people in each camp at any one time. The ANSLF claimed hundreds of people had been removed from the camps at night and executed.

At the same time, the formation of 'self-defence units', or militia groups, was being promoted among those villagers not arrested. Amnesty International identified one group established in East Aceh in August 1990, called *Laskar Rakyat* (People's Militia). According to Amnesty, they were given training and armed with knives and machetes, and told to act against suspected rebels. The militia group arrested 80 suspected rebels within the first two weeks of operation and handed them over to the military. Other groups were soon set up, with names such as *Bela Negara* (Defend the Nation) and *Ksatria Unit Penegak Pancasila* (Noble Warriors for Upholding Pancasila). They were given authority to kill suspected rebels, as the new Aceh military commander, Major General Pramono, told *Tempo* magazine in November: 'I have told the community, if you find a terrorist, kill him. There's no need to investigate him. Don't let people be the victims. If they don't do as you order them, shoot them on the spot or butcher them.'

The same strategy had been used in East Timor, forcing communities to turn on the rebels among them. There were always poor transmigrants from other parts of Indonesia who could be relied on to join such groups for financial gain, and the rest of the community – including many who had been detained for suspected rebel connections – was then forced to join such groups to prove their loyalty.

The military declared it would crush the rebels by the end of the year. But the killings continued into 1991. On a visit to the province in 1991, journalist Sonny Inbaraj reported the massacre of 150 villagers in Kota Makmur in North Aceh in November the previous year. They had been forced to line up and shot at point-blank range. Their bodies were then dumped in a pit constructed by the military especially for that purpose. According to rebel sources Inbaraj had quoted, the number of fighters in the field had increased to 750 armed men; he had also received documents from the rebels that showed 600 had done training in Libya.

Far from 'crushing' the insurgency, the tactics of the military only forced the population to support the rebels, and instilled in thousands of young men the thirst for revenge against the widespread abuses visited upon them and their families.

In 1993, Amnesty International issued a report on the violence that stated at least 2000 civilians had been killed in Aceh since the start of the campaign, and that more than 1000 had been subject to torture and detention by the armed forces of Indonesia.

It qualified these figures by saying that no thorough and impartial investigations had been carried out. The report cited the rebels' own estimate of 20,000 dead in those first three years of the military operation since 1989, and put independent observers in Aceh as citing the figure at 10,000. The lack of access to Aceh by any human rights groups meant that Amnesty could only quote the figure of 2000 from the testimonies of eyewitnesses and relatives their personnel had interviewed or who had been interviewed by other human rights organisations.

The comprehensive report detailed individual cases of torture, murder, rape and arbitrary imprisonment by the Indonesian security forces. It gave details of the campaign of mysterious killings and the existence of mass graves. It concluded, 'political killing may be a central part of Indonesian government policy'.

None of the recommendations of the report, such as the further investigation of the atrocities in Aceh and the accountability and prosecution of those involved, was ever carried out. And because access to Aceh was denied to journalists and human rights workers for the five years following the publication of the Amnesty report in 1993, the issue remained off the international agenda until the Acehnese themselves began to exhume the bodies in 1998.

Australian photographer David Dave Parker was dozing in the front seat as we came around the corner. I reached over and tapped him on the shoulder. Standing in the middle of the road, Brimob troops were aiming their guns at the oncoming traffic. Some had red headscarves covering the lower half of their faces, and they were positioned three or so metres apart, staggered along the bitumen of the Medan to Banda Aceh highway. On the edge of the road, a minibus was being searched and the occupants were standing to one side – guns aimed at them – as their belongings were searched. Our car stopped as ordered and two Brimob soldiers peered in the front windows, one on either side, with their guns pointing inside. We got out of the car and the terror on the faces of our driver and the young female Acehnese translator dissolved any bravado Dave or I had about having been through similar situations in other parts of

Indonesia. The young Brimob soldiers demanded to see our documents then studied them. Our press cards, issued in Jakarta, brought more barked questions, and our driver was now sweating and keeping up a nervous stream of explanations to the Brimob soldiers. Dave had a camera around his neck and took a few quick shots. The soldiers examining the documents didn't seem to notice or care. From across the street there was a shout and an older non-commissioned officer (a sergeant or a corporal) came charging over, yelling and pointing his gun at Dave, demanding he take the film out of his camera. At first Dave tried to protest, and I joined in saying we were press and pointing to the passes still in the hands of the other troops. The translator and the driver started talking and the enraged NCO (noncommissioned officer) pointed his weapon at Dave and slammed the bolt back, loading in a round with a loud metallic clunk, and there was total silence.

We all stood there on the hot road with our hands raised. The fury of the NCO whose authority had been challenged in front of the Acehnese by the foreign photographer – who stood about 30 centimetres taller than him – was obvious. The soldiers checking our documents had taken a step back and were now pointing their weapons at us with impassive faces. And the NCO was glaring up at Dave with his weapon aimed directly at his chest.

To everyone's relief, the NCO repeated his demand for the film in a loud voice strangely constricted by anger. We all smiled and Dave made a big show of opening his camera and handing over the film. The NCO appeared satisfied, and as Dave entered into another argument trying to prevent the two soldiers from taking his unused film, they told us to get out of there; they seemed as rattled by their superior's outburst as we were.

Back in the car, it was obvious the driver and the translator couldn't wait to get away. Despite it being Ramadan, the driver smoked one of my cigarettes and the translator looked straight ahead with a shocked, expressionless face. Dave admitted that he'd managed to save the shots he'd taken at the roadblock – he'd given them some other film – but doubted they would show much as he'd shot without even looking.

The incident had shocked us into realising the futility of our official press accreditation, which we had obtained after months of waiting back in Australia and days of running around in Jakarta. Despite having permission to travel to Aceh from the national police chief in Jakarta and the office of Indonesian Foreign Affairs, all the accreditation really seemed to have achieved was to let the officials know exactly when we were going to Aceh. It seemed that we would have had more freedom and aroused less suspicion if we'd been travelling on tourist visas.

Dave pointed out that there was a reason why no good photos came out of Aceh – and that we had been comparatively lucky at the roadblock. In that year, 2001, reporters had been regularly assaulted on the Banda Aceh to Medan highway. Correspondents from Reuters had been ordered from their cars at gunpoint and forced to lie on the ground while their identities were checked. A Fairfax journalist and his photographer had been harassed and their translator assaulted; the journalist's working visa was later revoked for what he had written while in Aceh. Torgeir Norling, a Norwegian freelancer, had been detained and expelled from Indonesia for working on a tourist visa in Aceh. They had hauled him off a bus, questioned him for five hours and kept him overnight. After nervous guards outside his door shot gunfire into the night to ward off GAM attacks, he was released and told to leave Aceh immediately. He passed through burning villages, empty except for TNI squads moving in formation. That was what he was not supposed to see.

An American photographer, Thomas Dallal, had also encountered trouble in November 1999 in the West Aceh town of Lamno. All of a sudden, about 20 TNI soldiers appeared, shooting wildly. Apparently there had just been an attack on the TNI by GAM and one of their men had been wounded. Discovering Dallal and a Japanese colleague in a street near where the attack had taken place, they screamed at them, fired above their heads, kicked them and hit them with their rifle butts. They threatened them and called them 'dirty journalists' as they marched them down an alley to what Dallal thought would be their execution. Luckily for the foreigners, a local shopkeeper was identified by the wounded man, and the soldiers began beating him, deflecting the anger from the American and Japanese men, who were told by the soldiers to get out of there as soon as possible. They returned to their car to find it full of bullet holes.

As the conflict intensified throughout the year 2001, foreign journalists' attempts to get into the field in Aceh were met with a bloodyminded refusal by the Indonesian military to accept that their government was allowing reporters from Jakarta to travel to Aceh. As far as the military in Aceh were concerned, foreign reporters were the enemy and were to be kept well away from any operations. When the Indonesian police colonel in

Jakarta handed us our official permission letter for our visit to Aceh, he said with a smile, 'This should be fine for the police, but I don't know if it will help with the army.'

We had entered Aceh by road from Medan the day before and the main difference I noticed from the previous December was the presence of tanks dug into position under camouflage netting on the side of the road. The terrorist attacks of September 11, 2001 had diverted any attention there had been from the outside world on Aceh, and it appeared the Indonesian military had responded by going on the offensive. The highway was now back in their hands. With the conflict in Afghanistan playing out in December 2001, media interest in Aceh, despite the past year having been the bloodiest since the end of the Suharto era, was very low.

All the indicators in Aceh were that, with the outside world distracted, the situation had deteriorated. In Lhokseumahwe you could still hear the sound of gunfire at night and the streets were deserted. In the evening, in the centre of town, the military and police were present with more force than ever and even Indonesians in civilian clothes would drive past and laughingly show the foreign reporters their pistols or small machine guns. There was an arrogance in the Indonesian presence that hadn't been there the previous year. Now with more troops, the end of the so-called humanitarian pause and the resumption of hostilities under Wahid's Presidential Decree Number Four, 2001, in April, the Indonesians in Aceh were re-asserting themselves. The decree had authorised the resumption of hostilities against GAM mainly in response to the lost revenues suffered by the central government after GAM, had successfully shut down the ExxonMobil PT Arun Liquefied Natural Gas Plant near

Lhokseumahwe for five weeks in March and April.

In Lhokseumahwe Dave and I hired a car and a driver and headed north. The young daughter of the vehicle's owner wanted to come along as a translator for us and we agreed. She seemed confident that there would be no problems, and she was a bit in awe of the press and kept asking why we didn't mark the car with tape like the CNN reporters did.

Travelling through the Pidie district on the way to Banda Aceh, Dave told me how in late 1999 he had met the leader of GAM, Tengku Abdullah Syafei, in a village just off the side of the highway. Back then, there had not been much of an Indonesian military presence in the area and he had just stopped at a village and asked around. It turned out that it was the GAM leader's local village and he was led to him by men in civilian clothes on motorbikes and carrying guns.

We passed a mosque where in 1999 refugees from areas where there had been fighting had sought shelter with GAM protection. Requests to stop the car and have a look around were greeted with a terrified expression from the driver and the translator's gentle suggestion that this would not be a good idea. Aside from constant convoys of military trucks and the occasional armed post, there didn't seem to be many people around and most of the houses looked deserted. It was then, somewhere before Sigli on the road heading north, that we hit the Brimob roadblock. After that it was obvious our translator just wanted to get rid of us and the driver just wanted to get his car safely back to Lhokseumahwe before it got dark.

OUTSIDE THE hotel in the middle of Banda Aceh, an Indonesian sergeant with wild bloodshot eyes talked of snipers. The soldiers had killed two of them that morning, he said. With an imaginary gun, he took aim at the top floor of a nearby building and demonstrated how his men had done it. He was obviously slightly unhinged or on drugs, or not dealing with the fact that here, in the middle of Banda Aceh, outside his well-protected barracks, someone had tried to kill him. Or maybe it was cumulative and happened every day and the guy had simply lost it.

Acehnese civilians avoided the Indonesian sergeant by crossing the street as he yelled about the recent combat to Dave and me. We had just arrived and had been walking down the street. His own Indonesian military comrades just laughed and refused to come out of their sandbagged post that was covered in cyclone wire as grenade protection. Situated in the middle of the main shopping district, previously the military post had been a small bench for soldiers to occasionally sit on.

The sergeant's hysteria was the only indication that something had happened in town that day. The bodies of those killed had been taken quickly to the morgue and then collected by the families. There were no funerals planned because they would draw a response from the military. Local human rights workers and journalists had no choice but to accept the military claim that the dead men were armed members of the GAM separatist movement, and that was what was reported in the newspaper the next morning. One local photographer managed to get into the hospital morgue, but his photo of a bullet-riddled corpse on a stretcher didn't reveal anything about what had happened and, consequently, no newspapers or wire services used it. It was simply another incident that would pass with no official explanation.

We got an explanation of sorts a few days later when we met a local GAM commander on the outskirts of Banda Aceh. After a series of phone calls and text messages in the company of some very frightened and nervous local reporters, we got in touch with the leader. He was close by but we had to be quick. A trusted driver was found and we went to meet him. We simply had to drive down the main street past the military barracks, with the soldiers manning their light machine guns, and past the Brimob headquarters with the armoured cars lined up out the front, then down a side street through some suburbs, and then we were out in the paddy fields.

A young man on a motorbike frantically waved down our vehicle and directed us along a small, raised dirt track built on a levy in the paddy fields, then he raced off in the other direction. We drove along slowly, feeling quite exposed on the bad track. By simply turning off the road we could not give any excuses to military we encountered, and the two Acehnese reporters with us were very nervous. We passed a small bridge and a man waved us forward from under it, then another man, who talked continuously into a hands-free mobile phone set-up, waved us down and ordered us to leave the vehicle and follow him on foot across the flooded rice field.

Less than a kilometre away there was a slight depression surrounded by reeds. A small, rough wooden-plank shack sat low in the waterlogged ground and outside it, sitting on palm frond matting to keep the mud off his immaculate clothes, sat Ayah Sofyan, the GAM spokesman for the Greater Aceh region that surrounds the capital. There were no guns visible, just the ever-present wearer of the mobile phone with the earpiece keeping up a constant dialogue with those watching the road.

Sofyan started by giving the figures. He claimed to represent 2000 men in Greater Aceh, out of a total GAM strength of 25,000 trained fighters throughout all of Aceh. The strongest area was North Aceh, near Lhokeumahwe, where he claimed there were as many as 6000 trained fighters under Sofyan Dawood. They had supplies of modern weapons – guns, mortars, grenade launchers – from Malaysia and Thailand. Mostly Russian weapons bought in Malaysia and Thailand by rich Acehnese abroad, he said. If the figures were not inflated, one got the impression that the majority of these fighters were like himself and his men who were present – unarmed or with their weapons well hidden, wearing civilian clothes and, for all intents and purposes, living normal lives among the population. He said they had no international support and, as he would repeat throughout the interview, 'GAM is not for war, we only want to survive'.

Ayah Sofyan was a typical GAM member. He had joined the movement in 1985 after having spent time working in Singapore and Malaysia. He said the worst time was the present, with the constant risk that was one of the consequences of being a spokesman. His motivation was, as he put it, feeling part of the Acehnese people: 'This movement is the Acehnese people.'

At the time, there was a concerted effort by the Indonesian authorities to somehow link the fight against GAM to the US war on terror post September 11. 'GAM can't accept it,' said Sofyan. 'The United States say they have nine countries on their list with terrorist connections and no GAM are on this list. Then the Indonesians say GAM is 25th on this list. But Indonesia has no basis for this. We can't accept we are terrorists. We never attack Jakarta. We just want our freedom. GAM just wants to survive in our own area. If we want to make bombs and act like terrorists, it is quite easy, but we don't want to behave like that.'

The real reason for the increased US support of Indonesian troops, said Sofyan, was to simply protect US assets in Aceh. 'For example, Exxon stopped their production this year. That is the reason why it is important the US will support the attack by the Indonesians,' he said. According to Sofyan, the Indonesian government was in trouble: 'In one position they put more troops here and they have more human rights abuses and the international community asks them why they use the military and not carry out peace talks if they want the funding from the IMF and so on. If there are still human rights abuses in Aceh, they get no support.'

In his view, the alternative for Indonesia was to take all the troops out of Aceh: 'If they take all the troops from Aceh in one day, all of Aceh will fly our red flag. That is the spirit of Aceh. Why? Because democracy in Aceh does not exist. If Indonesia were not here, the people can say they want independence.

'But right now, Indonesia make a trick. They can get funding if there is no fighting here, so they say Aceh is safe and there is no conflict. They say to the international community, we try dialogue, but the reality here is for you to see, like this morning a body was found near that bridge 400 metres from here.' He pointed back towards the road.

That morning, Sofyan's men had found a mutilated body near the bridge we had crossed to get to the GAM post. The night before, two cars had come from town, and in the morning there was a body. The commander didn't know who it was.

'Special autonomy and dialogue has not done anything,' he said. 'The international community should never believe Indonesian statements until they have observers in the field.' And then he repeated that Aceh would be safe and at peace if the Indonesian military left.

He was able to shed a little light on the shooting incident in Banda Aceh that had rattled the Indonesian sergeant. One of Sofyan's men, Sansor, had indeed shot and wounded two Indonesian military who were among a group of 30 searching for him and surrounding the building he was in near the Baiturrahman mosque. The same group then carried out a sweep in the area and the people ran to the mosque. One of those running, Zulkri, a civilian, was shot and died. He was shot 'because of the ratio of troops' Sofyan said. He was thrown together with the other body and they were both said to be GAM.

'The military claim every ordinary person they kill is GAM. They put bullets in the bodies' pockets, or guns, and claim they are GAM,' Sofyan said, adding he had lost about 30 of his own troops in Banda Aceh in the last three years.

Sofyan delivered his story in a deadpan way, as if he was surprised to be asked about the incident. His minders talked nervously on their mobile phones and Sofyan glanced at them constantly for any indication that we might be interrupted by the military. The light was fading, he terminated the interview abruptly and we headed back to the car.

His fears were not groundless. Almost six months to the day after that interview, Sofyan was ambushed and fatally wounded in a raid on a similar hideout 12 kilometres from Banda Aceh. As when we had met him, he was unarmed and only some GAM documents were found with him. He was taken to the police hospital in Banda Aceh where, according to Sofyan Dawood, another GAM spokesman, he died after being tortured and denied medical care. The Aceh police commissioner, Suparwoto, told the press Ayah Sofyan had been killed instantly in the raid when 15 police stormed the hideout and shot him in the waist.

THE DAY I visited Feisal Hamdi at the office of the Aceh NGO Coalition for Human Rights (*Koalisi Ham*), he had had only one visitor – the wife of a 25-year-old fruitseller from the capital who had been kidnapped in the middle of the day in Banda Aceh. The missing man had been selling fruit by the roadside when four men in plain clothes pulled up in an Isuzu minibus. At first they impersonated buyers, asking the price of his fruit, then they grabbed him and took him away. There was no other information. She had already lost one husband, in 1990, in East Aceh. She'd informed the human rights groups about his death then and she thought she had better do it again this time. There was, of course, nothing Feisal Hamdi could do. She was the only person who had been brave enough to approach the office recently to report a relative missing, and Hamdi was telling the story to illustrate the way things had changed for his organisation.

'If you look at the data,' he said, indicating the confusing printed graphs and statistics he was handing me across the table, 'you can see there has been a decrease in the number of incidents since the beginning of the operation in April. My figures show a decrease in incidents because people are afraid to report them now.

'TNI are shooting civilians – summary killings, involuntary detention. TNI are responsible for most of this and the Polri [Indonesian police], well, the counterinsurgency operation is led by Polri, in theory.

'The reality is, the TNI do what they want. Frequently something happens after a gunfight. There is an attack of the guerrillas against the police. They [the military] attack the villages, they beat and assault the people and torch the house.

'There is no change since Suharto, Habibie, Wahid and Megawati – only an increase this year in the level of violence. Massacres still happen . . . the last one was in East Aceh, more than 30 plantation workers. There is no statement saying this was done by the army, perpetrated by TNI. The soldiers were seeking information and taking revenge for soldiers killed.'

That massacre had happened on August 9, 2001, at a palm oil plantation owned by PT Bumi Flora at a place called Julok in East Aceh, and had received some media attention. A group of 20 soldiers had approached the plantation that morning and ordered the male workers out of their barracks. They were all told to squat on the ground with their hands on their heads. They were then shot dead. The wife of one of the dead men later told a local government fact-finding team investigating the killings: 'It was the military who did the shooting. It was not possible that GAM did it. They could not speak Acehnese. They asked me, "Are these Acehnese or Javanese?" I said, Acehnese. They only nodded their heads and did not speak more.'

The military claimed GAM carried out the killing, and GAM blamed the military, saying it was a reprisal for an attack they had carried out a few days earlier at a nearby military post. No further investigations or prosecutions were carried out.

A new development in the situation, according to Hamdi, was the increased use of theft and extortion by the military in plain clothes. He told the story of how a bus had recently been held up near the airport in Banda Aceh by armed men wearing civilian clothes and balaclavas. After relieving the passengers of their money, jewellery, watches and mobile phones, one of the men declared, with a heavy Batak (North Sumatran) accent, 'If we don't die here we shall leave rich.' Coincidentally, the Brimob unit stationed near the scene of the crime was about to be rotated back to its base in North Sumatra, with particularly bad consequences for the locals – theft and extortion was common when soldiers were leaving and when the new troops arrived. Because the new troops don't know the local people, they tend to be 'highly suspicious', and more civilian casualties result.

THE NATURE of the operations against GAM had become more sophisticated in the second half of 2001, according to Feisal Hamdi. There were more than 200 Kopassus personnel stationed in the province, although not officially. 'The people recognise them from the DOM era,' said Hamdi. 'Sometimes now they are Brimob or TNI.'

Reports from the six legal aid posts in Aceh indicate that the military and the police already knew the targets they wanted shot. INTEL (Indonesian state intelligence), Hamdi said, had succeeded in infiltrating the population right down to the village level, and GAM had been forced to move further into the forest.

GAM was guilty of abuses, he said, but in terms of scale they were not anywhere near what the military and police were conducting. For example, when the coordinator of the legal aid post in South Aceh was detained by some GAM troops at a roadblock in South Aceh, they searched his car and found a book on the autonomy proposal. He was escorted to meet the commander and threatened at gunpoint, but after explaining he was a lawyer and needed the book for research, he was released. But, Hamdi said, if GAM find real TNI at their roadblocks, 'they will kill them'.

However, almost on a daily basis, according to Hamdi, incidents like the following one involving Brimob were occuring. One day in early December 2001, on the remote west coast road between South Aceh and West Aceh, Brimob soldiers stopped a bus for a routine check. One young passenger had a bag of new trousers he was taking to the capital to sell. The soldiers took the bag, inspected it, but didn't give it back. So the young man stepped forward from the line the passengers had been forced to form. 'What you want, hot shit tough guy?' one Brimob soldier asked and slashed the passenger's arm with a knife. Then, as the young man tried to get back onto the bus, two more police – apparently drunk– joined in. One stabbed him in the back of the head and the other dragged him onto the bus and told him to get going.

By the end of 2001, the number of deaths from the conflict in Aceh was calculated by human rights workers and the media to be at least 1700 for that year alone; the victims were mostly civilian.

⊢⊷⊶⊙⊷⊶⊣

THE THREE GAM negotiators lounged in their room at the Kuala Tripa as though they were in a prison cell, which effectively they were. 'Our status now? Our status is detainees,' said Teuku Kamaruzzaman. There were two others with him, Amni Marzuki and Amdi Hamdani.

'They arrested us here at the office. We were detained for 40 days. We think they treated us inhumanely,' he continued. 'Amdi here, they pointed a gun at his chest and beat him, and the first night they threw water and dung on him.' Amdi looked up from where he was lying on the bed with a tired expression.

They had been arrested at the hotel for separatism after the talks broke down in April – whilst they were still supposed to be under the protection of the HDC as the official negotiation team. One of the other members of the team I had met last time, Zulfani, was now dead – shot by troops searching for him in his own backyard or, if you believed the authorities, shot dead fleeing a roadblock and carrying a pistol on October 14. He had avoided being arrested along with the other negotiators because he hadn't been present when the police came. Those who were and had been arrested had since not been allowed to leave the hotel, but were still supposed to be participating in the security monitoring committee that was formed by the HDC to oversee the humanitarian pause, which had ended in April with Wahid's decree. The situation itself was farcical. The committee still existed – the humanitarian pause didn't.

The negotiators said the process was deadlocked. It was very difficult for the HDC's security monitoring team to work in the current environment. They were supposed to be sending data on the situation to the HDC, to NGOs and foreign governments, but often they had no choice but to accept the version given by the TNI.

There was an atmosphere of tired resignation in the room. Kamaruzzaman kept talking but Amdi lay on the bed and Amni slouched in the chair. 'We still think the conflict should be solved at the negotiating table. We are aware we cannot solve conflict while the Megawati policy is that, publicly, they say they are willing to talk, but what they do in the field is different, and we continue to see that.

'It is impossible for the TNI to carry out the operation without the decree. [Wahid's decree authorising military action was extended by Megawati in October 2001.] But Megawati can't control what the army does here.

'What they do here is kill their own citizens and it will not be changed and it has not for a long time. The TNI still uses the same approach. So we believe their doctrine is fascism. The first Indonesian soldiers were trained by the Japanese and the practice of fascism will continue to happen here. It is war. They will do everything to defend the unity, to retain Aceh, it is very integral to Indonesia so they will do all they can.'

Kamaruzzaman was a practising lawyer in Banda Aceh, educated under the Indonesians. He had joined GAM as their negotiator in 1998 and was seen as something of a moderate. It was disturbing to hear him talk with such despair about the situation. 'For the Indonesian government, it is okay to do anything to make Aceh a part of Indonesia,' he continued. 'Violations of human rights? In DOM there was no follow-up to any of these. It is important for the international community to help. Lots of innocent people will be killed. The international community should be aware. We have the same rights. The international community must save the Acehnese.'

He went on to say how in 1993 Hasan Di Tiro had tried to get the UN to intervene on the basis of the widespread humanitarian abuse going on in Aceh at that time, but he had made no headway. The first international interest came with the HDC in 2000 but according to Kamarruzaman, they could not do anything.

The current operation, he said, would not wipe out GAM in the field: 'Basically, the situation is not changing. We use the weapons to defend ourselves, they use more tanks, we use guerrilla methods – it is the innocent civilians who get killed.'

Now, Kamaruzzaman said, the TNI had basically 'made conflict their business'. He talked of how certain generals had sent the Laskar Jihad fighters to Maluku and to Poso in Sulawesi in 2000 and 2001 to heat up the conflicts for the purpose of increasing their own influence. 'They make the conflict and they also play the conflict,' he said.

In the case of Aceh, when the military guarding the Exxon plant near Lhokseumahwe began aggressive sweeps against the GAM units in the area early in 2001, the GAM representatives in the HDC complained to the Indonesian police appointed to the same HDC security monitoring committee as part of the humanitarian pause. The police response was that they couldn't control this group of military, who were under North Sumatran command – the command that Exxon pays for the security of the plant. The disturbances around the plant created by the TNI were part of the negotiating strategy they used with Exxon, which, according to Kamaruzzaman, employs four battalions to protect its assets.

It was GAM's response to the provocations of the Indonesian military, eager to prove their worth to Exxon, that closed down the plant in March; an action that prompted Wahid to grant the TNI more powers to suppress GAM in his Presidential Decree Number Four, issued in April – powers that in turn authorised the onslaught of 2001.

Part of the TNI operation was to activate the militia groups that had been formed in Aceh, some as early as 1998. Javanese transmigrants were recruited into an organisation called *Puja Kusuma*, which had close relations with the military in central Aceh, who, from 2000 onwards, had a training camp in a place called Gunung Jati in the Singin subdistrict of Central Aceh. There were clashes there between the Acehnese and the militia in June, July and August of 2001, and then the TNI gave the militia orders to destroy the houses of local Acehnese people. According to GAM, this action created 25,000 internally displaced people in the Pidie and Lhokseumahwe areas, as the people fled towards the coast. 'The TNI force them to create conflict in their own villages by joining *Pemuda Panca Marga* [a militia group]', said Kamaruzzaman.

This program was under the command of Major General Igede Purnama from Kodam Medan, who had recently been reassigned from Bali, and Ari Kumaat from Bakin in Jakarta. The weapons, M-16s and homemade weapons, a familiar combination from East Timor's militia, had been distributed in mid-2001 by the local military commands in Central Aceh.

'The TNI say the violence is people defending themselves,' said Amni who was now getting interested in the conversation. 'Some speak Acehnese and they tell the people to say it is GAM burning the houses. But the people know it is not GAM.' He produced a report from two days earlier in the village of Tinkom in Central Aceh. Military from the Sri Wijaya battalion, based in Palembang in South Sumatra, visited the village, rounded up the people and told them to join the militia in their own interest and to maintain order. 'They did this in 1990 in DOM,' said Amni. 'The TNI called them to go to the militia base to report. They are doing things they have done before. They call them "*Jagu Java*". The people either join or have to leave. If they leave, the militia occupy the farm. There is a lot of coffee in that area.'

The significance of the emergence of militias in Central Aceh for GAM wasn't apparent at the time, and it was given barely any attention by the media. The almost daily occurrence of clashes and the ongoing civilian deaths, on average five a day in that period, took up what small international coverage there was of Aceh. The ambush and death of Greater Aceh GAM operational commander Sidom Apui (direct commander of Ayah Sofyan) and three of his men on December 12 was one such item on the wires.

Another typical action at this time was the incident in North Aceh in the village of Bukit Ujing in mid-November 2001. There was a clash between GAM and the military. GAM retreated and the village was shelled. Six civilians, including a small child, were killed. More often, however, there were comparatively minor incidents that nobody would bother reporting, which cumulatively produced a picture of widespread repression. In Greater Aceh alone in the two days of December 9 and 10, one civilian was shot dead while praying, another was shot and severely wounded, five were beaten and seriously injured, and three were arrested (never to be heard of again) – all in the course of a normal two-day search operation by the military and police. Another report from December 10 details a civilian being beaten, arrested and robbed by the police for refusing to hand over his money when a public bus he was on was stopped at a roadblock.

The frustrating thing was that these reports only illustrated a fragment of what was going on, and the only people prepared to speak the truth to a reporter were the very ones who were the targets of these operations.

Our plans to get into the field with GAM were complicated by the death of the leader closest to the capital. After gathering for the December 4 declaration of independence anniversary, many of the GAM groups had gone to ground, and Dave and I took a bus down to Sigli, 112 kilometres south of the capital, to try and make contact with some people there.

After an uneventful trip from Banda Aceh to Sigli, we waited for our contact at the bus station, trying to keep out of sight of the TNI troops who wandered around looking bored with their hands on their weapons. Despite the conflict, it was still not completely unusual for the occasional tourist to be travelling north to Pulau Weh or south to Medan, and people left us alone. When our contact, Ahmad, finally arrived, he chose the most comically attention-grabbing transport – three decrepit motorcycle *becaks*, where the passenger sits in a large open sidecar. In a procession that brought stares from the soldiers we had been trying to avoid, we roared off through the crowd into the narrow side streets of the town.

Ahmad's local GAM organiser hadn't been answering his phone, and Ahmad had no idea what to do with a couple of foreigners in a town full of soldiers and staring people, so he left us at the local office of PBHAM (*Pas Bantuan Hukum dan Hak Asasi Manusia Aceh*), a legal aid NGO. On the wall of the waiting room there was a huge portrait painted roughly on a cloth banner. It was of Suprin Sulaiman, a lawyer, who had been killed by Brimob for visiting a client – a woman who had been raped by Brimob. He was killed in March 2001, along with two other human rights workers, on the way back from interviewing the woman in South Aceh. The woman later changed her story to say she had been raped by GAM. Sulaiman and the two others were all members of the local security monitoring team for the HDC cease-fire committee back in the capital and were supposed to be protected against violence.

The waiting room quickly filled with people, all of whom were eager to talk about the current situation. Only one, Abdul Multali, was willing to give his name. It didn't bother him to be identified, he said. He had already been arrested once this year.

'The situation in Aceh now is this,' said Multali, 'important leaders get killed. Ordinary people get killed. People with protection get killed. Human rights investigators and lawyers get killed. In general, we can say that TNI and Brimob don't like us who are involved in humanitarian work.' He smiled wryly.

'I was arrested by the intelligence of the TNI in April,' he continued. 'They said I was a member of GAM. I said I was a human rights worker, and they said it was the same thing.

'Again last week there was an armed clash between TNI and GAM, and we tried to get there. The TNI kicked and punched us and pulled us out of our cars when we said we had nothing to do with GAM. They said they didn't care whether we were

GAM or human rights workers, and beat us anyway.'

Multali said the figures for human rights abuses in the Pidie district had declined since more TNI had arrived in the previous four months. 'It is because we don't dare go out in the field to get reports. Because of what happens,' he said, nodding towards the portrait of the dead lawyer, his former boss, on the wall.

Another lawyer, who wouldn't be named, told us that the Indonesian police would forbid local people from coming to the legal aid office. 'So victims of violence from Brimob have to make a report to Brimob if they want the matter investigated,' he said. 'They threaten the victims. They won't come and see us. They are afraid.'

He talked of a situation of deeply embedded corruption. Whether a person was found guilty or not guilty in the local courts, it would still cost at least 1 million rupiah (approximately AUD$200) to secure his or her release from custody. Those detained were often beaten until they admitted some link to GAM. 'If they suspect you are a member of GAM,' he said, 'you have to admit you are or it will be bad for you. They make you admit anyway by torturing you. There was one incident with a schoolteacher in Mutiara. They suspected him and went to his house and they beat him without any questions in front of his wife. But we know he is not GAM. He is a teacher.'

He said the increased presence of TNI and Brimob in the Pidie district had led to the widespread extortion of local businesses and civilians by the security forces, as well as violence. The roadblocks on all major roads where money was demanded were only the most visible form of this.

The area around the Pidie district was one of the worst for this kind of behaviour. It was impossible to say how many TNI soldiers were based there because the new arrivals didn't set up permanent camps; they moved around constantly on operations. Two days previously, some people had been arrested in the neighbouring Mutiara district and the lawyers were trying to arrange their release. The day before in Bireuen, one member of GAM was arrested by the TNI and the people who saw it were kicked and beaten. 'They said he was GAM, but we don't know,' said the lawyer.

Two weeks before, in the Inda Raja subdistrict, the TNI raided a house and killed two GAM suspects and arrested eight people, only two of whom had since been released. 'Once a prisoner escapes from them, TNI kills them on the spot in front of the public. This scares people. The psychological terror stops people reporting incidents,' said the lawyer. 'Sometimes it is difficult for us to get a report in this situation. There is a lot of risk to our volunteer investigators.'

Still, they managed to work, or to try to keep working. One man, a volunteer investigator, insisted on lifting his shirt to show us the bullet scars from when he was arrested, shot and beaten by the TNI in 1994, during the DOM era. Dave obliged him by photographing his scars, which by then were little more than small circular mounds of scar tissue, like healed tropical sores. He was accused of being GAM and had denied it and was tortured. The bullet fragments were still inside his body, he said. He still wasn't GAM. He was committed to this dangerous unpaid job for no other reason than the desire for the truth be known, and in this area it was inevitable that, sooner or later, he would become a victim of the violence he was trying to document.

The Indonesian strategy was clearly to terrorise the population into silence, and organisations such as this one, which worked to break that silence and protect the people from abuses, were targets. It was a very literal manifestation of 'shooting the messenger'.

The hoped-for meeting with the local GAM people in Sigli fell through and we managed to get onto a minibus that was leaving town before dusk. It was still Ramadan and the bus pulled over at almost exactly the appointed time for the end of the fast. After eating, the other passengers seemed to relax and became more talkative. After every roadblock a great deal of discussion went on about how much different types of vehicles had to hand over to whom. Local police seemed to get the least, followed by territorial troops and then Brimob. If you were pulled over by anyone else, namely Kostrad or the marines, you would be searched and have to get off the bus. If it was Kopassus, one passenger joked, you were in trouble unless you promised to later say it was GAM that pulled the bus over.

Along that 112-kilometre stretch of road from Sigli to Banda Aceh, I counted 28 military and police posts or roadblocks; there were probably more that I didn't see because it was dark or because they were stationed off the road.

As we approached one, the driver would either slow down and wave or stop and hand over some money. It seemed almost random, but there was an etiquette and an expectation of money at some roadblocks or posts and not at others. The people seemed to learn the ever-changing rules and adjusted to them, and a kind of normal life – interrupted by search-and-destroy missions by Indonesian soldiers in their own streets and villages, constant arrests and killings, demands for money, and frequent gunfights between both sides – existed.

In the last few days before the end of the fasting month, everything in Aceh seemed to stop. Shops and offices were closed. There was no transport available. There was nowhere to get anything to eat. People left the towns in droves to return to their villages and spend the Lebaran holidays at the end of fasting with their families. Despite the fighting and presence of Indonesian military in the countryside and the lack of security, people still left, and for the last two days of the fasting month the streets of Banda Aceh were empty. This happens all over Indonesia, but in Aceh – due to the population's extreme devotion to Islam – the shutdown is complete. Our constant attempts to organise meetings with GAM at this time were met with: 'It's Lebaran, the fighters will be going home to their families to observe the holiday. Wait.' In fact, the local papers announced that the fighting would cease for Lebaran. The military commanders' assurances were matched by similar statements from GAM, and for a day or two, there were no attacks by either side.

On the day the fasting finished, I went to the GAM room at the Kuala Tripa. Because they were unable to leave the hotel, the representatives' families had brought the feast there. The small hotel room was filled with food – fish, chicken, beef and vegetable dishes all cooked in spices and served with rice; there were colourful juices, cakes, bowls of nuts and rich, dark coffee. The traditional Acehnese food was served by the wives of the representatives, who were now laying back and enjoying themselves.

Although it still felt like visiting day at a low-security jail, the atmosphere was relaxed, for once, despite the subject of the conversation. 'The policy of the TNI,' Kamaruzzaman began, 'is they are preparing for a big operation in Aceh. They want to make a state of emergency and declare martial law.

'The stronger the chances of dialogue, the more intense the military operation here. That is what we expect. The process of dialogue is at an impasse. They plan to sabotage the process of dialogue in Aceh.'

After talking about it some more, he expressed his frustration with the whole HDC effort. He said they were allowing themselves to be used by the Indonesians to maintain the façade that they were trying to achieve peace through negotiation. It meant Indonesia could continue military operations on the ground and still say it was trying to bring peace to Aceh.

The HDC, for their part, were very hard to find in Banda Aceh at the time. Their low-key approach was so low key that they seemed, for the time being at least, to have disappeared altogether. They had a policy of not talking to the press, so they avoided me and Dave whenever our paths crossed, usually in the dining room of the Kuala Tripa. There wasn't any other foreign press in Aceh at that time and, to be honest, sitting in our cheap hotel room watching the news of the Americans attacking Tora Bora in Afghanistan, we began to feel the chances of selling stories and photos of an Islamic rebellion against a US ally rather slim. I think it was the intractable nature of the situation, with no solution in sight bar endless outrages against the civilian population by a military with an already atrocious record, that made editors and journalists reluctant to cover Aceh. There was also the fact that it was bloody dangerous and difficult to get out into the field; to get any outstanding images that would grab attention was near-impossible in a conflict that was directed against civilians in remote areas and carried out in a way that kept it hidden from attention.

There was one other foreigner there at that time, however. Lesley McCulloch, a Scottish-born academic, then working for the University of Tasmania, was trying to document what was happening to the Acehnese people in the countryside. She had spent some time there the previous year and was back for a two-month stint researching the military and their relation to business and also doing some reporting. On her visit the previous November, she told us, she had seen people shot in the street at the time of the attempt to hold another mass rally. She talked of how they had loaded wounded people onto military trucks in the centre of town. The enormity of what was going on in Aceh was not at all lost on her, as it was on some other foreigners who visited. And her connections with the Acehnese were already attracting the attention of the Indonesian INTEL operatives, who seemed to follow any foreigner (and with so few foreigners about, it was not hard for them to keep track of what people were doing).

In Banda Aceh, you always had the sense that your movements were being closely watched. Lesley, Dave and I would sit at an open-air restaurant and talk about the situation, and there was always someone listening or moving closer to catch what we were saying. Beneath the veneer of normality, there was a hostility

towards foreigners from the Indonesian businessmen and officials in the capital that expressed itself in a hundred small ways.
Knowing that you were a journalist, the attitude of many
Indonesians in Aceh was that you were there to destroy their
country, or at least make money from it, and even small things
like booking an air ticket or buying a meal became difficult
exercises. This was because many Indonesians in Banda Aceh felt
threatened by the current events and by GAM.

At that time in Indonesia under Megawati there was a kind
of state-led resurgence in pride for the military. Events like a
celebrity-studded Dangdut concert (a concert where the
Bollywood-inspired music that is very popular in Indonesia is
performed) to thousands of soldiers in Java were dedicated to
the troops in Aceh and simulcast on Banda Aceh television. On
a visit to the troops in Aceh to raise morale before the Idul Fitri
Muslim holiday, Kostrad Commander, Lieutenant General
Ryamizard Ryacudu, told the *Jakarta Post*, 'Remember, the
people love TNI. It's not true what some people say, that TNI
is not wanted here.' He told the troops in Aceh they were
carrying out state duty, to defend the Unitary Republic of
Indonesia against armed separatists. He visited Takengon, the
capital of Central Aceh, in the presence of the Kopassus chief.
Not suprisingly, community leaders in the area reportedly
requested the generals to provide more TNI in their area, not
less. But the community leaders introduced to the General
would hardly say otherwise, at least not to the press. In
Megawati's now often-quoted statement – made in an address
to military leaders and thousands of troops in Jakarta to mark
Indonesian Armed Forces Day on December 29, 2001 – she

reinforced this pro-military trend. 'Suddenly we are aware . . . of the need of a force to protect our beloved nation and motherland from breaking up,' she said, and told her audience to respect the law in the course of their duty. 'With that as your guide, you can do your duty without worrying about being involved in human rights abuses . . . Do everything without doubts.'

There were no doubts in Aceh at that time. Over the next few days there were many signs that military operations had resumed after the brief pause for Lebaran. These included the reported covert night landings of three battalions of troops on the coast near Lhokseumahwe; tanks being used against civilians in operations; and the blocking of roads to villages in Central Aceh, where there was a burgeoning refugee situation. The death toll quickly returned to an average of five a day, and our planned meetings with GAM commanders in the field were postponed repeatedly due to military activity.

It had been announced in Jakarta in late November 2001 that a further 32,500 troops would be deployed to Aceh and Irian Jaya to suppress separatist sentiments, and the consequences of that decision were already being felt in Aceh. GAM put the combined TNI and police figures at 50,000 to 60,000; the NGOs put it at a minimum of 50,000; and the authorities themselves gave a combined total of 30,000 TNI and Polri personnel in Aceh.

The airport was full of military returning home. The soldiers seemed happy and talkative. They spoke about how they were fighting terrorists – in line with the new post-September 11 rhetoric. There was a great display of camaraderie and lots of yelling, farewells and back-slapping in the coffee shop. But the impressive display of weapons on the tables symbolised the insecurity the officers felt when outside of their barracks; automatic rifles, sub-machine guns and pistols sat alongside cups and saucers as the officers and their families ate and drank. Outside in the carpark, armed and alert soldiers stood guard in groups of two and three. On the tarmac, a group of soldiers was loading two coffins into the cargo hold of the Garuda commercial plane that flew out every day. We watched another soldier lying on a stretcher with an IV drip attached being carried up the stairs before we were allowed to board. They strapped the stretcher in across two seats at the back of the plane. He looked heavily drugged for the one-hour flight to Medan. The Indonesian military has always been reluctant to admit their casualties in Aceh.

According to Matt Davies – a former Australian military intelligence analyst who compiled an open-source study of Indonesian casualties in Aceh from official Indonesian police and military records, GAM statements and Indonesian media reports – between March and May of 2001, a total of 300 Indonesian police and military were killed in the 95 clashes that took place. His figures were more than ten times what the Indonesian authorities admitted to for the same period.

Other internal Indonesian police documents obtained by Davies in the course of his research revealed that from January 2000 until October 2001, 40 per cent of the 120 casualties recorded by the police in Aceh among its own people were listed mysteriously as 'ill died normally'. Whether that means Indonesian police were subject to an unexplained epidemic in

Aceh at the time or, more likely, the deaths were the result of gunshot wounds from unrecorded combat, the document showed how the Indonesian authorities concealed their own casualties from the public and their own organisations.

Davies' research also showed the targeting of high-ranking officials by GAM. From the year 2000 until mid-2003, Indonesian media and government sources have recorded the deaths of 14 district commanders, seven mid-ranking officers and seven regional police chiefs; one retired major general was also killed, along with a lieutenant colonel and 14 party politicians. Even the most senior Indonesian officials in Aceh were not safe from GAM, and this policy of killing officials acknowledged that many retired or active Indonesian military personnel worked closely with the Indonesian military in trying to suppress the support for independence in the wider population. So it was no surprise that, at the only airport in Aceh with direct flights to Jakarta, these officials were taking no chances.

As we were flying back to Medan and on to Jakarta, another plane went down in flames at Lhokseumahwe airport. It was an Indonesian military Hercules C-130 transport that was hit by ground fire then crashed through a fence before being completely destroyed. Several of the 90 Indonesian military troops on board were wounded, mainly with broken legs from the impact. GAM claimed they had shot the plane down in an operation that involved 150 troops. In a statement to Associated Press, GAM spokesman Amri Abdul Wahab said, 'We did it and we will do it again if the Indonesian military insists on sending more troops to Aceh.'

The military denied the plane had been hit by ground fire

and said its brakes had failed on landing, causing it to crash through a fence and burst into flame. It was a big loss to the Indonesian Air Force, which at the time had only 24 Hercules C-130 transports.

PART II

Winning Hearts and Minds: Murder, Negotiation and the Creation of Conflict

As 2002 began, it was obvious from the bellicose statements from Indonesia's leaders, civilian and military, that they believed 'separatism' was the main threat to their country, and that it could be crushed militarily. It didn't take long for their campaign to enjoy what they called a major success, either. On the morning of January 22, 20 soldiers from Kostrad surrounded a house in the tiny village of Sarah Panyang, about 20 kilometres east of Sigli. They ordered the occupants to surrender and then opened fire, starting a 20-minute gun battle. When it was over, GAM's military commander in Aceh, Tengku Abdullah Syafei, his pregnant wife and five bodyguards were found dead inside the building. The military later said they found a satellite phone and documents with the bodies; the documents included a recently dispatched letter from Aceh Governor Abdullah Puteh calling on the rebel leader to participate in peace talks in Aceh. It was this letter that GAM later claimed had led the troops to Abdullah Syafei's hideout. They claimed the bulky envelope in which the invitation was delivered had been kept by one of the two bodyguards who managed to escape, and was later found to contain a sophisticated homing device of the type used by special forces around the world – a suspicion later echoed by a former Australian army intelligence employee who told me that the success of the operation to kill Syafei and the way he was tracked and executed reeked of foreign, possibly US, assistance.

The bodies were taken to the hospital in Sigli to be identified. Local reporters were shown photos of Syafei's body, which had bullet wounds to the head and chest, and Syafei's brother, a schoolteacher, was brought in to identify the corpse.

Syafei had been the military commander of GAM in Aceh since the start of the guerrilla campaign in 1989. He had been among the first recruits to GAM in 1976, and had worked his way up through the ranks. In the period following the downfall of Suharto, he had made himself available to foreign journalists from his base in Pidie, and had appeared secure and confident in his support.

Syafei's death was a major blow to the Acehnese and GAM, whose members tried to shrug off the leader's death. Ayah Sofyan, who would be the victim of a similar ambush five months later, told the *Jakarta Post*, 'One goes, ten come. The more the military kills rebels, the more Acehnese people will join GAM. Syafei's murder has produced deep sympathy from a majority of Acehnese people and all this has spurred the rebels' fighting spirit.' This interview was delivered by telephone from his hideout near Banda Aceh. He also told the paper that the new commander for Aceh had already been appointed – Libyan-trained Muzakkir Manaf – and that GAM would only negotiate with the Indonesian government if a third party was involved, as they no longer trusted them.

The Indonesian reaction was less subdued. In the Indonesian parliament, House Speaker Akbar Tandjung commended the Indonesian military for killing Syafei: 'We congratulate the military for its tough measures against those trying to secede from Indonesia.' The Indonesian foreign minister, Hassan Wirajuda, said that the government was eager to resume talks with GAM, even with a third party or mediator, but the basis for talks would be whether the 'separatists' would accept the autonomy proposal or not.

In Banda Aceh, according to a foreigner resident at the Kuala Tripa at the time, the military was ecstatic. The Kostrad soldiers involved in the killing were brought back to the capital and treated to a lavish party at the hotel, with prostitutes flown in from Medan especially for the occasion. They were later decorated for their part in the operation.

Syafei's death highlighted the contradictions in the policy being followed by Megawati on Aceh. The legacy of President Wahid's efforts had recently been officially adopted in the imposition of Syariah law in Aceh, a concession to the religious differences between Acehnese Islam and that followed by the majority of Indonesia. This made no difference to the daily lives of most Acehnese, as they observed strict Islamic customs and always had. The Autonomy law had just officially come into operation in Aceh as of January 1, 2002. The redistribution of revenue from the central government back to the provincial administration was the core part of this. But the fact was, the provincial government in Aceh was already deeply unpopular and it was also (according to the World Bank) the most corrupt provincial government in one of the world's most corrupt countries.

The daily reality of the people living in Aceh was the military operation being conducted around them, not the allocation on paper of funds for their province which would undoubtedly be siphoned off before they received any tangible benefit anyway. What the implementation of autonomy in Aceh did achieve was the creation of a diplomatic firewall for Jakarta, and for the governments who wished to deflect attention from the situation in Aceh.

But at that time, President Megawati's support for the US-led campaign in Afghanistan had helped the military and, by extension, its campaign in Aceh. The TNI was included in a counter-terrorism training program for officers in South East Asian armies that was passed in the US Congress in December 2001. The US$21 million training program sidestepped the restrictions placed on funding to the Indonesian military by US Congress following the involvement of the Indonesian military in the widespread and systematic human rights abuses in East Timor in 1999.

'The Pacific command is ready to work with the TNI now in multilateral missions such as the campaign against terrorism, peace-keeping exercises and mutual support,' US Pacific fleet commander Admiral Dennis Blair told a meeting of Indonesian business and military leaders in Jakarta in November 2001. 'We are ready to resume the full range of bilateral cooperation, when the military reforms which the TNI is undertaking ... reach maturity.'

—▸•◦•◂—

SYAFEI'S WAS just another in a string of high-profile leaders' deaths in Aceh that were traced back to the military. On September 6, 2001, Professor Dayan Dawood, the rector of the Syiah Kuala University, was shot in the head and chest in broad daylight in the centre of Banda Aceh. The assassination took place less than 100 metres from a military checkpoint on a road that was well patrolled by Indonesian troops who were preparing for the visit of President Megawati Sukarnoputri two days later. The military denied their involvement.

Not long before his death, Dayan Dawood had announced his willingness to mediate in talks between GAM and the military. A year earlier, the rector of the Islamic University in Banda Aceh, Professor Syafwan Idris, was killed in his home after making a similar offer to mediate between the two sides. These were just the two most prominent deaths in what seemed to be an emerging pattern – those who stood up to campaign for a peaceful solution to the problem in Aceh were being dispatched in suspicious and violent circumstances, while the government and the military continued to publicly support the negotiation process. It was obvious in Aceh, and in Papua with the death of independence leader Theys Eluay in November 2001, that the Indonesian military were pursuing the strategy of publicly negotiating with, but privately eliminating, the leaders they saw as threatening the two most resource-rich provinces in the archipelago. And, judging from the silence of Australia and the US, this policy was tacitly approved.

In February, the military reformed the Acehnese command for the first time since 1985. The Iskander Muda command, named after the famous 17th-century Acehnese sultan, would allow the military more independence in the conduct of its operations, as well as facilitating another increase in troops deployed to Aceh – which they did throughout 2002.

In May 2002, talks were held in Geneva between the Indonesian government and GAM with the HDC as mediator. The Indonesians continued to insist that the negotiations were strictly limited to the acceptance of autonomy by GAM. They accused the HDC of siding with the rebels and in August issued an ultimatum to GAM to accept autonomy within three months or the talks would be abandoned. Military operations had already been stepped up in Aceh, amid constant accusations by the military of terrorism on the part of GAM.

IN MEDAN, the military were partying. About to return for another 'tour of duty' to Aceh, they were up late in the hotel karaoke bar belting out, 'I love you baby, I love you more and more oh pretty baby'. It was like something out of the *Deer Hunter* or one of the bad 1980s crop of American Vietnam movies they tend to play constantly on Indonesian television. Indeed, the comparison to Vietnam was being thrown around a lot towards the end of 2002 – the Indonesian military was using it to justify its tactics in Aceh, the HDC was using it to try and get the Indonesians to negotiate, and GAM was using it to show how it could never be defeated.

Now the Indonesian military was publicising its latest operation in the area around Nisam and Cot Trieng, near the PT Arun Liquefied gas facility in Lhokseumahwe. It had begun in late October when the military surrounded an area eight kilometres long and two kilometres wide and began attacking it with rockets launched from helicopters combined with frequent bursts of fire from truck-mounted heavy machine guns. They had also deployed tanks and armoured personnel carriers, as well as setting up a ring of troops around the large area. They claimed they had the GAM leadership surrounded and then very publicly laid siege to the area. GAM alternately said they weren't there or taunted the Indonesians to attack. The military eventually gave access to the local and then the foreign press, and the 'siege' became something of a show of strength.

But what was really going on behind the scenes was that the Indonesian military, under pressure in the negotiations with the HDC to agree to a wide-ranging cease-fire, was trying to present the image that it had militarily forced GAM to reach the agreement and had in effect won the conflict. GAM had declared a cease-fire for the fasting month of Ramadan that began on November 4, but with the continuing operation in Nisam, that halt in hostilities had quickly broken down.

Working behind the scenes with the Indonesian military and GAM, the HDC had actually come up with an agreement that was to deliver a degree of peace to Aceh. At that stage, in November 2002, the negotiations and the jockeying for position between GAM and the military had kept the imminent arrival of international monitors to oversee the cease-fire a closely guarded secret. It was not until I saw two undoubtedly British ex-military men on the plane to Banda Aceh that I realised the negotiations had come so close to an agreement; these two advance 'logistics' employees of the HDC were already on their way.

There were other reasons why the events in Aceh didn't raise much attention at that time. On October 12, the terrorist organisation Jemaah Islamiah exploded the bombs in Bali that killed 202 people, incuding 88 Australians. The majority of the international press was still covering the aftermath of the bombing and the start of the investigations.

Another issue was the indefinite incarceration of Lesley McCulloch and her travelling partner from the US, Joy Lee Sadler. They had been arrested in South Aceh on September 10, on a bus they had just boarded after leaving a GAM area. They were travelling on tourist visas and were still being held in the police station in Banda Aceh. McCulloch was, of course, well known to the authorities through her writing on Aceh, and the military was determined to make an example of her. At that stage they were threatening to charge her with espionage. In the previous year, McCulloch had become a major source of information about the conflict in Aceh, and her articles, critical of the Indonesian military operations, had attracted the ire of the military. Now she had been silenced and faced a protracted wait for legal proceedings as they analysed the documents on her computer and tried to come up with a charge.

The trumped-up nature of her detention was an obvious signal to activists and journalists alike to stop reporting the military activities in Aceh. Despite the fact that I was travelling on a jour-

nalist's visa, I still panicked when, moments after I had checked
into a hotel in Banda Aceh, I looked out the window to see a
truckload of Brimob stop out the front and come into the foyer.
McCulloch's incarceration had been very well covered in the local
press, so the normal residents of the capital looked at foreigners in
a different light now – with a mixture of sympathy or suspicion,
depending on their own loyalties. And now people demanded to
see your visa and press card before even talking to you, believing
they were under threat of arrest and questioning over your activities if your papers were not in order, as had happened to
McCulloch's translator. The Brimob downstairs were already
checking my partner, Meredyth Tamsyn's (who was accredited to
a New Zealand magazine), and my visa details in the register and
it wouldn't be long before INTEL would be visiting.

The mood at the Kuala Tripa was upbeat. Things were
changing and, with the prospect of an agreement being struck,
the HDC and the GAM negotiators were trying to play down
the violence which, according to GAM, had resulted in the
deaths of 27 people in the first ten days of November. After
nearly three years of trying to end the violence, the HDC staff
felt they were getting somewhere. The HDC now had a public
information office run by Bill Dowell, an American academic
and former journalist. He had just arrived when we went to see
him and he began by talking about Quebec and how it, too, had
tried to secede but now was part of Canada. He spoke in broad
generalities – the negotiations, he said, were at the stage where
'eventually we have agreed that the military will reduce its force
and the GAM will put its arms in for safekeeping'. He admitted
that since he had just arrived, he had a few things to catch up

on, but he genuinely believed the deal was going to work this time. 'Indonesia cannot get rid of these people and they can't beat Indonesia. We are hoping the agreement and the implementation of the Joint Security Committee will be signed and upheld,' he said as his only on-the-record comment. The plan was to have at least 100 foreign monitors reporting back from the districts to the Joint Security Committee, who would then level 'sanctions' against parties who violated the cease-fire. What these sanctions were nobody could ever say.

The GAM negotiator Kamaruzzaman was still in the same room at the hotel, although he was allowed to come and go now, as long as he reported to the police regularly. He explained that when GAM had not signed the agreement and had asked for it to be rewritten, the Indonesians had begun the attack at Cot Trieng and Nisam. 'We wanted a cease-fire from November 4 to December 10 for Ramadan,' he said, 'and on October 28 they started the attack. They used the chance of a cease-fire to attack the GAM base. This is the main problem we face. One part of the military says we want peace and then they start attacking us. It is a double standard. Two faced.'

He went on to talk about the times Indonesia had done this before. The area around Nisam was actually the GAM main base area at the time and their leaders were inside the encirclement when the attack began. They escaped after the first few weeks, leaving only a handful of fighters inside the area.

But he admitted things were not going as well for GAM in the field as they had in the past. 'This year is much harder. This year they are using tanks and helicopters to attack all over Aceh. The TNI have become much more numerous.' He said they had information that Kopassus had been bringing in many more people disguised as civilians. But he wouldn't be drawn on specifics. He had become a lot more guarded – his comment that 'we cannot defeat them and they cannot defeat us' echoed the HDC line and it seemed now, at this stage in the negotiations, it wasn't the time to condemn the TNI.

Amri was also still living in the same room and gave me a printed report of recent violations by the TNI. As well as the operation in Nisam, where local people were trapped inside the encirclement and nobody – including the Indonesian Red Cross – had been allowed into the area to confirm casualties, the TNI had also been active in South Aceh. GAM claimed 300 people had been detained by TNI in a school building in Sawang for two days in early November, and 200 people had fled to the forest to avoid the TNI. One hundred houses had been burnt down in the village of Simpang Ulim, and the population had become refugees. A total of 27 people had been killed in separate incidents in the first ten days of November. In North Aceh, military involved in the Nisam operation were preventing people leaving the town of Lhoksokun, and they had stolen eight motorcycles and burnt down 55 houses. Things had quietened down. For Aceh this was peaceful.

I got a text message from Muhammed Nazar telling me to get down to a religious college in the centre of town. They were going to have a free-speech forum and were expecting a response from the authorities. It was the first time I had met Nazar, the head of the pro-referendum group SIRA. Every other time I had been in Aceh, he had been in jail. He had been arrested twice for subversion – on November 20, 2000, after the rally, and then again on October 9, 2001.

On the occasion of the meeting, he had only been out of jail for six months. It was a simple affair with about 200 people milling around in a hall where a plain banner declared the meeting to be a free-speech forum. The plan was to have two speakers and then everybody would pray and break the end of the day's fasting together.

Before the meeting began, Nazar quickly outlined for me what he and his organisation SIRA stood for: 'We have representatives from 106 Acehnese organisations, in Malaysia, Canada, the Philippines and here in Aceh. We support the cease-fire as the first step to stop the violence in Aceh. First stop the violence and then comes a democratic peaceful process. We don't want our future determined by Indonesia. We send recommendations from 17 civil society organisations to increase the involvement of international monitors here. This is a good step to come to the next big step. First stop the violence then we can talk about the political problem comprehensively. We never stop calling for a referendum. Now we try lobbying to empower the people for a referendum.' He came across as calm and reasonable, even as the police arrived in large numbers outside the gate; SIRA hadn't received permission from the police for the meeting.

Nazar went on to tell me how in May 2000, UN Secretary General Kofi Annan had made a statement supporting the right of the Acehnese people to engage in negotiation about Aceh's status. SIRA had sent representatives to New York the previous November to meet the decolonisation committee. 'I think they appreciate the right of Aceh to choose self-determination,' Nazar said.

That was why they were having the meeting on that day – they wanted to talk publicly about the rights of the Acehnese people. 'Today we just want to appreciate our freedom of speech,' said Naza. 'Before 1945 our leaders joined with the Indonesians to fight Dutch colonialism. The future belongs to all Aceh people, not GAM, not Hasan Di Tiro, not Indonesia. We must all decide in a democratic referendum.'

Our attention was distracted at that point. About 50 metres away, the heavy steel main gates had been swung shut by a group of police who had just arrived. They didn't say anything, just shut the gates and stood outside with their automatic weapons. Initially I counted 15 in uniform, armed with military automatic weapons, but then a group of Javanese men with short haircuts and carrying walkie-talkies arrived. One of these men approached me and bluntly said he was INTEL and demanded my ID. After checking my visa, he waved me away. More of his kind started arriving.

Nazar indicated we should go inside as the meeting was about to begin. The crowd was seated in rows – men of all ages, women with their headscarves on, and children. They all sat in silence as the first speaker, seated at a large table on the stage, began. The uniformed police walked into the hall. Some walked directly up to the stage, some stayed by the doors and others walked up the side passages between the walls and the seats. Another group, which included an officer, walked straight up the central aisle. Then the police grabbed the speaker from either side and carried him away.

Nobody said anything. There was no protest from the crowd, who just sat in their place, and the police, who now stood guard at all the exits, were also silent. The next speaker, another young student, stood up, took the discarded microphone and began to talk. The police at the front of the room walked up to him, grabbed him from both sides and carried him away. Nazar then declared the meeting over.

The two students who had tried to address the meeting were marched away and taken for questioning. The INTEL and police were still blocking the gate and some of the people inside the meeting hall began to pray while others started laying out packages of food. 'The police try to undermine the program by terrorising the community to not come here,' said a resigned Nazar.

American reporter Billy Nessen arrived then, and was arguing with the INTEL men to let him into the school. They were standing around, basically to check those leaving the meeting. Another one approached me and claimed to be a journalist for the local paper, *Serambi*, and showed me his ID, but from the way he was taking orders from one of the other INTEL guys, it was clear he was one of them.

It was now getting dark and the atmosphere in the hall was becoming tense. Just by attending this small thwarted attempt to discuss a referendum in Aceh, these people had made themselves targets.

>-+>-0-<+-<

NESSEN HAD just returned to Aceh after marrying an Acehnese woman. Earlier that year, he had been the first reporter to go into combat with GAM. Later he showed me the footage. Because it was quite shaky, he'd had trouble selling it, but there were so many bullets flying around in the ambush he'd filmed, it was a wonder he managed to capture anything at all. GAM had ambushed an Indonesian military truck, and it was terrifying to watch as Nessen and the GAM fighters, literally running for their lives through the jungle following the attack, were almost encircled by the responding Indonesian troops.

He had spent some two months with the fighters, and it said a lot about media interest in Aceh that Nessen couldn't sell his story, which he'd got at such huge personal risk. Ironically, the fact that he hadn't made a big splash with the story meant that the authorities were unaware of what he'd done, and so he had been able to return to Aceh.

———•———

LESLEY McCULLOCH and Joy Lee Sadler had finally got a court date for November 25 so I stayed in Banda Aceh waiting for the trial. The *Times*, the *Guardian* and the BBC all sent journalists up to Aceh for the case and there were a lot of Indonesian media representatives.

The publicity surrounding the unprecedented courtcase had forced the Indonesian judge to drop the absurd charge of espionage and the prosecutor was left to argue that McCulloch and Sadler had violated the conditions of their tourist visas by travelling to South Aceh and meeting with GAM. The maximum penalty for this was five years in jail and a $5000 fine. But the pair was hoping that the matter would be dealt with quickly and they would be deported.

When the day of the trial arrived, they had been in detention for 72 days. They were keyed up to get a decision and smiled for the cameras. McCulloch looked thin and pale. Sadler looked ill – she had recently revealed she was HIV-positive and she had been sick from the poor food.

The two were led into the court by armed guards and put in a barred room at the back where the Indonesian media filmed them through the bars. One of McCulloch's legal team, Rufriadi, expressed what most people in the court hoped would be the outcome: 'This is a simple case under article 50 of the immigration law. The prosecutor will use the laptop files and the pictures to say McCulloch violated it. Her defence is she was forced. They force her to go to the village. Her defence about the material on the laptop is it belongs to Tasmania University.

'They are not really interested in Joy,' continued Rufriadi, 'It is McCulloch they want to get.'

Hopes for a quick outcome were dashed immediately by the prosecutor when he asked for a two-day adjournment in McCulloch's case as his witnesses were not present. Then the charges against her were read out. She had gone to the Kuala Tripa and spoken with Kamaruzzaman. She was collecting data about GAM. She had talked to people in a GAM village. She had photos of burnt houses. She had met the commander of GAM in Tapaktuan. Her case was adjourned for two days.

Sadler came forward and her case was read out. A 57-year-old nurse from Iowa, she said she had come to Aceh to look for humanitarian work. She had worked previously for Save the Children and had approached some NGOs in Aceh about work. She said she travelled on a motorcycle to the village where they met the GAM people. She saw no GAM flags and took no pictures and saw McCulloch talking to the commander. The defence called for McCulloch to be brought out as a witness. The defence lawyer started his barrage of questions; McCulloch replied, 'I met her in a guest house in Banda Aceh where we talked about travelling somewhere for a holiday. We went south.'

Then came the part where they went to the village of Mangammat, and McCulloch was asked what Sadler did there. 'Joy helped some villagers – women and children, some with gunshot wounds, shot by the Indonesian military.'

There was an immediate reaction in the court, something between a groan and a sharp intake of breath. The prosecutor smiled, the judge's head snapped up to attention, and some of the Indonesian journalists busily whispered to each other. Some of the Acehnese women who had come to support McCulloch looked shocked and scared.

It was a horrible moment. McCulloch would now be on the record again for accusing the Indonesian military. Some of the journalists present would blow it out of proportion, with the effect of increasing her sentence. By telling things as they happened in this highly politicised court, McCulloch had sunk her chances of getting off. But the situation was so absurd – the people who needed treatment had been shot and McCulloch was damned for saying who had done it.

She tried to qualify what she had said: 'Joy was helping to give medicine to villagers. I am not thinking of which side. She is going there to help people. I didn't watch closely what Joy was doing but I saw many women and children victims.'

The defence lawyer tried to get her out of it. 'Was Joy carrying any medicine?' 'No,' said McCulloch. 'Did she have a meeting with the GAM leader?' 'Joy didn't meet him,' said McCulloch, 'I met him. I spoke with him but I did not have a meeting. I spoke with him.'

A camera was produced and shown to the judge as evidence they had taken photos.

'It was never our intention to go to the villages,' said McCulloch, trying to get back to the original defence. But then she said it again.

'There were many people with gunshot wounds and other injuries sustained in a military operation – by the military.'

This time it was no slip. She had said it loudly and clearly, almost in defiance of the absurdity of the questions – questions the police had been asking them for months.

The defence finished by asking if GAM had forced them to go to the village. It was a loaded question in the circumstances. If she answered yes, the Indonesian press would trumpet GAM had kidnapped them. If she said no, they would be guilty of agreeing to go.

'They did not push us, but they had guns and we thought it was a good idea to go with them,' she said evenly. 'In my country, there are no people with guns, so when an armed man asks me to do something, I am not likely to say no.'

The case was adjourned for two days.

⊳—◦—⊲

TWO DAYS later, the first witness for the prosecution was a surprise – a man from the Aceh tourist ministry. He began by stating there were 113 designated tourist areas in Aceh, including some in South Aceh, especially the beaches on the islands of Pulau Banyak (a group of islands known as 'many islands').

Sadler was close to tears when she spoke to reporters: 'I request this process to be dealt with quickly. I am sick. It is all getting too much emotionally.'

Then the questions and answers began again. 'I'm a nurse – I wanted to provide any kind of help here . . . In August I met McCulloch . . . We were going to Pulau Banyak . . . then Medan . . . We thought we were going to the police then they took us to the field . . . They told us they were police . . . then they took us to this village and I was very very busy . . . They told me they had very many sick people – 100 to 200 people . . .

I was very busy . . . The children were covered with sores, gunshot wounds, some had been beaten, they were very sick . . . They had medicine . . . I cleaned the wounds and gave help to the children . . .'

Then she burst into tears. 'Did you give them injections?' the prosecutor asked.

'Yes,' Joy replied.

'Well, what about the injecting equipment?' he asked.

'They had very good equipment, but they didn't know how to use it. I work as a nurse, I know what to do. I did nothing else . . . I took no pictures . . . No, I don't speak Indonesian.'

'Did you meet GAM?'

'No, I don't know what McCulloch's activity was,' she said, still crying.

'Did you see the burning house, the IDPs [Internally displaced people] and the GAM flag?' asked the prosecutor, triumpantly waving the folder of photos and handing them to the judge.

'I don't know who took the pictures. I didn't even know they were taking pictures. I was busy.'

She went on describing the situation – the men with guns, the sick people, how the people in the village wanted their stories told; how they were dropped off at the highway after three days in the village, how the bus came and then how the TNI stopped them shortly after.

They asked her if she knew that McCulloch had met Hasan Di Tiro (there was a photo on McCulloch's laptop) and if she had seen the document McCulloch had on the laptop about the military.

'I didn't know anything, I thought it was a bad dream', Sadler said, exasperated by the questioning.

Then he asked her to describe the GAM flags she had seen. It was a cruel performance, with Joy obviously distressed and the prosecutor relishing it.

When it was McCulloch's turn, the prosecution went through everything. They had downloaded everything on her computer and printed it out – research papers, stories she had written, material she had downloaded from the Internet about Aceh, photos from previous trips. They also had her notebooks as evidence, with the accounts of ill treatment by the military of the people in the village she had visited before her arrest.

Basically, the majority of her work on Aceh was being used as evidence against her. She had just been held in custody for months because of who she was. The maps on her laptop of Indonesian military positions in Aceh were the main source of the espionage allegations but, as McCulloch pointed out, they had come from a website owned by the Indonesian government.

Technically, McCulloch and Sadler had broken no law.

But the prosecution even got a representative from the immigration department to swear in court that when a foreigner arrives in Indonesia and is given a tourist visa, what they can and can't do is explained to them. McCulloch immediately refuted the truth of that, and anyone who has ever been to Indonesia for a holiday would know that not to be the case. Even more absurd, McCulloch actually had a valid working visa in her passport which she had been planning to use on a subsequent trip. But now they had her and they weren't going to let her go, and if that meant locking up Sadler as well, then so be it.

McCulloch told the court how she had been sexually harrassed and how a knife had been held at her throat while she was being questioned shortly after her arrest. When the two were actually arrested by the army in South Aceh, McCulloch said Sadler had been punched in the mouth in a scuffle as the troops tried to seize their bags.

The case was adjourned until December 19, after the Idul Fitri holiday and Sadler, in tears, vowed to begin a hunger strike. The two were taken back to the police headquarters next door to the court where they were being held.

BRIGADIER GENERAL Bambang Darmono was in charge of TNI military operations in all of Aceh from the Iskander Muda military headquarters in Lhokseumahwe. It was a large, freshly painted building with a wide, shady veranda, which the general and my partner Meredyth and I sat on as we chatted, away from the harsh midday sun. He was second in command only to General Djali Yusuf, who was in charge of all forces, including the police and Brimob.

Bambang Darmono was a well-travelled man who spoke excellent English. He had trained in Australia at the Joint Service Staff College in Canberra in 1989, and at the Jungle Warfare Training Centre, an army establishment, in Conungra, Queensland. In March of 2000, he had attended an international human rights symposium in San Remo, Italy. And, noticing that Meredyth was from New Zealand, he mentioned what a beautiful city Auckland was – unfortunately, he had only been there for a short time. Where did he stay? 'At the Sheraton

. . . such a beautiful hotel.' And, he added, he was especially fond of New Zealand as the people cared so much about the environment.

After the small talk, I asked him about the situation in Aceh. He explained the encirclement operation in Cot Trieng. The TNI had been there for over a month. 'Just to push them we will do like this.' Darmono said. 'One, we encircle the area. Two, we announce with loudspeakers for them to surrender, and we drop leaflets. Three, we fire the missiles from helicopters. Four, we set fire to the area.'

He said they were still at the psychological phase of using loudspeakers to make GAM surrender, but he conceded that there weren't very many of them left in there, 'No more than 60, maybe less than 40.'

He said there were still around 1200 of his troops involved in encircling the area, and that the operation had nothing to do with the cease-fire agreement that was due to be signed in Geneva the next week on December 9.

The military had surrounded the area to put pressure on GAM to sign the agreement, but the GAM fighters had basically slipped away. The military were left with a very public operation that hadn't achieved its result and after the army chief of staff, Ryamizard Ryacudu, had declared the imminent capture of GAM's leaders and told the press he would fly to Aceh to accept GAM's surrender, the military could not for the time being declare the operation over. So they allowed the press in to see the new TNI conducting an operation with no human rights abuses, against an enemy who by then, in late November, was far away. 'We say to the Indonesian Red

Cross, come and see, and as you can see, we are open to the press,' said Darmono.

Bambang Darmono said he was concerned with human rights issues: 'We review what we conduct here. We believe there were some mistakes. We start with the basics of human rights. Our philosophy now is to win the hearts and minds. GAM, they are trying to build a nation within a nation. Sometime they force the people not to support us but now they like TNI here because the situation here is better and they can improve their lives.'

He again expressed his current mission in point form. 'One, to conduct a counterinsurgency operation. Two, to support the local government. Three, to support the people and deal with social and economic problems. Four, to secure national vital objects.'

Of these, the TNI was definitely conducting a counter-insurgency operation, and the only national vital object was the ExxonMobil plant, which four battalions of his men, the best-equipped in Indonesia, were guarding not very far from where we were. As far as local government was concerned, the area of North Aceh (which had the highest concentrations of his men), 358 out of 390 villages had no functioning government at all. And I couldn't see how the TNI had been supporting the people with their social and economic problems, because in Aceh they were the cause of them.

According to the brigadier general, the military's main aim was to separate the people from GAM. 'We try to conduct psychological war to do this,' he said. I asked him what would happen to his operation if the agreement went ahead in Geneva. 'If they sign, we will follow what the agreement says. We have to follow what the international community agrees upon. If they don't sign, we will follow what the government says about Plan B. We just prepare for that,' he said, smiling. Plan B was the military elimination of GAM.

According to Bambang Darmono, his men had suffered no casualties in the current operations and they had captured a 50 kilogram bag of rice, some ammunition, some documents and some equipment used by GAM from the encircled area. They had also captured 1.4 billion rupiah which he said GAM were going to use to buy weapons 'from outside'. As he said this, he pointed towards the sea. GAM were still in there, he was sure, and in one day his men would wipe them out. How did he know they were there? His men had intercepted their mobile phone calls, he laughed. But for now he had told his men to hold their fire 'because of journalists and international pressure' he said, smiling.

'And now I have a question for you,' he said. 'Why is the press so interested in this operation? All the world's press have come here to talk to me.'

He was right. The *Guardian* and the *Times* had come down and the *Asahi Shimbun* correspondent from Japan was waiting to talk to him. I mentioned the peace process, the donor conference in Tokyo that was about to happen, with countries pledging funds for Aceh's rehabilitation, even the new openness of the TNI. I didn't mention the TNI's appalling human rights record.

'And you, why do you come here? What do people in Australia think of Aceh?'

'Nothing,' I replied truthfully. It was the answer he wanted and he shook my hand and insisted we accompany the armed guards he was sending out with the Japanese journalist to inspect 'our' operation at the Cot Trieng encirclement.

The cars that escorted us the 20 kilometres to the Cot Trieng encirclement raced through the streets of Lhokseumahwe at high speed, honking their horns. They were the newest Indonesian military vehicles I had ever seen. Brand new military Land Rovers, undoubtedly paid for with the proceeds from guarding the ExxonMobil plant. We turned off the main road and passed soldiers on foot in full combat gear. The soldiers became more and more numerous, camped out in small tents made from their military ponchos.

At the command post was Brigadier Nasution, who was in charge of the operation itself. There were several tanks and armoured cars parked around some large tents and soldiers, all wearing flak jackets and helmets, milling around with a few Indonesian television journalists. There was not much happening, in fact the troops looked like they were having a day off. The road that stretched around the perimeter of the restricted zone was dotted with the small poncho tents with two or three soldiers in each who seemed to be comatose in the hot early afternoon sun. Every few hundred metres there was a small tent with guns poking out in the direction of what were basically rice paddies and swamps.

The Indonesian journalists were all talking about the discovery of some rice and documents by a patrol that had been sent into the encircled area. It was the most exciting thing that had happened in a few days. There was an almost permanent contingent of Indonesian reporters in Lhokseumahwe now. They all stayed at the hotel Vina Vida, across the road from the military headquarters in town. Most of them had a healthy scepticism about what the military told them at their increasingly common briefings, but their copy was read by the military and they were open to intimidation, which would in time get much worse.

The local journalists were also quite scared of GAM, as they knew how unkindly some of their coverage was viewed. At that time it was quite a simple procedure to contact GAM in that area – GAM had mobiles and satellite phones and often could be reached for comment after a clash, each area having a designated spokesman.

The local media was in a very difficult position and it would get worse. With the resurgence of Indonesian nationalism taking place under Megawati, there was a growing demand for their reports and images, and most of the reporters were more or less permanently in Lhokseumahwe covering the military. But what they saw the military doing and how they reported it would later cost some of them their lives.

The troops at the encirclement were also among the best equipped I had ever seen in Indonesia. They were there for the cameras but also if you looked at the grafitti on their flak jackets, it said 'Ambon, Papua, Aceh' – the three current trouble spots in Indonesia. There were some Kostrad strategic reserve men, the troops deployed to conflict zones, and some who could be identified as Kopassus by their shoulder badges. They loved the cameras, posed aggressively for the photographers and joked around a lot. The presence of armour made them very confident and when we spoke to the colonel of the group about the situation he said, laughing, his men could crush GAM any time.

It did look like an exercise, but a remarkably relaxed one, with the regular troops in their small, hot tents complaining of boredom and asking the Indonesian journalists for something to read. The few civilians still in the area kept away.

The next day we headed back to Banda Aceh. We spent a long, hot day on a rundown and almost empty local bus to Sigli, about half way back to the capital. At a small village along the way, Brimob troops in a fanned-out formation blocked the road, stopped the bus and ordered everybody off. The locals were ordered to one side and we were told to stand on the other. It was very aggressive, and unexpected after the welcome we'd received from the brigadier general, and I told them, stammering, that was what we had been doing – talking with him, their commander.

The Brimob guy in charge had a hard, angry manner, and I kept thinking of Lesley McCulloch, who was still in custody. There was no-one around save a few passengers who were also being searched. They were lifting up their shirts and emptying their bags, surrounded by troops who had their weapons trained on them. As the Brimob guy handed back our passports, press cards and the *Surat Jalans* (police permission to travel) form, I noticed my hand was shaking. He noticed it too, and looked at me harder, as if for a moment doubting my story. I was relieved to get back on the bus and away. The atmosphere among the few passengers on the slow-moving, rattling bus had changed to one of silent and sullen fear.

In Banda Aceh, the intimidation of those involved in the peace process took a more familiar form than the military show in Cot Trieng and Nisam. On November 30, six armed men kidnapped a 26-year-old human rights worker, Musliadi, as he was sitting down to break the Ramadan fast with his evening meal. He was due to travel to Geneva the following week to represent Acehnese 'civil society' at the talks to negotiate a peace deal. His body was found floating in a river four days later. Witnesses to his kidnapping identified the car involved as belonging to Brimob, whose right to carry assault weapons and conduct operations against GAM was one of the sticking points in the peace deal.

Muhammed Nazar, the head of SIRA, was back working in the SIRA office. He said that Musliadi was not the only person who'd been kidnapped recently. On November 22, Nasri, an assistant lecturer in engineering at the Syiah Kuala University in Banda Aceh, had been kidnapped on his way home by men with guns whom Nazar believed were TNI or Brimob. He said there were mysterious Kopassus agents studying incognito at the university, who were controlled directly from Jakarta. Many students linked this to the deaths of the rectors in 2001 and 2000 – respected people who also stood for nonviolence, a democratic referendum and a cease-fire.

Forty members of SIRA had been arrested in the previous year, but the organisation still carried on with its activities. The present level of harassment was at least better than in November 2000 when 2000 SIRA members had been arrested following the attempt to hold the rally in Banda Aceh. Nazar himself received an 11-month sentence at that time for sedition.

A few days earlier SIRA had sent recommendations to the Indonesian government, the GAM leadership in Sweden, the HDC, the UN, the World Bank and the US and Japan that the peace process be supported as a step towards allowing the Acehnese people the right to self determination. 'We support a comprehensive peace in Aceh which will come by giving freedom for the Acehnese to express their right for self-determination,' said Nazar, referring to the recommendations.

The Tokyo donors' meeting had resulted in the allocation of 8 million dollars for reconstruction and rehabilitation in Aceh if the Cessation of Hostilities agreement was signed and implemented. Nazar was worried that the summit in Tokyo had been exploited by Jakarta for propaganda purposes, as they had presented the peace agreement as the endorsement and acceptance by GAM of the autonomy package and an end to calls for independence.

'The United States and Japan cannot just accept information from the Jakarta government without checking it here on the ground in Aceh,' said Nazar.

SIRA's aim now was to prepare for the local elections due in mid-2004 and to use the elections as a vote for self-determination by fielding their own candidates. But he knew it would be difficult. 'The military have become a colonialist, terrorist, mafia organisation protecting their own interests here in Aceh,' he said.

As our meeting was winding up, my mobile phone rang. It was Billy Nessen giving me Nazar's phone number, which I wrote down before asking whose number it was. As I wrote down his own mobile number in front of him, Nazar's eyes widened and he quickly pulled out his phone and removed the SIM card. In Aceh, where phones were traced and assassinations made on the basis of that information, my receiving a call and identifying his number had freaked him out.

Everybody remembered the death of GAM leader Abdullah Syafei. Stories of the surveillance powers of the Indonesian military intelligence abounded and multiplied until many credited the military with a lot more control than they really had, which was the intention of the rumours. Even though I tried to explain the reason for writing down his mobile number, Nazar still looked at me suspiciously.

December 4 was the anniversary of Hasan Di Tiro's declaration of Acehnese independence with 27 supporters way back in 1976. Every year, the GAM fighters in the field had tried to have some kind of parade to mark the date. These had grown to huge affairs after the fall of Suharto, but the previous year's had been relatively small due to threats from the military. Photos I saw of those parades never contained more than 20 or so fighters in uniform at any one place. This year, however, with the imminence of the peace deal, the presence of the HDC and the higher than usual media interest, GAM was preparing to mark the day in full style. The Indonesian authorities knew this and had made their preparations as well.

THERE HAD been many false starts but finally, on December 3, Meredyth and I hired a driver and a translator, and travelled along the Banda Aceh to Medan highway, which was even more heavily patrolled than it had been a few days before when we had travelled along it by bus. The area appeared to be firmly in the hands of the Indonesian military and Brimob, who had placed petrol drums in the middle of the highway which forced the traffic to slow down as it passed their sandbagged and barbed wire-covered posts. Armoured personnel carriers and trucks with armour plating bolted to the sides patrolled the highway, escorted by UK-made Saladin armoured cars. Near the town of Sigli, all traffic was stopped again and searched by Brimob. But there was hardly anybody travelling on the roads that day; the military had warned people not to attend any commemorations, and the extra security reinforced that warning.

We had been told by text message to drive to the town of Juenib in the Bireuen district. When we got there, another text message told us to confirm our registration number and sent us further on past the next police post. Only about a kilometre further on, two men on a motorcycle flagged down the car and pointed to a side road that ran off through the rice paddies. On the rough dirt road, more men on motorcycles and carrying automatic weapons came out from behind trees and shacks, and rode alongside the car then pointed to another side track. The driver pulled over and more uniformed and armed guys surrounded the car and started talking, as well as some laughing and smiling civilians. This all took place less than 100 metres from the heavily patrolled highway.

Two of the GAM soldiers who had AK47s got into the back of our four-wheel drive. It was interesting to watch the reaction of the driver, who suddenly started saying 'Merdeka!' (freedom) and punching the air with his fist. He chattered and joked incessantly with the two guys in the back. He seemed nervous, but more worried about the car than anything else, as the two soldiers in the back ordered him to drive back into the open down a very rutted road. The translator, who had insisted on studying our visas and documents, and bringing her husband with her, sat in the back of the vehicle looking nervous. They were city people, and the GAM guys, who looked wild with their long hair, weapons and sunglasses, scared them.

The GAM guys on motorcycles were showing off, standing up and waving their weapons above their heads and shouting as the four-wheel drive and motorcycles moved to the protection of the trees through the open paddy fields that were visible from the Indonesian-controlled highway. Then the whole procession came to a stop – a large ditch blocked the road. Still in the open, two planks were produced and laid down and first the motor-cycles crossed, then, under careful directions, the car.

The GAM fighters were highly organised and very confident that they could meet any problems they might encounter from TNI. And as soon as we entered the cover of the trees, we saw the reason for their confidence. Men wearing fatigues or civilian clothes and carrying M-16s, AK47s, light machine guns with belts of ammunition slung around their necks and rocket propelled grenades (RPGs) lined the road through the trees. They smiled and waved at the car and at the motorcycles escorting us, and shouted 'Merdeka!' and punched their fists in the air. The whole thing had a bit of a special event atmosphere, with the main celebrations planned nearby for the following day; the huge numbers of armed men increased the sense of security.

The road led to a small village at a crossroads. The square was crowded with civilians and GAM soldiers who milled around or sat outside the small shacks that served as shops. Across the road was a large meeting hall that was raised off the ground. We came to a stop in its shadow and the car was surrounded by children and a few GAM soldiers. A tall Acehnese man in civilian clothes and carrying a hand-held satellite phone came over and introduced himself as Commander Darwis Juenib.

Plastic chairs were produced and we sat there, half in the shade and half in the scorching sun, surrounded by a throng of villagers, children and GAM soldiers. Darwis explained he had been commander of the area since 1999 and had been part of a GAM battalion in this area since 1990. Like many GAM members, he had escaped the Suharto 'shock therapy' killings in the early 1990s by travelling and working in Malaysia, Singapore and Holland. He claimed to now have 5000 GAM soldiers in the Bireuen area under his command, but wouldn't say how many were armed.

The clashes between TNI and Brimob in the Bireuen area were frequent and mostly due to theft and extortion by the Indonesian forces. 'If the TNI come to the villages and steal things, like motorcycles and cars, we will attack them,' said Darwis. 'The TNI don't have a right to attack Aceh people. To shoot Aceh people. To kill people. We have a right to get independence. This time it is very unpredictable if they come to the villages. GAM will attack them.' The most recent incidents he described were all related to money, and in his district he had lost only nine of his men that year, as opposed to the 100 civilians he believed had been killed in the Bireuen district.

According to Darwis, on November 30, TNI troops had rounded up all 300 inhabitants of the village of Cot Plieng in front of the mosque, beat them with pieces of wood and demanded money. Two days earlier, elite troops from Kostrad had rounded up the villagers from nearby Blang Kuta and shot three children, aged eight, 14 and 17, in front of the crowd. The reason, according to Darwis, was that the TNI had found out that the villagers were paying more money to the Brimob police than they were to the army.

Two days before our arrival, it had been reported in the Banda Aceh newspaper, *Serambi*, that there had been a GAM attack in the centre of the town of Bireuen and one of the attackers had been killed. I asked Darwis if his men were responsible. 'The victim in that case was just a local tailor,' said Darwis. 'The TNI come to his shop asking for the money. One month for 500,000 rupiah ($100). The tailor was sick of the demands and pulled a knife, and they shot him. We had no GAM in the city. We don't go to the city.'

The TNI still flew over the Bireuen area in helicopters on average twice a week. Groups of troops in armoured personnel carriers came through the area maybe three times a week, but they hadn't ventured very far from the main highway recently. As for the peace discussions due to start in Geneva, Darwis said only that 'Jakarta makes a trick. The dialogue is not relevant to the real situation in Aceh today.' He would welcome the international monitors if they were deployed, he said, but he had heard nothing about warehousing his weapons or renouncing the goal of independence, which is what the Indonesian press were saying was the aim of the negotiations. The main problem in his area was the Brimob and TNI stealing rice and kidnapping people whenever they came to the villages.

Darwis invited us to stay for the celebrations the following morning, but our translator and driver insisted we go back to Banda Aceh that day. They were plainly scared of spending the night in the villages, and in a way you couldn't blame them. The military commander of Aceh, Major General Djali Yusuf, had been reported in the press that morning to have said that he would bomb any gatherings from the air if they took place on December 4: 'No ceremonies, no flags. We're searching for their positions wherever they are.'

It annoyed Darwis, who was confident there would be no problem, that we could not stay. He insisted, instead, on a military parade before we left and lined up almost 200 of his men; there was almost the same number still stationed around the town square and along the road back to the highway.

Their weapons were impressive. As well as all the standard TNI weapons – M-16s, Indonesian-produced SS1s, AK47s – there were many other models I had never seen in Indonesia before. I had seen the kind of Chinese copy AK47s and light machine guns before in Burma, and the RPGs as well. They told me they had been smuggled in from Thailand and Malaysia. In truth, their weapons came from wherever they could get them, and most often that was from Java, from corrupt Indonesian military officers.

The unit we were visiting, at least, was as heavily equipped as the Indonesian military, and probably better armed than the police. But even though it was the day before the big parade, and they probably had on show a lot of what they possessed, it was still more than I had expected. The men themselves looked liked they were never apart from their guns, and the wear on the weapons indicated they got a lot of use.

For the civilians in the village, the military parade was another form of entertainment, and they gathered around watching as the fighters presented arms. They weren't afraid. Some of them laughed at the seriousness of it or at someone they knew in the parade, but it was obvious they were very relaxed with having that many GAM fighters in their village, and in that area considered them as their army.

The same motorcycle escort that had brought us there led us back to the highway, and they couldn't resist riding up and down on the asphalt, waving their guns and standing up on the bikes. There was traffic on the highway that could have been anybody, but they were just making a point that it was their area. Within minutes of being back on the highway, we were slowing down to the first sandbagged Indonesian police checkpoint.

The celebrations went ahead the following morning. Sofyan Dawood, the commander of the Passe region in North Aceh and the main spokesman for GAM in the field, attended a ceremony close to where we had been. A thousand fully armed fighters paraded and raised the GAM flag. A few small gun battles were reported in the area and GAM flags were raised in the villages near Banda Aceh but quickly removed. The only reported casualty of the day was a TNI soldier who was wounded trying to remove a booby-trapped GAM flag in North Aceh.

The capital was quiet on December 4, with hardly any shops open. The big news of the day was that Musliadi's body had been found in the river, with signs of him having been tortured.

Bill Dowell, the HDC information officer, had obviously changed his personal opinions on the conflict and seemed shaken by the grisly death of Musliadi, a delegate who had been working with him. The HDC, GAM and Acehnese civil society representatives were preparing to travel to Geneva for what at that stage were still negotiations for the peace deal on December 9. Kamaruzzaman, who was going to Geneva for GAM, said the December 9 talks were merely a starting point. Dowell was cagey about what he thought would happen in Geneva: 'The whole thing is like a poker game, everybody is holding their cards close to their chest.' But he would admit that the international monitor team would eventually number 50 and that the six-member advance team of mostly former British military were already on the ground in Aceh.

Arrangements for the rest of the team's arrival were being made. They would join 50 representatives from GAM and 50 from the government to form 24 teams of the Joint Security Commission, the JSC, which would monitor the cease-fire. Off the record, though, Dowell admitted to the problems that were inevitable even if the cease-fire were implemented. He talked of the 'predatory nature' of the police and the military in terms of their constant extortion demands on the local community and how that would be a problem if the shooting ever stopped.

The HDC had been sending teams out to the regions, along with local journalists, to explain the process on a regional level. In some places, the reception to the HDC by local officials had been obstructive and hostile. Dowell no longer mentioned Quebec; instead he now talked of the situation in the countryside in terms of Vietnam, comparing the Indonesian military with America and GAM with the Vietcong. After seeing the countryside and speaking to the people, he privately admitted to the impossibility of the Indonesian military securing places such as the one mountainous road to the central Aceh town of Takengon. After roughly three weeks in Aceh, Dowell now saw the conflict in a much more realistic light.

THE MILITARY had announced their intention to launch a large-scale offensive against GAM if they failed to sign the agreement in Geneva on December 9.

A few reporters from Jakarta began arriving in Banda Aceh, to be there when the signing in Geneva took place. We hitched a ride with Ian Timberlake from Agence France Presse back down to Lhokseumahwe, where there were still reports of clashes.

The military in Lhokseumahwe was blaming GAM for the latest death. A 42-year-old sergeant had been shot from his motorcycle near the town of Bireuen that morning by two men with AK47s who then stole the bike. The military was still in Cot Trieng, and they had produced from inside the encircled area a blue bag containing 603 M-16 bullets. A TNI patrol had followed some footprints, or so the story went.

The Indonesian journalists at the Vina Vida hotel insisted the bag must prove GAM was still in there. 'The bag is blue. It is not a TNI bag, their bags are green,' said one, excited by the new development. It seemed like they were being fed tidbits of information to keep the story of the encirclement alive to save face for the Indonesian military. What seemed more ominous was the arrival in the harbour three days earlier of 2900 fresh TNI troops who were now to be seen driving in armoured trucks in convoys through the town. It looked like the military was trying to boost its numbers before the agreement was signed, which would theoretically freeze troop levels at their current numbers.

The next morning, December 8, there were troops in convoys heading out of town to the north. GAM told us that we could not go and meet them as planned, as they were engaged in a fire-fight, so instead we went down into one of the villages to ask some people what they thought of the agreement.

The village was just a small collection of wooden huts down a side road near Lhokseumahwe, near the half-finished concrete shell of the shopping plaza on the way out of town. As soon as we got there, a small crowd formed and took us to a spot on the road outside a small wooden shack that served as a shop, and began telling us how people had been shot there. Grisly photos of bodies lying where we were standing were produced, and it turned out the incident had taken place some months earlier. The local people wanted to re-enact the deaths for us; we were the first journalists to ever ask them anything, so they described the incident in minute detail.

A young man sweating heavily raced up on a bicycle and called himself the local GAM commander. He quickly dismounted and began giving a confused speech about how they would never give in to the 'Javanese colonialists and imperialists' and how they would fight to the death rather than live under the hated Javanese. He was sweating heavily, his chest puffed up, and flecks of spit flew from his mouth as he spoke. It was quite a performance – more for the local people gathered around than for us. We had to excuse ourselves as the GAM commander in the field had called and said that the firefight was over and we could go and see them now.

'What did you make of the guy on the bicycle?' Ian asked as we drove away. I could only reply that it must be a GAM area and he was kind of the block leader, a minor GAM official representative for that particular set of wooden houses – or maybe just a local hood trying to impress his neighbours.

Heading north on the highway, we passed four TNI trucks speeding in the other direction. At the mosque just outside of Bireuen – the place we'd arranged to meet GAM – a man wearing a white robe flagged us down and pointed to some guys on motorcycles who were waiting behind a shop across the road. They told us to get on the bikes and we headed off and passed through a small village. There were people around who looked shocked to see three white people on motorcycles so soon after a clash.

Commander Darwis was sitting in a small raised meeting house surrounded by about 30 of his men. The TNI and Polri had come in shooting to the nearby village of Abu Dinha at about six in the morning. They shot one person in the leg, a boy. The GAM soldiers who were camped about 500 metres away moved in and the gunfight that ensued lasted for about five hours – until the TNI pulled out after, according to Darwis, five of them had been wounded. Three were critical, he said.

Darwis immediately admitted to killing the TNI sergeant near the town of Bireuen the day before. A businessman had reported the sergeant to GAM for demanding money from him four or five times a week. Every time the sergeant wanted 500,000 to 1 million rupiah ($100 to $200).

'We don't want to fight but TNI are always coming into the villages,' Darwis said. 'We want the international peacekeepers.' It seemed both sides were taking advantage of the last few days before the meeting in Geneva to tidy up a few loose ends – the TNI by deploying more troops and GAM by getting rid of the TNI sergeant accused of extortion.

It was impossible for his men to accept the peace agreement, Darwis said, if the other side kept to the four conditions – a one-sided disarmament, forcing GAM to accept autonomy, the sending of additional troops and the setting up of police posts in every town. He joked about disarmament – how could he disarm his men when, in this area, he had to deal with some of the worst human rights abusers, the Indonesian army. He told us the story of how currently in a village close by there was a girl of 12 who had been raped by 30 TNI soldiers in Banda Aceh. When I asked him why, he looked at me as if I were a fool and said, 'Just because she was pretty.'

Since we had met Darwis the previous week, he and his men had been forced to move because, after the December 4 celebrations, the army had sent in 1000 fresh troops to the area. The GAM fighters used the main highway to travel further south, simply going around the military and police posts on back roads. They were now back in smaller, more mobile, groups and had a few more motorcycles with them.

Darwis told us how one of the Acehnese men sitting with us was a former police officer. When he joined GAM, he'd made off with 18 weapons and a motorcycle while the rest of his unit were praying – the story got a lot of laughs. Another man there told how he had been in the TNI, which he had joined to get training. After being sent to Java, he had deserted and returned to Aceh to fight with GAM.

When we made moves to leave, Darwis wanted to make a final statement – that he thought the peace agreement in Geneva would not work. 'Just a referendum for self-determination can solve the Aceh conflict. Not guns, not violence. Referendum is the peaceful solution for Aceh.'

Ian asked if he could take some pictures and the parade was formed again. Not all of them were wearing uniforms this time, but they were very well armed and posed on the back of their motorcycles with their grenade launchers and machine guns. Once again there were children and civilians standing around, but not as many as before – the fighting that morning had made the people a little more nervous.

It was starting to get dark but getting out of there wasn't going to be a simple exercise. Accustomed to living with the TNI nearby, the GAM fighters hadn't really thought about how we would leave their area. We headed off on the motorcycles and rode away from the highway then cut across behind the treeline. The military was patrolling the road and it wasn't safe to return as we had come. After leaving us on a side road with some villagers who didn't know what we were doing there, the GAM soldiers returned on the motorcycles and took us around to where the trees ended and the rice paddies began beside the highway. They were quite blasé, holding their weapons in view of the road with the trees behind them. At that distance, with the light coming towards them, they knew the soldiers in the military trucks we could see passing on the highway couldn't see them, and they stood around joking. As we waited for what seemed a long time for our car to come around, we watched more military vehicles pass.

When our car finally showed up, three civilians rode us on the backs of their motorcycles across the open ground of the paddies. It seemed to take forever to reach the car; we felt very exposed crossing open ground from the direction of the GAM positions. When we finally got there, we frantically leapt off the bikes and into the back of the car before more military traffic came along. As the three bikes fled back across the rice paddies and out of sight, the driver slammed down the car bonnet – he had been pretending to tinker with the engine as an excuse to be there beside the road – and jumped in. We sped off back to Banda Aceh.

The Geneva meeting took place on December 9, 2002, and – to the surprise of many in Banda Aceh – the Cessation of Hostilities Agreement, the COHA, was signed. Due to the time difference, it was late in the day when I heard about it in Banda Aceh. Even the staff at the HDC office at the Kuala Tripa seemed surprised by the speed of the signing, and they didn't have enough copies of the agreement on hand to give out to journalists.

The COHA was a simple agreement that called on both sides to immediately inform their troops to cease all hostilities, acts of violence and destruction of property. This was deemed to include attacking, shooting, torturing, killing, abducting, robbing, extorting, threatening, terrorising, harassing, illegally arresting or raping people; as well as bombing or burning property and conducting illegal searches. It was a revealing list, showing the tactics used by the Indonesian military and, to a lesser extent, GAM, in the conflict.

The next five points of the agreement attempted to reduce proxy violence: both sides were to cease all forms of violence and acknowledge they were in full control of all their forces on the ground; they were to take joint action against third parties violating the agreement; neither side was to increase military strength and they were to redeploy forces (GAM was supposed to gather its troops together and TNI was supposed to reconfigure itself into a defensive force only); they were both to acknowledge the HDC's right to facilitate the agreement; they were both, in theory, to respect the right of civil society to express its democratic rights.

The time-frame for enactment of the agreement was five months – the first two months as a confidence-building period and to allow the deployment of the 150 monitors, 50 of whom would be foreigners (Filipino and Thai former and serving military officers). This would be followed by a reduction in the TNI presence and the warehousing of GAM weapons by the HDC. The police and Brimob were to be responsible for the maintenance of law and order in Aceh, but would be reinvented to perform to regular police activities; Brimob would no longer be used to track down GAM, which until then had been its primary role.

It was a comprehensive agreement that reflected the problems of Aceh and the HDC's familiarity with the situation in the field. The clause about third parties was directed at Indonesian-inspired militia or elements of GAM acting outside of central control.

The problem of TNI and Polri's extortion of the local people had been addressed and, in theory, the people were going to be given back their democratic rights in the lead up to elections in 2004. That would again, in theory, stop the arrest, harassment and kidnapping of people like Nazar and others in his SIRA organisation. The redeployment of TNI into a defensive role would also in theory reduce civilian deaths in the field. But the questions nobody could answer involved the enforcement of the agreement. Who would enforce the sanctions? Who would deal with violations? Especially in the case of the Indonesian military, what would the sanctions be?

After the signing, much was made of the involvement of the so-called 'team of wise men'. A retired four-star US marine general, Anthony Zinni; the former ambassador of Yugoslavia to Indonesia and the UN, Bodimir Loncar; and Thailand's former minister of foreign affairs, Surin Pitsuwan; were involved in brokering the deal. Zinni, who was quoted by Associated Press as saying that the US State Department had requested his involvement with the talks, had toured Aceh in August 2002.

At that time he had met with the Indonesian commander Major General Djali Yusuf and GAM officials in the Pidie district. As a Vietnam veteran and former Middle-East peace envoy, Zinni's involvement was seen as critical to deal with the military of both sides, and of course he carried the weight of the US in the negotiations. Many believed he had a lot to do with the Indonesians accepting the foreign monitors into Aceh for the first time.

The HDC, on the surface, had succeeded in doing what had become anathema to the Indonesian military since the UN went into East Timor in 1999 – getting them to accept scrutiny from officially sanctioned foreign observers inside a conflict zone in Indonesia.

In the immediate aftermath of the signing, the situation did seem to get slightly better. People weren't exactly dancing in the streets over the news, but there was a cautious optimism in Banda Aceh. Travelling back down to Lhokseumahwe the day after the agreement was signed, there was the normal tension when young TNI soldiers flagged down the car near Bireuen. But, to our relief, the soldier who smilingly looked over the car offered us some oranges. It made us laugh. We had all been prepared for another confrontation.

At other roadblocks, the soldiers merely waved the car through. But there was not much traffic and Lhokseumahwe was, as usual, virtually deserted at night. Still, it was quiet, and with nothing else to report from 'on the ground', when the BBC called me in Lhokseumahwe later that night, I was forced to relate the story of the TNI handing out fruit.

⊶─◦─⊶

SOFYAN DAWOOD sat imperiously at the centre desk of a rural schoolhouse about 30 kilometres from Lhokseumahwe. In front of him the desk was piled high with microphones and tape recorders, and around him more than 100 fully uniformed GAM fighters sat at the rows of school desks cradling their weapons between their legs, GAM flags tied around their necks. The schoolroom had simple Indonesian hygiene and alphabet cartoons on the walls, and the sight of the GAM men, with their worn automatic weapons and hard, weatherbeaten faces, sitting at the small desks was a strange one. Outside, children, civilians and other GAM fighters crowded around the open cyclone-wire windows to get a look at GAM's first televised press conference in the field.

It had been a morning of farce in Lhokseumahwe. Brigadier General Bambang Darmono had heard about the GAM leader's plans to call a press conference and had ordered the Indonesian press at the Vina Vida to attend a briefing at his headquarters. Some of them did. They were warned not to attend the GAM briefing, but most of them did anyway. Many arrived wearing bullet-proof vests after travelling in a long convoy of vehicles to the site. Some of the local journalists expressed their fear of GAM and others admitted their fear of the military as we all set out.

With theatrical flair, the small bridge on the side road leading into the GAM territory was guarded by probably the largest Acehnese man I have ever seen. Dressed in black, he was holding a heavy machine gun and was draped in ammunition belts. For added drama he had a GAM flag wrapped around his head and wore reflector sunglasses. He was an imposing sight and the Indonesian press all stopped for photos, causing a traffic jam on the bridge.

Sofyan Dawood began his address to the Indonesian television cameras with the announcement that the TNI had broken the cease-fire. 'Since the ninth there has not been big contact but there are people who have been captured, there are people who are shot, in several places there has been shooting. The TNI who are guarding ExxonMobil are responsible. I got information this morning from my members in the field that there has been two more victims.'

He said, in regard to the COHA, there had been no decisions taken yet about warehousing of GAM weapons. 'The Indonesians can't carry out sweeping [armed patrols and identity checks] if they want GAM to warehouse their weapons,' he said. And it was true the Indonesians were still carrying out checks on the population. That morning on the way to the press conference, outside of Lhokseumahwe, they had been doing just that. 'The Indonesians are distorting the terms of the agreement,' he continued. 'They are saying TNI and Polri are the only ones who have the right to carry weapons. 'But we are the army of Aceh.'

When asked if GAM still sought independence, he replied, 'The agreement didn't discuss independence or autonomy. It just talked about security.'

He said the agreement was a good one, but 'now the people of Aceh are asking for independence from Indonesian colonialism. Don't let Indonesia think it can finish this rebellion off like the way they finished off the Darul Islam rebellion in '59. That's their idea. They want us to surrender to them. There are no ideas among my men to become members of the TNI or civil servants under Indonesia. We're still in the Free Aceh Organisation.'

The military situation was unchanged, Dawood said. The Indonesians were still carrying out sweeping operations.

Then he mocked the Indonesian claims over the Cot Trieng encirclement. 'I was there for seven days and then I went back in and the TNI couldn't get me, even using tanks and helicopters. They were going in the wrong direction. They had the wrong targets. There were no GAM victims. There were some TNI and Polri victims and I got information one was from Kopassus,' he said triumphantly.

He said GAM would respect all aspects of the agreement in Geneva, however 'we still guard like the TNI too – they can't be on the streets. But if we are attacked we have a right to defend ourselves.'

The questions from the Indonesian journalists kept coming. You had the feeling that an opportunity like this was extremely rare. Here was the most-wanted leader in Aceh, second only to the Libyan-trained field commander Muzakkir Manaf (who never allowed the press to interview him), and the Indonesian press wanted to know everything. Had GAM split in two? No, said Dawood, 'GAM is one body and we are all still loyal to Hasan Tiro.' Then who was responsible for burning down the schools? 'There are those who try to destroy the GAM name. They are the bad eggs of TNI and Polri. There are also those who cause chaos in the name of GAM and they are from TNI and Polri. The ones who burn the schools are from TNI and Polri.'

The GAM leadership was making sure all the men were in their barracks and, Dawood said, they would not let them do anything to break the Geneva agreement. He said that as of 8 pm on the night of December 9, his men had ceased action. As for the TNI, 'They are still looking for the place where we had the ceremony on the fourth.' There were still convoys of troops going into the area, he said. One of 24 trucks, another of 33 trucks, another of 45 trucks.

In the end, Dawood said, it remained to be seen if the Indonesians would respect the agreement and that was the job of the international monitors. According to their leader, GAM would accept any sanctions the Joint Security Committee imposed for violations of the agreement and, he said, the heavier they were the better chance they would work. But, he added, 'We still live for independence or die as martyrs. The Indonesian side has to think about how to fix the problem. Can they do it with military operations or not?'

The problem of disarmament was raised again and Dawood revealed his true thoughts on the matter: 'Under the leadership of Indonesia, since 1998, ten people die every day. There should be human rights investigations. International bodies should be investigating. In East Timor the problem is over. Who violated human rights? Indonesia. In Aceh, who has human rights violation? It's proven. Indonesia. There are human rights violators still in Kodim in Lhokseumahwe. They ask us to hand over our weapons. We can't do it.'

Dawood was becoming exasperated with the questions and the press conference. 'Indonesia is trying to wipe out the history of the nation of Aceh to make their new history since 1945,' he continued. 'Megawati I think is only remote-controlled by the Indonesian military. There is no policy for Aceh. The officials, the generals all have business in Aceh so they can add forces here. The soldiers who come here don't know anything about the country's history. They were increasing the forces before the agreement.

'The situation has got to become normal. The people must be free to give their opinions to GAM or the TNI.'

The press conference was declared over and everybody walked out to watch the obligatory parade. For some reason, some of the troops were wearing cheap plastic motorcyle helmets painted in camouflage, which only made it obvious they didn't have the real thing. They still had the same array of weapons, but the plastic imitation helmets revealed their real poverty.

Many of the Indonesian journalists wanted to be photographed with an arm around Sofyan Dawood, or shaking his hand, or holding a GAM flag, many of which GAM gave away as souvenirs. All of this was strange – even more so when you considered some of the things these journalists had written about GAM. But at that moment, surrounded by more than 100 armed GAM men, they were punching the air with their fists and shouting 'Merdeka!'

A small knot of people hovered around Dawood and he invited all the press to the next village for coffee and something to eat at a small restaurant.

><+>-0-<+><

DAVE GORMAN was the coordinator of the HDC mission in Banda Aceh. He was the only staff member who had been there virtually since they first arrived in early 2000 – and he looked like it. He was rake-thin and had a kind of jumpy nervous energy. But he was ecstatic. The whole team had just arrived back from Geneva. They had pulled it off. After two years of broken agreements on all sides, continual violence, constant lies and crackdowns by the Indonesian authorities, and near irrelevancy for his organisation in Aceh, the HDC had finally brought it all together. And Gorman was pretty much the architect of the successful agreement. He was going to be in charge of the expanded HDC presence, and he was the perfect choice because, having lived in Aceh for almost two years, he knew exactly the difficulties they were going to face

He was excited at the prospects and when I asked him about the details, the answers just spilled out. Twenty people were already in Bandeh Aceh working on the logistics and providing technical support to the monitoring teams, and a further ten were working as assistants. There were already five temporary monitors, among them the British contingent we'd already seen around, and they would be heading out into the field straight away.

The monitoring team was going to be made up of 25 Thai and 25 Filipino members. They were all serving or retired military officers who would be seconded to the HDC under the command of a Major General Thanon Suhn from Thailand. Other staff would come from Britain, Sweden and Australia. Norway, Australia and the European Union had all pledged $2 million each to help pay for the operation.

When I asked why the monitors were coming from Thailand and the Philippines, Gorman said because they were the only countries acceptable to the Indonesians. 'GAM first suggested Australians and New Zealanders! Can you believe it?' he said. 'We sent it back to them and said try again. We didn't even suggest it to the Indonesians.'

Gorman seemed almost disbelieving that they had secured the deal. I had tried to speak to him before he'd left for Geneva, but he'd only given me the vaguest outline of what had been going on. He hadn't wanted to jeopardise anything and the whole thing had still been up in the air.

'There was a lot of negotiation,' Gorman said, 'Right up to the eleventh hour.' The security system for the warehousing of weapons was a sticking point, apparently until a two-lock system with the keys held by GAM and the HDC was suggested. 'Look,

this is a confidence-building process,' said Gorman. 'The important thing is that there's a reduction in violence. But the spirit of
the agreement is understood by both sides.'

The sanctions were something that had to be worked out by
all sides, he said. The monitoring teams' results would be
published weekly and would list any incidents and how the JIO
responded to them. Major breaches would have to be taken to a
joint council made up of the HDC and the leadership of both
sides.

The acceptance of this agreement, Gorman believed, brought
with it a better chance of bringing peace to Aceh than ever
before. 'There is a strong international focus on this,' he said.
'You've got the World Bank, the UN.'

Gorman outlined some of the problems they would face if the
agreement was to work. 'The election law will have to be
reviewed, we will have to review the autonomy law, the law for
local elections; we will have to have an all-inclusive dialogue to
formulate and implement the agreement at the Joint Security
Committee.'

What had changed the Indonesian government's position on
Aceh was, he believed, the involvement of the so-called 'wise
men' – Zinni of the US and Loncar and Pitsuwan, the former
ambassador and foreign minister of Yugoslavia and Thailand,
respectively. Not long after Megawati had assumed power, he
said, it was impressed upon her by General Zinni that there was
going to have to be some kind of international involvement
in Aceh. Then, according to Gorman, two days after the Bali
bombing on October 12, the Indonesian police chief, Dai
Bachtiar, announced that Aceh was a priority, a civil society had

a right to express itself, and human rights issues had to be addressed.

But there was still a lot to be agreed upon. The so-called peace zones – where GAM would be able to exist unmolested – would have to be established. The TNI would have to withdraw to defensive positions; only then could demilitarisation begin, with the placement of GAM's weapons in storage and the military returning to barracks. The police, in particularly Brimob, would have to be reformulated to a peacetime police force to maintain law and order.

Gorman predicted the initial stages of the agreement, such as the deployment of the monitors, would be carried out unhindered by the Indonesian authorities. But the problems would start later, if the peace held, when the income streams of the Indonesian military and the police began to dry up. 'Then we are very likely to see some big problems,' said Gorman. 'But we will just have to face that.'

KAMARUZZAMAN HAD also just returned from Geneva. He looked exhausted but invited Chris McCall, from the *Economist*, Meredyth and me back to the same room at the Kaula Tripa he had occupied for all the years of negotiation. 'There is a difference in this process, which is quite strong,' he said. 'It is the coming of the international monitors.' He looked happy, but said the negotiations had got stuck over the lock set-up for the weapons warehouses. 'The Indonesians wouldn't come to the negotiating table until that [the lock arrangement] was there. The Indonesians put this back in suddenly and they made the situation tense,' he said.

According to Kamaruzzaman, the Indonesians had already started to misrepresent the deal by declaring that GAM's renunciation of weapons was part of it. In his mind, the significant part of the deal was that the Indonesians had to withdraw *their* forces from operations. 'We don't know how long the military will adhere to the agreement. They are still going to have operations,' he said.

He said that it was impossible to predict what would happen because 'the government in Jakarta say one thing and the TNI don't obey'. His opinion was that the process's only hope of success was if the international community gave it priority. 'I think without pressure from the international community the Indonesians would not have signed and without pressure they will try and sabotage these points,' said Kamaruzzaman.

He was probably being more open because the deal had been signed, the monitors were on their way and – possibly – 'I don't think their [the military] intentions are good. In the Aceh problem the only ones that are left out is the military. The only way they can do anything is with guns. Certainly they have tactics which we are going to see.' He laughed at the notion of a regular peacetime police force. 'Normal police functions . . . like UNAMET. Bang, bang.' He fired an imaginary automatic weapon in the air. It was a reference as to how the Indonesian military had run the first UN mission, UNAMET, out of East Timor in 1999 by surrounding their compounds and shooting above their heads.

'There will be more Javanese militias in Aceh, that is my prediction.' Why did they sign then?' one of us asked. 'Whatever. We have to try first. I think the international community hopes there is an agreement,' he said. 'Indonesia cannot be defended anymore. Indonesia is a military country. There is no hope . . . with the Bali bomb I was hoping the Balinese might try to leave. If Aceh leaves it will be certain that Indonesia will disintegrate.'

As he warmed up, Kamaruzzaman started to reveal what he really thought of an Indonesia dominated by Java. 'Nietzsche said, "It's not possible for a country with a lower level of culture to lead another with a higher level of culture." Killing for them is normal. A king in Java is like a messenger of god. For us a king is respected. An unfair king is brought down.

'Why not have a sultan, Hasan Di Tiro? There are plenty of kingdoms in the world that are democracies.'

He made a joke about Australia still having a queen before talking about the historical links between the British and the Acehnese sultanate before the Dutch arrived. He pointed out that the current GAM prime minister in exile, Malik Mahmood, had served in the British navy as a young man due to his Singapore citizenship.

He then asked me the same question Brigadier General Bambang Darmono had asked, but from the opposite side. What does Australia think of Aceh getting independence? I replied there were many in the Australian government who were very afraid of Indonesia breaking up, that they thought it would bring chaos and instability to the region.

'The people in Australia who say the break up of Indonesia will bring chaos,' said Kamaruzzaman, 'Well, I think it is not going to happen – the chaos they predict. Through the trade and if the borders are there, if the communication is there. A country like Australia and countries which are democratic can give ideas, they can give advice.'

Concerns such as those of Australia seemed frivolous to him. 'The ones who have a disaster are the people of Aceh because our culture has been destroyed by the Indonesians. It won't be long now until Aceh is independent. Thirty years of war with Holland and they always said it was near. For Acehnese, death is not a problem at all. What is important is how we die.'

He went back to talking about how Kopassus and the Indonesian Combat Intelligence Unit (SGI), recruit young unemployed Acehnese to create enmity among the people and create problems with Acehnese businesses. He was very negative about the immediate possibility of peace in Aceh, and pointed to the activities of the Indonesian intelligence services in Aceh as a sign of things to come. He looked exhausted and we said goodnight.

Back in the middle of town, Chris, Meredyth and I went for some dinner. It was late and there wasn't much open so we went to a small Chinese-run restaurant with outdoor tables. As we ate, a young man with long hair and wearing greasy camouflage pants sat down and stared hard at the three of us. The expression on his face was halfway between a leer and a scowl, but it had a kind of vicious ferocity that scared the hell out of me. He reminded me of militia I had seen in East Timor in 1999 – all wired up with a combination of hate, booze, drugs and indoctrination by some military intelligence operative. Maybe he was just some local drug-addled kid, but he didn't look Acehnese and he was grinning in a twisted manner – as if he was about to do something. The Chinese owners tried to get rid of him but he refused to move and it looked like there would be a scene, so we paid our bill and left.

I couldn't help thinking of what Kamaruzzaman had said and how plausible it was that the Indonesian military would not let Aceh go – and what they would do to keep it. I also thought about how easy it would be for them to hide behind the deniable screen of organised thugs, just like they had done so many times before.

><del>·<del>·O·<del>·<

FIGURING THAT the first HDC monitoring team had gone to Meulaboh, the capital of West Aceh, Meredyth and I headed down there the following day. The minibus was crowded as it left the capital but quickly emptied on the outskirts, and soon it was just the driver, his two friends and us. He drove fast and talked about how there were always problems on this road, which hugged the coast and was flanked on one side by the sea and on the other by a high, forested cliff. At a few points it turned briefly inland and we travelled along the floor of deep ravines. It was just before one such turn that the driver swivelled around and said that there were always problems at this place and that he would wait for the military convoy we had just passed to come through. The driver and his friends were worried about ambushes but when I asked them if it was GAM who was doing the ambushing, they wouldn't say; they just said there were always problems here.

We passed through along with the convoy without incidents. Our driver said it was very common for GAM or the military to cut the road to West Aceh. There was no road across the mountains to the west coast, and the area had a very isolated, back-water feel about it. In former times it had been a tourist desti-nation favoured by European backpackers seeking the ultimate jungle and beach hideaway experience. We passed a few aban-doned and falling-down resorts – thatch huts that ranged along the pristine white beaches could be glimpsed through the palm trees from the road. Now, only the occasional traveller passed through, and would invariably be harassed by the police or military when he or she arrived at one of the towns on this road, which led all the way down the west coast of Aceh and back to North Sumatra.

Meulaboh was a dusty, broken-down town with wide streets full of shouting rickshaw drivers. We were directed to the Tiara hotel – which was actually the Mutiara but the M and U had fallen off the sign so long ago it was now referred to as the Tiara. The only contacts we had down there were some people involved in the same student organisation that the recently murdered Musliadi had been the representative of. When we called them, they invited us to a prayer meeting they were having that evening in memory of their friend who had just died.

About 30 people had gathered in a small room in a private house. We sat cross-legged with them on the floor in a large circle. Dark coffee was served and the group, mostly men, told us about what they knew had been happening in West Aceh. There had been no real change in the situation since the peace deal was signed.

There was still a military operation going on in the subdistrict of Beutung. On December 11 and 12, they said, troops from Battalion 521 had beaten and slashed 12 people in the village of Pantai Chermai. Two days before the agreement was signed, GAM had shot and wounded two Brimob soldiers in the village of Panya Pucuk, and the reprisals were continuing. Around 2000 people from the area had fled to the closest regional centre of Panga after a TNI operation on December 10 and 11. Two new military bases had recently been set up in Panga, which was about 75 kilometres from Meulaboh on the road back to the capital, and in the first two weeks of December at least six people had been badly beaten by the military at their new checkpoints near the town. We had seen some of the refugees as we travelled through the town earlier that day; they were camped out in the grounds of a mosque by the side of the road.

The people at the memorial gathering explained how in West Aceh there had not been a lot of GAM activity until 1998. The traditional lands of the Tiro leaders and the real GAM strongholds were over on the other side of the province, along the main highway and near the strategically important gas field. But now, they said, there were at least 1600 TNI troops based permanently in West Aceh, and there were frequent operations.

The local GAM leader, Abu Arafah, had been killed in October 2002. He had been taking a bath and had been surrounded and murdered by TNI soldiers. A few months earlier, on August 16, operations to find the GAM base resulted in the murder of seven sleeping GAM members during an early-morning raid. Two days later four more GAM members and eight civilians were killed nearby. But those deaths hadn't stopped the operations – four women had been arrested 30 kilometres from Meulaboh by Brimob the week before the peace deal. One of them had had a shotgun in her house and they were all still being detained.

Some of those present at the gathering had met with the HDC team who had come down to Meulaboh the previous day. They had given them the same information about the situation, particularly about the new refugees in Panga. But it didn't seem to be a big deal to anyone – these things happened all the time and the current situation was quiet compared to the past. TNI and Brimob were still behaving as they had done before the agreement, and there was little expectation that things would change, even though the international monitors were about to be deployed.

We stopped talking and prayers were chanted for their dead colleague. We were then told it was time to go. It was getting late and the local people didn't want to be picked up by the military who patrolled the town, so we were taken via a round-about route back to the centre of town, which, by 8 pm on a Saturday night, was totally deserted.

⊱⊰

BACK IN Banda Aceh, there was more information from GAM about breakdowns in the cease-fire, mostly in North Aceh and involving the area surrounding the ExxonMobil plant.

On December 10, 50 Brimob had arrived in the village of Batu Fat Baranto and surrounded the mosque. Then, by firing into the air, they had forced the people into a truck and taken them to attend a rally to support the government. On the same day, TNI in Lhoksukon had arrested a small boy at his house (they probably believed he was involved with GAM or had some information) and taken him away, then carried out an operation at the local bus terminal where they demanded 5000 to 15,000 rupiah from every passing vehicle. Meanwhile, about 1000 TNI soldiers in 100 trucks were patrolling near the previously encircled area of Nisam. Later that same day, December 10, 400 of these troops carried out foot patrols in the same area.

The next day, the forces protecting ExxonMobil shot at people who had fled Nisam and the TNI stole a motorcycle that was left behind. That night, an unidentified body with fresh gunshot wounds was found in the same area. For the rest of that week, TNI and police carried out searches near ExxonMobil with tracker dogs, and Brimob blocked the main road and demanded between 20,000 and 100,000 rupiah from every truck, and 5000 to 10,000 rupiah from every motorcycle. Two people were arrested – a 28-year-old and a 50-year-old man – and were being held in the local military base where they were reportedly being tortured with electric shocks.

This had all taken place after the signing of the agreement and demonstrated how little attention the authorities had paid to the deal, even in the area directly surrounding their headquarters in Lhokseumahwe.

Back at the Kuala Tripa, the monitoring teams were not available for comment. Dave Gorman, the HDC coordinator, was temporarily out of town and Bill Dowell, who ran the HDC public information office, had left for good. A stand-in spokesperson said the peace deal was holding and there had been no reported violations.

In the dining room, there were many new faces – European

and American NGO workers wearing the trademark uniform of the foreign professional in conflict zones (cargo pants and vests full of pockets). The Joint Security Commission (JSC) was yet to have its first meeting, but a new building down by the river had been found to house the HDC operation and that was the main topic of conversation.

The logistics team was busy arranging accommodation and transport for the Filipino and Thai monitors who were about to arrive, and the carpark was full of new rented vehicles with HDC stickers on the side. There was an air of excitement and motivation as the sunburnt foreigners ate their meals and drank beer in the comfortable air-conditioned dining room. But outside the situation continued largely as it always had, with the TNI and the police making full use of their positions to extort as much money as they could from the local population before being sent somewhere else in Indonesia.

Even as the HDC mission was being set up and before the JSC had met for the first time, Indonesia's national police chief, Dai Bachtiar, was announcing the need for more Brimob in Aceh. With only one police officer for every 1000 Acehnese, he deemed the forces insufficient and sent more, in direct contravention of the agreement that had just been signed.

Similarly, the military announced it was sending 1800 more marines to Aceh, and the navy said it was assigning 11 warships to be stationed in Aceh's waters.

On the same day, December 14, it was reported that two men had been shot dead near Bireuen the day before, and a woman had been murdered earlier in the week in South Aceh.

In the wake of the peace deal, international media interest in Aceh had declined. It seemed that because the Indonesian government was at last trying to address some of the ingrained problems in Aceh by allowing the HDC to bring in the monitors, the continual incidents didn't warrant much attention. There seemed to be a consensus among foreign governments, the HDC and some sections of the media to allow the Indonesian government to claim success and to commend them for allowing the peace process to begin. It seemed that the situation on the ground was being temporarily ignored in order to allow the monitors time to get into position and begin their work.

⊢◄►─◦─◄►─┤◄

BUT THINGS did start to calm down in the field. By early January 2003 it was peaceful enough for GAM to have a meeting of 2500 of its officials from all across Aceh to discuss the cease-fire. The meeting, held at a secret location in North Aceh, was guarded by GAM troops and passed without incident. It was the first time Muzakkir Manaf had met most of the GAM officials since becoming the commander for Aceh after the death of Abdullah Syafei the previous year. According to Sofyan Dawood, the main spokesman for GAM in the field, the meeting was held to formalise arrangements for a GAM police contingent to enforce the cease-fire among their own people.

At around the same time, Dave Gorman of the HDC was quoted in the *Jakarta Post* on January 8 as saying the average level of fatalities in Aceh had fallen from 87 per month to 11 per month after the peace deal. There were signs that things were going well. It was reported GAM had begun recalling their troops to their bases and some had already returned to their villages to resume life as civilians. The monitors, under the command of Thai Major General Tanonsuk Tuvinun, had begun arriving on December 28 and were beginning to deploy to the areas most affected by the conflict near Bireuen, Pidie and Greater Aceh. There were already 28 cases of violations for the JSC to investigate by January, but the outlook was hopeful that they would be addressed.

By mid-February, the JSC had announced the establishment of seven peace zones in accordance with the agreement. No GAM troops or Indonesian military were supposed to be carrying weapons in the areas in West, South, North and East Aceh. This was the point at which GAM was supposed to begin warehousing its weapons in accordance with the agreement, the TNI was supposed to adopt a purely defensive role, and the Indonesian police force was supposed to revert to a civil police role.

Kamaruzzaman declared GAM was ready to lay down 20 per cent of its weapons immediately in the 32 locations outlined by the HDC, and committed GAM to completing the disarmament within the next five months.

At the same time as the peace zones were announced, coordinating minister for political and security affairs, Susilo Bambang Yudhoyono, a former general and the third most powerful man in Indonesia, began accusing GAM of violating the agreement. Ominously, he told reporters in Lhokseumahwe that 'there are too many violations and irregularities and distortions [of the accord], most of which have been committed by GAM'. He added, 'Now we have to make sure whether we will all comply with all the agreements drawn up in the peace pact or not.'

Despite the accusations flying between GAM and the Indonesian government, conditions for average Acehnese people did improve throughout February. Trucks and public buses resumed travelling at night. Restaurants and cafes in the major towns began opening later and local markets reported upturns in trade. The fear that had kept people indoors in the evenings and made Banda Aceh virtually deserted after dark began to dissipate, and much was made in the local press of the success of the peace deal in allowing people to return to a more normal existence. Oxfam, USAID and the World Food Program increased their staff and programs in Aceh, and Japan quickly made good on its promise to provide reconstruction aid in the form of a US$5 million grant to the Consultative Group on Indonesia. Japan also provided US$1.2 million to assist in the establishment of the JSC.

As the demilitarisation period began in mid-February, the HDC had recorded nine GAM deaths in the two months since the truce was signed; four security officers and 24 civilians had been reported killed in the same period. This was hailed in the local press as evidence that the cease-fire was working.

However, there were some things that the Indonesian authorities just weren't ready to accept, and these revealed the huge gulf in expectations between the Acehnese and the Indonesians over what had actually been agreed to in the peace deal.

On January 9, SIRA held a rally for free speech in Lhokseumahwe. According to SIRA, around 15,000 people tried to attend the rally but those coming from outside the town had been turned away by the police. As a reminder of what had happened in November 2000 when those trying to attend the rally calling for a referendum in Banda Aceh were killed, four people were shot and badly wounded by the police for refusing to turn around. The rally went ahead with only about 3000 people in attendence.

Despite a specific provision in the peace agreement that stated, 'Both parties will allow civil society to express without hindrance their democratic rights', the police issued an arrest warrant for one of the organisers, the well-known activist, Kautsar, on January 27. He was charged with 'convening a public event without police permission' and went into hiding.

Nazar, the head of SIRA, was not so lucky. At 1.30 am on February 12, six police officers kicked down the door of his house outside Banda Aceh and arrested him for holding a rally without a permit. The police major in charge of the arrest told Associated Press that Nazar had made speeches at the Lhokseumahwe rally that 'caused anxiety to the people'. Dave Gorman, now in charge of the HDC mission, said, 'I think giving a public speech is not wrong.' But for the time being, the HDC was powerless to do anything about the arrest. And despite continued protests from international human rights groups such as Amnesty International and the London-based Indonesian human rights NGO, TAPOL, Nazar remained in police custody. The police announced they were also issuing arrest warrants for three other SIRA activists involved in the demonstration.

Two days before Nazar's arrest, Lesley McCulloch had finally been freed from the police headquarters in Banda Aceh. Her trial had dragged on until December 30, when she was finally convicted to five months imprisonment for violating her tourist visa. The time she had already served since her incarceration in September was deducted from the sentence, and she was released on February 9, 2003.

Joy Lee Sadler was released one month before McCulloch after serving four months in detention for the same offence. During her incarceration, McCulloch had conducted interviews in which she spoke of the appalling beatings and mistreatment of other prisoners at the police headquarters, relaying how Sadler, as a nurse, would often be called on by the police to treat inmates they'd beaten.

McCulloch's release was accompanied by statements from security minister Susilo Bambang Yudhoyono that questioned whether foreign academics should be present in either of the Indonesian provinces wracked by separatism – Papua and Aceh. It seemed the silence of Australia, the US and the UK on the incarceration and treatment of McCulloch and Sadler had only emboldened the Indonesian authorities to announce that such measures were justified and indeed desirable to keep unwanted foreigners out of their 'conflict' areas.

It was from mid-February onward that the differences in the interpretation of the agreement by GAM and the Indonesian government began to become clear. As the terms of the warehousing of GAM's weapons were thrashed out, it became obvious that they had no intention of disarming fully, as the Indonesians had publicly declared they should. GAM only intended to store their weapons under the supervision of the HDC. And the TNI and police showed no indication that they were ready to withdraw their forces from the field and adopt a defensive stance as outlined in the agreement. GAM, not unreasonably, thought this aspect of the agreement would involve the dismantling of hundreds of military and police security posts throughout Aceh, and the relocation of these troops back to their regional barracks. The TNI, on the other hand, saw it as a matter of moving only a few of the posts located in the proposed peace zones and leaving the rest in place. The police, for their part, continued to act in a counterinsurgency role, arresting activists such as Nazar, and continued to conduct intelligence-gathering operations among the population. Brimob was still present in the province and still manning checkpoints and extorting money from the population. They were also involved in several violations of the peace accord during this period.

The people at HDC continued to put on a brave face despite all the problems they were facing in achieving any kind of compliance to the terms of the agreement from the Indonesian side. In an article published in the *Jakarta Post* on February 28, Martin Griffiths, the director of the HDC, pointed to the sense of hope and normalcy the peace deal had brought to the lives of the Acehnese. He talked about young couples enjoying the beach near Banda Aceh, people staying up late at coffee shops in the capital and the fact that after 4000 deaths in Aceh in the previous two years, the violence was finally slowing down. He spoke of the commitment of both sides to the continued peace. He said that the fact there had been several weeks in Aceh without a conflict-related death was a sign of progress, and that all parties had to keep their 'eyes on the prize' of a peaceful Aceh. The article ended by acknowledging the most difficult part of the process was still in the immediate future, with the five-month demilitarisation phase having only just begun.

But the demands this phase would make on the Indonesian military and police based in Aceh would, as Dave Gorman had predicted in December, prove too much for them too bear.

⊳⊶⊙⊶⊲

ON MONDAY, March 3, the HDC got an indication of the limit of its authority when around 4000 people besieged its office in the central Aceh town of Takengon. They burned down the three HDC vehicles parked outside and injured two monitors; then the crowd ransacked the office and held seven HDC representatives as hostages for several hours. The violence continued for most of the day, with the Indonesian military eventually dispersing the crowd at 4 pm.

Ostensibly, the crowd had gathered to demonstrate against the collecting of taxes by GAM in the area. They were demanding the HDC disarm GAM in Central Aceh immediately. The Indonesian state news agency, Antara, quickly reported that the crowd attacked because they were enraged by GAM taxes and the alleged kidnapping of a local businessman by GAM.

Antara has a long history of being a conduit for Indonesian intelligence misinformation that dates back to the Indonesian takeover of East Timor in 1975. And in this case it was almost as if the script had been worked out beforehand – mob angry at so-called GAM abuses attacks HDC then military steps in to restore order, removing HDC to the safety of the local military post.

The fact that Central Aceh had been a training centre for pro-Indonesian militia for the last two years and that the attack had come at a time when the HDC was pressuring the military to withdraw to their barracks was not lost on any observers.

The TNI had employed exactly the same tactics four years earlier in East Timor to put pressure on the United Nations. As the UN deployed in East Timor in mid-1999, militia attacks on UN posts in Maliana, Liquiça and Viqueque greatly reduced their capacity to function. It was what Kamaruzzaman had been talking about in December when he laughed at the concept of 'normal police function' and made a shooting gesture in the air.

Back in Banda Aceh, HDC head Dave Gorman could not confirm the veracity of the Antara report.

The following day, GAM issued a clear statement blaming the military for the attack, saying it had been carried out by Central Aceh militia under military direction. 'This incident was the work of militias trained by the Indonesian military,' rebel spokesman Sofyan Dawood told Associated Press. 'Their aim is to expel international monitors from Central Aceh so no-one can see what the military is doing.'

The military responded in time-honoured fashion. The spokesman in Banda Aceh, Lieutenant Colonel Firdaus Komarno, told AP, 'The rebels can accuse all they want. We had nothing to do with it. It was a spontaneous and genuine reaction to extortion by the rebels.'

The HDC, for their part, issued a strong statement calling on the perpetrators of the attack to be brought to trial, but nothing came of it.

The Indonesian NGO for missing persons and victims of violence, Kontras, released a report two days later in which they said the military was responsible for organising the attack. The report stated that 500 militia, some of whom were serving members of Kostrad, had been transported under escort to the office to join the civilians gathered there. Firdaus Komarno told the *Jakarta Post* the Kontras report was 'absolute rubbish'. He added that, 'The Indonesian military did not engineer that incident. The accusation of a military-trained militia is nonsense. It is untrue.' The report also said the militia had been involved in forcing the people to attend the demonstration.

The attack on the HDC prompted GAM to announce a delay in the planned warehousing of weapons on the grounds that the military had not yet made any move to withdraw its troops from the field and adopt the defensive positions outlined in the agreement. The military acknowledged that they had not done this, simply saying that this would take time.

The HDC kept maintaining that the process was still on track and that the delay would be overcome. But the signals from the Indonesian side continued to be negative. General Ryamizard Ryacudu, by then TNI chief of staff, told Kostrad troops in Jakarta that GAM was not only the enemy of TNI, they were also the enemy of the Indonesian state. The spoiling tactics had worked, and there was little doubt among any of the participants in the peace process about what was really going on. The point at which the process was impinging on the interests of the Indonesian military in Aceh had been reached after only two months and the warning in the form of the 'spontaneous attack' on the HDC rang loud and clear. Even as the last of the Thai and Filipino monitors arrived in Banda Aceh at the end of the first week of March, the process was in serious trouble. Central Aceh had been declared a no-go zone for the HDC and its office had been closed. The process continued with the declaration of more peace zones in traditionally strong GAM areas in North Aceh, but the crucial questions of demilitarisation, storage of weapons and the withdrawal of the TNI to their barracks had not been resolved. The honeymoon period of the agreement was over.

On March 13 it happened again, this time in the East Aceh town of Langsa. A mob of several hundred people surrounded the JSC office and demanded the GAM representatives hand over 70 million rupiah they said had been paid for the release of some local hostages. The six GAM representatives said they knew nothing about it and fled the office in fear for their lives. They went first to the local TNI barracks, then fled Langsa for their own camp in East Aceh. The office was abandoned and the local police and military did nothing to stop the situation.

The next day, Indonesian military chief Major General Endriartono Sutarto publicly urged the JSC to adopt police escorts while carrying out their monitoring duties. He said the military could not protect GAM delegates, as it would give the impression they were detaining them. It was a familiar pattern – threaten the international monitors and then offer them the protection that would limit their ability to carry out their job. If the monitors were forced to conduct their activities in the presence of the authorities, there was a significantly reduced chance that the local Acehnese would be able to let them know exactly what was going on. Once again, it was a method that had been used to great effect to thwart the United Nations' investigations in East Timor four years previously.

Sofyan Dawood issued a press release on March 19 outlining what GAM in the field knew about the program the Indonesian military were running to derail the peace process. He claimed the TNI was 'mobilising a number of trained civilians to demonstrate and harass the JSC and the peace process in Aceh'. In the previous few days, demonstrations against the JSC had taken place in the towns of Sigli and Bireuen, as well as the attacks in Langsa and Takengon. In Lhokseumahwe, a grenade with the pin half removed had been left outside the JSC office. Dawood said admissions by the demonstrators themselves and the similarity in the jargon used on banners to condemn the JSC proved the TNI had organised the protests. The GAM statement then sent a very clear message to those Acehnese who had been involved in the demonstrations and who were involved in the TNI militia groups – their own intelligence organisation was compiling lists and the 'provocateurs and manipulators' would be dealt with. 'Very firm actions will be taken against them in due course. The TNI/Polri will not be able to protect these traitors of peace from the long arms of the revolutionary laws of GAM,' the statement warned.

Dawood also reminded those who chose to work with the military that if the peace process was destroyed, they would be used by the Indonesians to fight GAM; in the end they would be forced to fight on the front line by their Indonesian bosses. The statement then called on the TNI to respect the peace zones and to cease the extortion of vehicles that had continued unabated on the Banda Aceh to Medan highway.

The JSC issued a statement on March 20 which called for a complete investigation of the Takengon attack and the prosecution of those found responsible for it. The report also claimed the Indonesian authorities in Takengon knew about the attack on the office several hours before it took place. The HDC immediately issued a press release saying it applauded the JSC's strong report and also recommended an investigation into the incident be carried out by the government of Indonesia and law enforcement officers prosecute those involved. It was clear that both the JSC and the HDC staff in Banda Aceh believed the Indonesian authorities were behind the attacks.

The military responded to these claims by announcing a meeting of all its leaders in Aceh to be held in Lhokseumahwe to coincide with the visit of the army chief of staff, General Ryamizard Ryacudu. As SIRA reported two days before the visit on March 25, preparations were underway to provide the general with the appropriate reception when he visited the Pidie district. According to SIRA, the TNI was exerting pressure on dozens of village chiefs to organise mass rallies on March 27. The villagers were being told to rally outside the JSC office and the military command in Sigli. Transportation and food would be provided, as would the banners, which had already been handed out by the local military. They read: 'We love peace, but we love the red-and-white [Indonesian flag] more', 'Please protect us, army chief, from GAM terror', 'We love the TNI and want more army posts here' and 'We don't want outsiders interfering in our affairs'. Every village chief was instructed to bring at least 20 people to the demonstration or the village would be declared a suspected GAM area. Houses along the route the general was to follow were instructed to hang khaki cloth as a sign of support.

SIRA concluded that this was a dangerous move by the military that 'will disrupt the peace process, and force local inhabitants to support the security forces by being used as militaristic thugs. It shows that the Indonesian government is not behaving honestly towards the agreement.'

The meeting went ahead at the multipurpose building complex at the PT Arun gas-processing facility outside of Lhokseumahwe, with all 12 regional military commanders from Aceh in attendence. There were problems with the demonstration planned for March 27, however. Most of the village heads (*Guechiks*) didn't attend, they simply disappeared. The TNI responded by claiming 56 of the village chiefs had been kidnapped by GAM – which Sofyan Dawood quickly refuted in a statement on March 28 which said the village heads had chosen to flee to the safety of the GAM area or to elsewhere in Aceh rather than be forced to attend the rally. He invited journalists to come and speak to the village heads in the GAM areas, to prove they had not been kidnapped. Dawood also alleged that the main purpose of the TNI meeting in Lhokseumahwe was to outline the plan for the formation of Acehnese militia by the Indonesian military. General Ryacudu was proposing that ten to 20 people be recruited from each village and trained by the TNI as auxiliaries.

<hr />

PROBLEMS KEPT appearing in the peace process. On April 4 at 2 am, a group of men tried to kidnap Amri Abdul Wahab, the GAM negotiator and JSC member, from his house in Banda Aceh. Amri fled by foot as the attackers smashed in the front door. He said the attackers were a group of Indonesian special forces soldiers who had come to assassinate him. The previous day, six Swedish HDC employees were forced to leave Banda Aceh when the Indonesian authorities refused to renew their visas.

On April 6, a mob attacked the empty JSC office in Langsa and burned it to the ground. The remaining JSC representatives in Langsa, unable to work, took shelter with the military. On April 7, a mob of several hundred people surrounded the JSC office in Tapaktuan in South Aceh and demanded the JSC leave town by the end of the week. In Bireuen on the same day, 40 members of Brimob occupied the office for eight hours and kicked and punched a GAM representative. They demanded GAM return a supposedly kidnapped comrade. The HDC and the JSC ordered all the monitors in the field to return to the capital on April 9.

The situation had become untenable. The militia were racking up the protests against the JSC. 'They were demanding Indonesian government's sovereignty over Aceh,' said Dave Gorman, shortly after the attacks. 'They said they disagreed with separatists . . . they want the Joint Security Committee – if it can't do its job effectively – to leave.'

'It's clear these demonstrations, threats and attacks against the teams are organised and they all have a consistent message,' Gorman told Reuters news agency. 'That message has been anti-GAM, anti-JSC and anti-peace process.'

The military's accusations that GAM was violating the agreement intensified, despite the fact that GAM operatives were those being abducted and killed. The day after the monitors were recalled to Banda Aceh, nine GAM members were killed in four separate incidents throughout Aceh. Sofyan Dawood issued a statement saying 34 members of GAM had been kidnapped and killed by the Indonesians since the deal was signed.

The Indonesian government and military stuck to their script, regardless. Susilo Bambang Yudhoyono told Associated Press, 'We've agreed to honour the peace deal and bring the issue of serious violations to the meeting. Should the situation worsen, we may reverse our position. The president has ordered troops to be prepared to enforce the country's territorial integrity.'

More troops started arriving in Aceh. According to GAM intelligence reports, 8500 fresh Indonesian troops arrived on three ships on the night of April 12. GAM claimed the Indonesians had plans to deploy a total of 28,000 new troops. Three days later in Jakarta, on April 15, President Megawati Sukarnoputri met with the heads of all branches of the military and the police, the foreign and defence ministers and the vice-president. The subject of the closed-door meeting was the resumption of a military campaign to wipe out GAM.

The details of that meeting have never been released. But from that point on, every statement and action of the Indonesian government and all branches of the military relating to the Aceh situation led to the inevitable. Whatever the cost, GAM was going to be eliminated through force. Over the next month, every opportunity was taken to create in the domestic and foreign press an image of GAM as criminal, unreasonable and brutal. Every opportunity was taken to prepare public opinion in Indonesia and in the international community for the coming military campaign. The inalienable right of the Indonesian state to use all means at its disposal to protect its 'territorial integrity' became the pillar of Indonesian policy towards Aceh, and the denigration of GAM and the institutions involved in the peace process began in earnest.

Amien Rais, speaker of the People's Consultative Assembly (MPR), Indonesia's highest legislative body, spoke to the Antara news agency the day before the meeting: 'All along, I have said that the HDC is a small NGO in Europe. How could we have raised it high above our republic? I can frankly say that our attempt to find the best possible solution in Aceh by asking for a decision, a policy and a way out by the HDC was a big mistake.'

He said the Assembly would support a military option to wipe out GAM and there was no more role for the foreign mediators. 'The government should directly ask GAM leaders, "If you want peace, let us make peace. If you want secession from the Republic of Indonesia, no way",' he said. This statement was published the day of the closed-door meeting.

The next day, the commanders of Kopassus and Kostrad weighed in with their remarks, which were published in the national daily, *Kompas*. 'Of course the army is ready; 100,000, 200,000, whatever. Don't think about how many men are needed to deal with the rebels. The quicker, the better,' said Major General Sriyanto, the Kopassus commander. The Kostrad commander, Lieutenant General Bibit Waluyo, when asked about the likelihood of civilian casualties in such an operation in Aceh, added, 'If we were to have to think about the casualties, it would be difficult for us, so the best thing to make sure there are no casualties is not to rebel.'

The national police chief, General Dai Bachtiar, told reporters that GAM should be given until the end of that month to surrender its weapons. 'We would still give GAM leaders time to surrender their weapons. We will take swift action if they fail to do this,' he said.

The nation's largest Muslim organisation *Nahdlatul Ulama* (NU), also supported the government's moves in response to

GAM's perceived use of violence. 'Whether there's a military operation or otherwise will depend on GAM. If the movement resorts to military actions, the government must respond to them by military operations too,' said NU chairman, Hasyim Muzadi.

The Indonesian government, represented by security minister Susilo Bambang Yudhoyono, said military action would not be launched until after the next round of talks with GAM, which were scheduled for April 25. Army chief Endriartono Sutarto also said no military action would be ordered until after the talks. But the implications were clear. If GAM did not drop its aim of independence and agree to disarm publicly, the whole process was off, regardless of whether the TNI or Polri obeyed the agreement or not, which after four months they had shown no inclination to do.

Bickering between all sides – the government, GAM and HDC – began over where the next round of talks were to be held. The Indonesians wanted Bali, then Tokyo. GAM insisted on Geneva. Meanwhile, the Indonesian military continued to build up their troops in Aceh and the number of violent incidents started to escalate to pre-agreement levels, with 50 people killed over three weeks in April. Two days before the proposed talks, Susilo Bambang Yudhoyono was in Jakarta inspecting two marine battalions that were about to be dispatched to Aceh. 'We have to anticipate the worst-case scenario should our efforts to promote dialogue bear no fruit,' Susilo told reporters. The navy chief of staff, Admiral Bernard Kent Sondakh, was also there. He told reporters the navy was preparing between 14 and 17 warships to be sent to Aceh to join the ten already on duty there.

Later in the day at Brimob headquarters, the retired General Yudhoyono reviewed 6000 Brimob troops who were also being dispatched to Aceh, regardless of the outcome of the talks. Major General Djali Yusuf had said earlier in the month that at least 50,000 personnel would be required for the Aceh operation, and the new troops would be added to the 26,000 TNI and 14,000 Polri already in the province. More reports of troops arriving by sea and air kept coming from GAM and from official Indonesian sources.

On the same day that the military leaders announced the build-up, GAM requested that the talks, which had finally been planned to go ahead in Geneva, be delayed for two days. The reasoning was simple. 'After we have been in the aircraft for 18 hours in economy class, when we arrive in Geneva of course we cannot go straight to the meeting room,' GAM negotiator Sofyan Ibrahim Tiba told AFP news agency. He added that they also wanted time to consult with the exiled leadership in Sweden before the talks.

The Indonesian response was immediate. They cancelled the talks. 'The Indonesian people have dignity and honour, which cannot be humiliated by anyone, including the separatist Free Aceh Movement,' said Yudhoyono, who, it was reported, had consulted President Megawati Sukarnoputri before pulling out. Yudhoyono said GAM had been irresponsible in pulling out of the talks and the military preparations continued.

The GAM commander in the field, Muzakkir Manaf, responded immediately to Indonesia's withdrawal from the talks with a statement that pointed out that the GAM delegation hadn't been scheduled to leave Indonesia until 11.55 pm on

April 24, like Yudhoyono himself, and that the cancellation of the talks was 'childish, egotistic and most likely with a hidden agenda behind it'. The statement went on to say that GAM's request to delay the talks was being misrepresented as a cancellation and used to justify the military operation.

Muzakkir Manaf said in his statement: 'The TNA [*Tentara Nasional Aceh* – national army of Aceh] does hereby request the international community not to let the GoI [government of Indonesia] act as it pleases in trying to solve the conflict in Aceh. It was the GoI that orchestrated the condition leading to the stalling of the JSC machinery, it was also the one that asked for the convening of the JC [Joint Council], and it is now this same government that has cancelled the planned meeting of the JC.'

BUT THE international community was not listening. The US advance on Baghdad in Iraq was in progress, and Indonesia's deft footwork in creating pretexts for their own military operations went unnoticed. The only international reaction of any sort to the breakdown was from Australia's foreign minister, Alexander Downer, who told ABC radio: 'The GAM must work hard to be involved in the peaceful settlement of the Aceh issue, which should not be resolved through a military operation.' His comments were run on Antara and widely published in Indonesia inferring Australian support for the government position. It was hardly the international response GAM was calling for. It was a green light for the Indonesians to go on thinking that not only was Australia accepting their machinations, it was going to back them up.

Meanwhile, the public relations campaign to demonise GAM continued. None other than Susilo Bambang Yudhoyono told reporters that GAM's chief negotiator, Sofyan Ibrahim Tiba, once asked him for US$50 million to sign the peace deal. But according to Tiba, it was Susilo who offered *him* the money. As he told the *Jakarta Post*: 'I met Susilo in Singapore last year, just before the signing of the peace agreement. I asked him whether the government was serious about the offer, and he said yes.' Tiba continued, 'I never asked for US$50 million in compensation; they offered [it to] me. Three officials from Susilo's office made the offer to me before the peace deal was signed,' he said. Then some bombs went off in Jakarta and the finger was pointed at GAM.

On Sunday, April 26, a bomb exploded near the Kentucky Fried Chicken outlet at Jakarta's airport, wounding ten people. Within two days, national police chief Dai Bachtiar told the *Jakarta Post* that GAM was responsible: 'Our investigations are leading that way . . . The evidence at the scene was similar to that from the incidents at the back of the UN office and in Medan.'

A small bomb had exploded near the UN office in Jakarta the week before. It was convenient timing, to say the least, and there was a history of bombs being intentionally linked to GAM by the intelligence services. Sofyan Dawood immediately denied GAM was responsible, saying the government was just trying to increase public support for its offensive.

The rhetoric from the Indonesian side began to harden. No longer were they calling for a resumption of the peace agreement. They began to call for the renunciation by GAM of its goal of independence, the acceptance of the autonomy law as the final solution to the question, and the disarmament of GAM. No mention was made of the troop build-up or the requirement that Brimob withdraw and the TNI adopt defensive positions as was agreed back in December. All government and military leaders reiterated the existence and legality of the military option as GAM tried to restart the negotiations from the original standpoint: 'GAM seeks to enter negotiations. On the storage of weapons, GAM is ready to comply with the points in agreement at the same time Indonesia complies with their obligations,' Kamaruzzaman told Reuters.

In Central Aceh on May 1, a 'spontaneous' demonstration in the town of Takengon saw 8000 people rally in support of martial law and a new military operation. Near Banda Aceh two days later, six GAM members of the JSC were briefly detained by the military, despite their official role in the peace process. Another 1200 troops marched off a ship in Banda Aceh on May 5, and the head of the Indonesian Air Force, Air Marshall Chappy Hakim, announced that 2079 air-force personnel were on standby for the Aceh operation to guard airfields, in addition to the C-130, Fokker F27 and Boeing 737 transports, Skyhawk fighters, F-16s and Puma helicopters that were ready to deploy to support the TNI build-up.

I started receiving sporadic text messages from GAM in the field at this time, reporting the consequences of the increased presence. '2 DYS AGO TNI RAPED A 14 YO GIRL IN BIREUN NOW IN HOSPITAL.' 'AT THIS MOMENT IN BIREUN, INDON SF IS BEATING UP PEOPLE. SOME OF THE VICTIMS ARE TIED TO A SLOW MOVING MILITARY TRUCK AND

DRAGGED ALONG THE CITY ROADS.' 'INDON SF IS USING REFUGEES AS SHIELD WHEN CONDUCTING MIL OP IN ALUE KRUEP, PEUSANGAN.'

The small reports kept coming over the next few days. Many were about individual deaths in villages I couldn't even find on the map. I was by then back in Australia and remembered giving my Australian mobile number to 'Jamaica' at Sofyan Dawood's press conference. 'Jamaica' was the code name used by a young Acehnese man who had been in charge of trying to contact journalists. I knew he was with Sofyan Dawood's group somewhere near Lhokseumahwe. He was now trying to update journalists inside and outside Indonesia on the deteriorating situation in the field. Previously he had sent email updates, but that was obviously out of the question now that operations had begun and the only email facilities were in the towns. He said that as soon as Megawati had announced the possibility of military action in Aceh, the brutality of the Indonesian troops had increased.

FROM EARLY May 2003 onwards, there was no longer any doubt that the province would soon be at war again. The Indonesian military continued their build-up as their leaders maintained they were open to negotiations but requested such strict conditions that they knew there was no way GAM would comply. A May 12 deadline was announced for GAM to accept autonomy and disarm; if not, the military operation would go ahead. The Indonesians also insisted that the negotiations be held at a location inside Indonesia.

GAM specified through the HDC that negotiations take place in Geneva, where they always had. Indonesia refused and announced their plan to carry out what they called an 'integrated operation' that would combine humanitarian assistance, law enforcement and the return of local government control with a major military operation involving 50,000 troops.

But, as Sofyan Dawood told *Tempo* magazine, 'Call it humanitarian operation, law enforcement operation, or shadow operation, it's still war. The words put it gently, but it is war.' Which is how most Acehnese and foreign observers interpreted the move.

With the deadline looming, GAM continued to point to the agreement and reiterated its intention to disarm as soon as the Indonesian military reconfigured its military and police from offensive operations to defensive positions as was stipulated in the agreement. But this was brushed aside and the demand from the Indonesian side continued to be disarmament and a renunciation of the goal of independence.

As they continued to build up their forces, the nationalist sentiment being drummed up by the military in the media began to work in the government's favour. Susilo Bambang Yudhoyono publicly discussed releasing the HDC from their role as facilitator and army chief Endriartono Sutarto talked of the need for a presidential decree so that the integrated operation could proceed. The Indonesian foreign ministry announced it would campaign to have the Swedish-based GAM leadership extradited back to Indonesia to face charges of terrorism. No-one was talking of peace any more as another batch of 1300 rapid-reaction troops left for Aceh from Surabaya, complete with amphibious tanks and heavy equipment, as the advance force of another 2300.

⊶⊷◦⊶⊷

GAM FORCES in the field released their own guidelines for civilians in what they were now calling Aceh's 'Second Colonial War' (the first being the fight against the Dutch that began in 1873). They issued a statement on May 8 recalling all their personnel to their bases and defensive positions. They told all Acehnese that, in the event of an outbreak of hostilities, they should shut down and boycott all public offices and facilities – except hospitals, Red Cross and International Committeee of the Red Cross (ICRC) offices, water and electricity providers, international humanitarian agencies, NGOs, media offices and their transport.

They called for the shutdown of the ExxonMobil plant, which they called 'con-combatant', and within 24 hours of the start of hostilities, the draining of all the chemicals and fuel from the plant's storage tanks. They called on all Acehnese to avoid Indonesian military, offices, posts and vehicles, and called on them to refrain from using private vehicles except in an emergency. In such an emergency, civilians were instructed to wind down all the windows and, if travelling at night, to leave the interior lights on for identification.

When the government of Indonesia made clear its intention to restart the conflict in Aceh, there was some muted opposition. On May 7, 25 ambassadors met at a Jakarta hotel where they expressed their opposition to the end of the peace agreement. But they were mostly European and simply agreed to inform the Indonesian government of their concern over the situation and express their desire to see the peace process continued and the resumption of military operations avoided. US ambassador Ralph Boyce was quoted by the Acehnese daily newspaper *Serambi*, as saying that the US would be deeply disappointed if the peace process broke down but that they did support the territorial integrity of Indonesia. With the war in Iraq still demanding the world's attention, the US had very little leverage to object to the Indonesian operation even if it had wanted to.

Prominent Acehnese people in Jakarta under a grouping called the Forum for Aceh Concern met with Akbar Tandjung, speaker of the Indonesian house of representatives, the DPR, to urge the legislative body to oppose military action in Aceh. The same group attempted to meet President Megawati, but she refused to receive them.

Major General Samsuddin, a former special forces officer, publicly urged the government to reconsider its decision. He pointed out in an interview with the *Jakarta Post* that the government only needed to look at the experience of the DOM period to realise that a military solution would not work; he also cited the examples of East Timor and Papua to provide similar evidence of the futility of a military operation. But the military wasn't listening. 'The government should make a political decision, whether it is civil emergency, martial law or war status for the province,' urged TNI chief Endriartono Sutarto on May 8.

They were waiting for the presidential decree that would allow them to begin what would be Indonesia's largest ever military operation, with more than 40,000 troops already in place in Aceh.

What little international protest there was regarding the forthcoming operation didn't seem to concern the Indonesian government. 'All countries support Indonesia's integrity,' foreign minister Hassan Wirajuda told the Antara news agency on May 8. 'No document on my desk protests [the government's policy on] Aceh. There is no bad comment. All international laws, including the United Nations' charter, highly respect the integrity of any country.' And he was right – no country was strongly protesting the unfolding Indonesian operation. After supporting the US-led war in Iraq, the stocks of Indonesia, as the world's most populous Muslim country and a supporter of the US in Iraq, were high with the Bush administration and consequently criticism was muted.

GAM didn't respond to the government ultimatum and on May 12 the 50 Thai and Filipino monitors left Banda Aceh. A majority of the Acehnese people followed GAM's instruction to go on strike. Businesses were closed, students did not attend schools and public transport stopped running. In an attempt to restore normality, government buses were brought in to use as public buses but, reporters in the capital noted, not many people chose to use them as they were being driven by fully armed soldiers. Troops patrolled the capital in tanks and armoured vehicles, and the main hospital prepared 40 beds for expected casualties.

In Jakarta, the military asked the government for 1.23 trillion rupiah to pay for the military operation. The deadline for GAM to accept autonomy and disarm was extended to May 17 by what was said to be heavy international pressure on the Indonesian government. On May 15, GAM agreed to attend talks in Tokyo.

The prospect of a last-minute breakthrough brought praise from none other than George W. Bush, who said he was impressed by President Megawati and her 'willingness to go the extra mile' in pursuing the talks. But as the GAM negotiators were leaving the Kuala Tripa hotel on May 16 on the way to the airport to catch their flight to Tokyo, their car was stopped by police. According to a witness, the police searched the delegates' luggage, took their mobile phones and led them away to be questioned.

The Banda Aceh police intelligence chief, Surya Dharma, told reporters shortly afterwards, 'Of course they may not go. They are not allowed to go because they don't have a letter.' He said they were not included as delegates in Tokyo and they were going to be held for questioning. Three of the five GAM negotiators had been arrested the previous week and questioned over their apparent links to the bombing in Medan. It was just an attempt to derail the talks, carried out in such a way that the Indonesian government didn't have to take responsibility for it.

The Tokyo talks went ahead despite GAM's objections concerning their detained negotiators, with GAM representatives from Sweden attending on their behalf. And so did the Indonesian military preparations for the planned offensive. After two days, the talks were declared a failure. GAM's prime minister in exile, Malik Mahmood, was the head of their team. He told reporters that Indonesia was 'looking for a way to declare war. They asked us to abandon our independence . . . They asked us to surrender.'

The representatives from the US, Japan, the European Union and the World Bank, who convened the talks, said, 'The co-chairs do not believe the obstacles to a peaceful solution are insurmountable, even at this late hour.'

In Banda Aceh, the military was champing at the bit to begin the operation. 'These are the final minutes,' Aceh military spokesman Lieutenant Colonel Firdaus Komarno told Associated Press. 'We are waiting for instructions from Jakarta.'

At midnight on Sunday, May 18, Indonesia's security minister, Susilo Bambang Yudhoyono, held a special press briefing in which he announced that 'the President has ordered an integrated operation to begin'. The province was to be under martial law as of midnight on May 19 for a period of six months, to be extended if necessary under the authority of a presidential decree. He added that President Megawati had made the decision after the rebel delegation rejected the conditions laid out by the government in Tokyo. He said all the Indonesian efforts to achieve special autonomy, their comprehensive approach to Aceh's problems, their consideration of development needs and their dialogue had not succeeded in halting GAM's intentions to separate Aceh from the Republic. He also claimed that the level of armed violence had increased and accused GAM of involvement in terrorist activities. The operation began the next morning.

PART III

Martial Law: Strangling the Media and Silencing the Acehnese

On the morning of May 19, 2003 in Banda Aceh, the Indonesian military put on an expensive show: 468 fully armed paratroopers floated down above the capital to land safely within the grounds of the airport. The airfield had always been very heavily guarded and it was a bit like US troops storming JFK airport in New York or Australian special forces 'capturing' the Sydney airport. But the choreographed event – accompanied by rockets blasted from two US-supplied OV-10 Bronco ground-attack aircraft at some bushes outside Banda Aceh – was well used in the media to signify the commencement of this new style of operation by the Indonesian military in Aceh. This was the image the Indonesian generals wanted to convey. They wanted to show the Indonesian public and their foreign critics a professional and disciplined force carrying out a task integral to national unity, essential to the very survival of the Indonesian state itself. The continual footage of the US forces in Iraq over the previous two months had made its mark. Now the generals wanted the same coverage of their own war and they wanted to be proud of it.

The parachute drop was accompanied by the landing of a force of amphibious tanks and 500 marines further down the coast near Bireuen. Unfortunately, one tank sank in the choppy seas and one marine died – the first Indonesian casualty of the planned six-month operation that Indonesian army chief Major General Endriartono Sutarto told reporters in the capital would 'suppress the power of GAM to operate to a minimum'.

These events were well covered. Never before had Indonesian journalists had such direct access to their own military while it was conducting operations, and around 50 of them had been embedded with military units in Aceh – in a similar way to the US approach in Iraq. The operation was considered to be the largest undertaken by Indonesia since the 1975 invasion of East Timor. The authorities didn't seem to mind the comparison, despite the obvious negative outcomes of the East Timor operation – terrible suffering by civilians, and the eventual defeat of Indonesia and the withdrawal of its forces.

Ironically, the officer in charge of the military training the Indonesian reporters had to undergo to get accreditation to cover the 'new' conflict in Aceh was none other than Lieutenant Colonel Tono Suratman – the former head of East Timor's military command in the final year of Indonesian rule who was indicted for war crimes by the UN's serious crimes unit in East Timor. This man was now in charge of the TNI information unit.

Despite the images being provided by the Indonesian military, the 'new' war in Aceh had similar effects on the Acehnese as all the Indonesian military operations that had come before it. According to the People's Crisis Centre group in Banda Aceh, May 19 began in the capital with the discovery by local people of an unidentified body with gunshot wounds and showing signs of torture. Public transport was not running and the shops remained closed. In the Pidie district, a man was shot from his motorcycle when he refused to stop when ordered by soldiers. His two-year-old child was also shot and killed, and his wife shot in the thigh. Another man was beaten and robbed and one other person nearby at the time was shot dead by the soldiers. Gun battles between GAM and TNI erupted for several hours near Bireuen, and a civilian was wounded and another shot dead by troops in North Aceh. Schools and public buildings were also burned down in communities all along the Banda Aceh to Medan highway on the first day of the operation. The streets were reported to be deserted in all the regional towns as troops patrolled all the main highways in the province.

In remote South Aceh, GAM reported that, on May 19, 17 people had been burned alive by the soldiers from Kopassus and the Brawijaya battalion – they were locked in a house in the village of Djambo Keupok which was then set on fire. The name of the owner of the house and the names and ages of the 17 victims were provided to the media by GAM, but the report was never verified by the journalists. GAM also confirmed that a four-hour gun battle had taken place near the town of Peusangan and that five Indonesian soldiers had been shot dead in the exchange. They also claimed that five teenage Acehnese women had been raped by TNI troops in the area of the clash.

GAM admitted that the people of the villages in the area no longer felt safe as the Indonesian military was threatening them to reveal GAM positions, and they were fleeing to the internally displaced person (IDP) camps set up by the government.

Isolated incidents of military abuse were also reported by the foreign press in Aceh at the time – bits and pieces of what was going on throughout Aceh as the operation began; basically what the reporters could find out as they drove up and down the main highway. Matthew Moore, correspondent for the Fairfax group, wrote of two men taken from their homes by Indonesian troops 12 kilometres from Lhokseumahwe on the first day of the operation and, according to family members, shot. In true TNI style, gold had been stolen from the house of one of the victims.

John Aglionby of the *Guardian* reported three days later that Indonesian troops had killed a total of 18 civilians in raids on the villages of Cot Raboe, Cot Bate, Pata Mamplam and Pulo Naleng, near the town of Bireuen. He reported how villagers had woken in the early hours of the morning to find more than 100 Indonesian soldiers sweeping through as a helicopter flying overhead directed the operation. The bodies of those killed, including a 12-year-old boy, were discovered after the troops left. An AFP correspondent also saw six civilian bodies in Cot Bate, two of whom had been shot through the eyes, and the DPA correspondent reported that ten civilians had been killed in the Peusangan subdistrict near Bireuen. The military insisted no civilians had died but that nine separatists had been killed. The local people denied their villages were a source of GAM activity.

The burning of school buildings continued for the next week throughout Aceh, and by May 28 it was reported that more than 425 had been destroyed. Who was responsible, however, was never really clear. The military blamed GAM and GAM said it was part of a TNI counterinsurgency program to discredit GAM in the eyes of the Indonesian public and justify the operations. Two of the correspondents who actually witnessed the burning of schools in the town of Juempa near Bireuen – John Aglionby of the *Guardian* and Marianne Kearney of the *South China Morning Post* – both noted that the terrified local population had implied to them that the military was responsible, saying that the soldiers were the only ones present when they had arrived in the towns where the schools were still alight. Footage of burning schools featured significantly on Indonesian television in the first few days of the operation, the destruction being attributed to GAM.

As the reports of the foreign and Indonesian press in the field began to contradict the military version in the opening days of the operation, the military reacted. Major General Endang Suwarya, the Aceh martial-law administrator in Banda Aceh, announced on May 21 that journalists in Aceh were no longer allowed to quote GAM representatives. 'They are turning the facts upside down,' he said. Aceh was currently 'ill' he said, as his justification: 'There should be no news that confuses the people.' The new guidelines were spelled out very clearly: there would be 'no reports from GAM and no reports that praise GAM' Endang Suwarya told reporters in the capital.

The attempts by the Indonesian military to manage press coverage – the unprecedented access through embedded local journalists, provision of regular military briefings and even the establishment of a media centre in Lhokseumahwe – were not having the desired results. Journalists were quickly finding evidence of the real nature of the operation as they drove along the deserted highways of Aceh and spoke to the terrified population.

THE FIVE GAM negotiators in Banda Aceh had been arrested again and collected from the Kuala Tripa as soon as martial law was announced. The well-known pro-referendum activist, Cut Nur Aiskin, had been arrested at her home on May 21. The authorities announced they would arrest all members or suspected members of separatist organisations without warrants and hold them for 20 days without charge; they would seize public facilities and limit air and sea traffic to the province, and seize, alter and destroy news publications as they saw fit.

On May 22, the social welfare ministry announced it was opening 80 refugee centres with a capacity for 100,000 internally displaced persons. Indonesian military chief Endriartono Sutarto was in the capital by Wednesday exhorting his troops to 'exterminate' GAM if they did not surrender.

The international reaction from the quarters that mattered was muted. Australia's defence minister, Robert Hill, told the *Sydney Morning Herald*, 'Indonesia's got the perfect right to maintain its internal integrity and we regret those that are in armed revolt.' Similarly, Foreign Minister Alexander Downer told the paper, 'The violence perpetrated by the separatist movement is absolutely unacceptable.' The role Australia played in first supporting the incorporation of East Timor into Indonesia, then withdrawing that support, then leading a peace-keeping force into the territory after the UN-sponsored ballot in 1999, had revealed Australia's diplomatic influence when it came to Indonesia's international support.

The US regarded Indonesia as Australia's responsibility in matters concerning intelligence and regional security. It was the pro-Indonesian military line regarding events in East Timor in 1999 that Australia had passed on to the US that had prompted the Clinton administration to make Australia responsible for leading the peace-keeping force when things fell apart – when the Indonesian military set to destroying East Timor when the people voted for independence. The US had basically said at the time that it was Australia's mess and Australia had to fix the problem. Now, only four years later, as the Indonesian military were aiming to wipe out another separatist movement at the expense of the local population's lives, Australia responded by blaming the separatists. Which was exactly the same tune the Indonesian military were playing.

This support was an extension of the policy of renewed coop-eration with the Indonesian military and police as a result of the October 2002 Bali bombing. Defence Minister Robert Hill not only supported the Indonesian military actions in Aceh, but wanted to train the very units perpetrating the violence under the guise of counterterrorism. 'We have taken a decision to work with that part of Kopassus that has a counter-terrorism capability toward protecting the mutual interests of both Australians and Indonesians against terrorists,' Hill told the *Age* newspaper, adding, 'We accept that Aceh is part of

Indonesia and that they're [the Indonesians] right to protect their interests.'

Unfortunately for the minister, the same Kopassus unit that had a responsibility for counterterrorism, the 200-man squad known as Group V, was also responsible for political assassinations. Their most well-known operation was the murder of Papuan independence leader Theys Eluay in November 2001; seven members of the unit were later jailed by an army court for that murder, but the army chief of staff, General Ryamizard Ryacudu, described them as 'heroes' after their trial, revealing how their convictions for murder would not damage their careers.

Even a former Australian ambassador to Indonesia, Richard Woolcott, who had spent his career defending Indonesia's right to invade and oppress the population of East Timor, was wheeled out from retirement to defend Indonesia's actions in Aceh. 'Most Indonesians I know think we have no credibility in suggesting how they might deal with what's seen as a domestic conflict within a nation state,' he told the *Age*. Coming as it did directly after the US move into Iraq along with Australia's token support, Woolcott was implying that Australia had no right to criticise Indonesia for killing civilians in Aceh given its own actions in Iraq.

The US, meanwhile, responded with a brief statement from State Department representative Richard Boucher: 'We deeply regret that the government of Indonesia and the Free Aceh Movement forfeited a rare opportunity to advance a peace process with the assistance of the international community.' He added that Washington 'does regard the problem of Aceh as one that is not amenable to a solution by use of military force'.

The British foreign secretary, Jack Straw, called on the

Indonesian armed forces to show maximum restraint and respect for human rights in carrying out operations in Aceh. But that was as far as it went. Neither the US nor Australia nor the UK made any reference to the machinations of the Indonesians – including the virtual expulsion of the international monitors of the HDC – in resuming the military option in Aceh from an environment of comparative peace under the COHA agreement in January and February. No blame was apportioned and, if it was, such as by Alexander Downer, it was laid on the rebels for simply existing. The whole response to the Indonesian offensive by the nations in a position to prevent it was that it was a totally justifiable but somewhat regretful development.

Some sections of the media picked up and ran with this line. the *Australian* newspaper published an editorial stating, 'None of the factors that militated for Australian support for East Timorese independence – including the ethnic and religious identity of the East Timorese, and the fact they were colonised within the living memory of most Australians – apply to Aceh.' The editorial concluded that, 'Given all that, there is little we can do beyond what Alexander Downer did yesterday; lament the probable humanitarian disaster of a full-scale civil war, urge the resumption of talks, with both sides willing to negotiate on core demands, and secretly hope cool heads prevail.' In other words, the newspaper was telling the Australian people that the deaths of civilians at the hands of the same Indonesian military whose abuses had caused widespread public support for Australian intervention in East Timor in 1999, were in this case not significant. The reasoning for ignoring the atrocities in this case was given that the victims were Muslim and the conflict had started before we could remember.

In the same week the newspaper's own correspondent in Lhokseumahwe was writing that civilian casualties would without doubt be posthumously made GAM members by the military.

Editorial in the *Age* newspaper in Melbourne was more blunt: 'Two things are certain about the newly resumed war in Aceh; a lot of innocent people will die and not many people will care.'

The well of empathy for the victims of the Indonesian military had dried up in certain sections of the Australian media, much to the relief of the Australian Department of Foreign Affairs and Trade (DFAT) policymakers, who had become accustomed to belittling the abuses of the Indonesian military in Aceh, West Papua and East Timor since their careers began in the time of President Suharto.

By Saturday, May 24, the Indonesian Red Cross – the PMI – in Banda Aceh told reporters they had collected 80 bodies, mainly in North Aceh, since the start of the week. They mentioned, diplomatically, that most of these bodies appeared to be dressed in civilian clothes.

But the big story became the claims and counterclaims over the deaths of the civilians in the villages of Cot Batee, Lawang Peudada and Matamaplam near Bireuen. The deaths of at least 14 people, including two 12-year-old boys, were widely reported in the Indonesian media, which forced the Indonesian military to announce on May 24 that it was launching an investigation into the incidents. These were credible claims since the Agence France Presse correspondents had actually seen some of the bodies, and the BBC and the *Guardian* had interviewed some witnesses, as had a journalist from the Indonesian daily newspaper *Koran Tempo*. And this had infuriated the military – particularly Brigadier General Bambang Darmono in Lhokseumahwe. In response, the military quickly moved to further control the media.

Army spokesman Major General Syafrie Samsuddin announced in Jakarta that the media in Aceh would be required to 'work within the framework of the Unitary Republic of Indonesia'. 'We require all media personnel [to work within the framework] because news reports from the field may disturb the ongoing restoration of security,' he said. He invited the media to be involved in the investigation of what had happened in the villages of Cot Batee and Matamaplam, but added that 'if reports over [alleged abuses] by TNI members could not be proven, TNI leadership would take action against the media'. It was no idle threat. The TNI was threatening to sue *Koran Tempo* over the story and later threatened to sue AFP because its report was included in the *Koran Tempo* article. The TNI had only recently successfully forced the *Washington Post* to issue a retraction to a story that had said the TNI was responsible for an ambush in which two US citizens were killed near the Freeport gold mine in West Papua on August 30, 2002. The lawsuit, which was taken to the US courts, was settled out of court.

On the ground, the military's displeasure with the media was expressed in a more direct way. The AFP correspondent responsible for the report from Cot Batee was repeatedly summonsed by the military to its headquarters for interrogation, and in the field, reporters' cars were fired on after troops told them that their safety could not be guaranteed. The New York-based Committee to Protect Journalists detailed six incidents of

Indonesian and foreign journalists coming under accurate fire while driving along the highway between Lhokseumahwe and Banda Aceh. A car carrying journalists from Indonesia's *Metro TV* had its back window shot out and bullet holes were found in the drivers' door. The bumper of another Indonesian television crew's car was struck by bullets; another was chased by men firing from motorcycles when they stopped to film some footage.

All these incidents took place near a post manned by Brimob troops. Journalists in Lhokseumahwe were also harassed by the military who demanded to know the identity of their sources. By the end of the first week of the operation, many journalists were leaving Aceh. One colleague later told me how it reminded him of when all the journalists were chased out of East Timor after the UN-sponsored ballot was announced in September 1999. The same threats and near-miss shooting incidents, and the constant requests for journalists to leave for their own safety by the same authorities who were attacking them.

IT WAS announced by the Minister for Social Welfare, Jusuf Kella, that as many as 200,000 people would have to be moved to camps to protect them from the fighting – a program with similar overtones to the strategic hamlet operations run by the US military in the Vietnam war in which the population was removed from areas where they might offer support to the guerrillas. The same minister announced on May 25 that all foreign aid organisations and their staff would be banned from the province. The minister told the Detik news service the reason for the ban, which included such organisations as Save the

Children and Oxfam, was to avoid misinformation about what was happening in Aceh.

According to reports received at the time from GAM in the field, there was plenty going on that the military were trying to keep hidden from both the journalists and the foreign aid workers. One report told how, on May 27 in the late afternoon, the TNI shelled the mountains behind the villages of Juenib, Pandrah, Samalanga and Plimbang in the Bireuen district – the same area where I had met Commander Darwis Juenib the previous December. The local people were then ordered to raise the Indonesian flag or their villages would be burned down, then they were told to evacuate and the TNI soldiers proceeded to loot their homes.

The following morning, aircraft dropped 70 bombs in the area and the tanks continued the shelling. Troops also attacked the villages of Lhok Kulam, Cot Mane and Samalanga for the second time. The population fled and 17 shops were looted. Later the same day, according to the same GAM report, there was a major clash between GAM and the TNI, with the Indonesians responding with aerial bombing and tanks. GAM claimed a number of TNI were killed in the counterattack that forced them to pull back.

Clashes were also reported on that day by GAM near Meulaboh in West Aceh and in Tapaktuan in South Aceh. In West Aceh, GAM claimed to have killed five TNI troops. In Tapaktuan, four Acehnese men were shot dead by Indonesian marines for failing to raise the Indonesian flag, which was eventually raised after several other inhabitants were tortured. The report listed the names and ages of the dead.

Bits and pieces of information regarding the fighting came through in other reports from different GAM units. In the Peureulak district in East Aceh, the operation had begun on May 19 with the destruction of 51 houses by the Indonesian military. Thirteen villagers were beaten, two were arrested and two had disappeared, presumed dead, as the TNI searched for GAM on the first day. Nineteen clashes between GAM and the military were recorded by GAM in the area, including two ambushes in which TNI trucks were destroyed with RPGs. The TNI response was usually to round up villagers in the area of the clashes and beat them, then arrest suspects, whose houses were usually looted and burned down. In one incident on May 24, ten villagers were shot through the thighs by TNI troops responding to GAM activity in the area.

GAM also reported continuing operations against civilians in the Peusangan area; reports of the young boys shot there earlier in the week were still making headlines as the TNI first denied the incidents had happened, then claimed the boys were GAM spies, and then announced an investigation.

A fish farmer and a 60-year-old man were also shot dead by TNI troops on the morning of May 28 in that area, and another three civilians, including another 12-year-old boy, were shot two days later.

According to GAM, on May 31 in the village of Lawang Puedada in the Bireuen district, troops from Kostrad tortured three men, shot another dead and raped a 16-year-old girl. All the vicitims were taken to the local military post where later on the same day a 65-year-old woman was detained and relatives were asked to pay a 5 million rupiah bribe to have her released.

The journalists who managed to visit the area despite the restrictions reported more accounts of killings by the same troops in the Lawang village that week. *Tempo* journalists reported that a man was taken from his home on the Tuesday morning and shot dead. At least three villagers were also reportedly beaten with rifle butts, the victims so badly injured they were not able to move when interviewed by the *Tempo* journalist.

It seemed in almost every small village in the Bireuen area where journalists visited in that first week of the operation – when they could still get in – there was some further incident or killing. A reporter from the *Los Angeles Times* told how in the village of Garut, the military had called a meeting at which they were going to discuss 'security' with the local residents on Sunday, May 18. The soldiers surrounded the mosque, where the meeting was held, and ordered the men outside. They dragged two of them out and beat them severely, breaking one of the men's legs. The soldiers then ordered four men to carry the two injured men down the road where they were shot in the head.

In the next village, another man was killed on the same day. According to the *Los Angeles Times*, the man was beaten so severely his left eye was dislodged. The same soldiers who had beaten him carried him away and then, within earshot of the other villagers, shot him in the head, then dumped his body. The soldiers then went from house to house, taking money from the villagers and ordering the women to undress; according to the *Los Angeles Times*, they molested at least three girls, including one who was 12 years old.

The coverage of the killings that week in Peusangan was a deep embarrassment for the Indonesian military. The execution of eight unarmed males reported in *Time* magazine, one of them as young as 11 and the oldest aged 20, was also well covered by the foreign and local press based in Lhokseumahwe. Athough the military was forced to announce an investigation into the incident, its tactics didn't change – the military leaders just became more determined to rein in the press and scare them away, to prevent any more detailed accounts of the exact manner in which the operation was being conducted getting out.

⊷◦⊶

THE OTHER source of information on the situation in Aceh, domestic Indonesian human rights NGOs, were soon targeted by the authorities. On May 26 a paramilitary youth group attacked the central Jakarta headquarters of Kontras – the Commission for Missing Persons and Victims of Violence. The attackers, wearing military fatigues, were from the group *Pemuda Panca Marga*. The group, made up of the sons of veteran soldiers, surrounded the office, supposedly enraged by Kontras founder and human rights lawyer Munir's opposition to the military campaign in Aceh. Kontras had been involved in the first exhumations of the DOM-era mass graves following the fall of Suharto, and had said that the current integrated operation would have a similar result – widespread civilian casualties and even more resentment towards Jakarta's rule.

The mob called for Munir to come out of the office. A member of the executive board, Ori Rahman, came out to tell them Munir was not present. He was seized and forced to sing the national anthem. When he got the words wrong, stones were thrown at him and he was jostled by the mob, and punched in the head, ribs and legs.

After attacking the Kontras office, the crowd moved to the office of the PBHI, the Indonesian Legal Aid and Human Rights Association. They called for Johnson Panjaitan (who had been in charge of the defence for Lesley McCulloch) and Hendardi, two prominent human rights lawyers. The PBHI had issued a statement when the operation began on May 19 saying Megawati was repeating the mistakes of Suharto in Aceh. Hendardi came out of the office and addressed the crowd before they dispersed.

The crowd returned the following day and completely destroyed the Kontras office, leaving five of the staff injured. The reaction of the authorities to this attack left Indonesian human rights workers in no doubt about where they now stood – Indonesian defence force chief General Endriartono Sutarto told the Detik news service on May 28 that if 'Kontras no longer feels that it is part of this nation, the best thing for them is to leave the country'.

'Those who were attacked should be retrospective, because they are part of the nation' said Sutarto. 'GAM is an enemy of the nation. Despite that, the attack was a violation of the law and must be dealt with in line with the law.'

The Laksamana news service, however, quoted Central Jakarta Police Chief Sukrawardi Dahlan saying that it would be difficult to arrest the attackers, as *Pemuda Panca Marga* were protected by the military. Two of the attackers were later arrested but no charges were laid.

The attack on Kontras and Sutarto's flippant response about its legality were part of a wider campaign to move against anyone suspected of supporting GAM. This movement involved every arm of the Indonesian government in the first weeks of the operation. The shooting of the unarmed boys in Puesangan was just the sharp end. In Jakarta, Indonesian police chief Dai Bachtiar, later to be awarded an Order of Australia for his role in the Bali bombing investigation, announced on May 24 that he had called on Interpol to arrest Hasan Di Tiro in Sweden on charges of terrorism. He had also called for the arrest of Zaini Abdullah, chief negotiator and foreign minister of Aceh's government in exile, who had been involved in the peace negotiations.

Foreign Minister Hassan Wirajuda declared to the *Jakarta Post*, 'We hope that legal action would paralyse GAM's organisational structure'. On the same day, President Megawati asked Thailand's visiting minister of foreign affairs, Surakiart Sathirathai, to curb arms-smuggling from southern Thailand to Aceh; Foreign Minister Wirajuda claimed this was one of the routes by which GAM received weapons purchased from Cambodia.

THE GOVERNOR of Jakarta, the retired general Sutiyoso, announced that 18 residential areas where Acehnese people lived in Jakarta were being placed under surveillance by the security forces. He told the Detik news service that the heightened state of security was necessary because experience elsewhere in the world had shown that when rebels come under pressure, they try to distract attention by carrying out acts of terror. He appealed to residents of Jakarta to be the 'eyes and ears' of the security forces. The human rights group TAPOL speculated that the real reason for the surveillance was to make it more difficult for Acehnese fleeing the crackdown in Aceh to hide themselves among the tens of thousands of Acehnese people who were living in Jakarta. Suspected GAM operatives had already been arrested in Medan, Jakarta, West Java and on the island of Riau, close to Singapore, as the Indonesian authorities moved into action against Acehnese all over the country.

Pressure was also being exerted on Malaysia to monitor the large Acehnese exile community there. TAPOL reported that three Acehnese community leaders in Kuala Lumpur were picked up by the Malaysian police and told not to demonstrate against the military assault or seek asylum at the foreign embassies there, or they would be deported. The Indonesian navy had announced it had 12 warships patrolling the Malacca Straits to prevent Acehnese people fleeing to Malaysia and arms coming across by boat. Under pressure from Indonesia, Malaysia announced on June 3 that it would deport all people from Aceh caught entering the country illegally, regardless of whether they claimed to be refugees fleeing the fighting in Aceh. 'We will treat them as we do other refugees. We will detain them and send them back,' Malaysian Information Minister Khalil Yaac told reporters in Kuala Lumpur.

<hr />

THE OPERATION continued unabated in Aceh. Sofyan Dawood from GAM told the AFP news agency in Jakarta on May 24 that more than 30 people had been killed in a village called Bukit Sudan near Bireuen. Reporters trying to get into the area had been blocked by the military, who later admitted the clash there had been the worst of the operation so far. They lost seven men in one day.

The clash apparently involved some of GAM commander Darwis Juenib's group, and the American reporter Billy Nessen who had opted to cover the conflict from GAM's side in the field. Not long after the clash, Nessen's equipment was captured by the Indonesians as they attacked a GAM position and he was forced to flee without even shoes.

A *Tempo* report of the clash told how the unit commanded by Darwis Juenib was one of GAM's special units known as the Singa Mate and was made up predominately of men who had trained in Libya.

Indonesian Major General Bambang Darmono told reporters shortly after the evacuation of the bodies of his troops that it had been the most heroic exchange of the operation to date. GAM spokesman Sofyan Dawood told *Tempo* that it was a taste of things to come.

The fight was basically a GAM ambush of a TNI patrol. It began with a rocket-propelled grenade attack by GAM against the TNI trucks and became a firefight as the Indonesians chased the GAM fighters up a hill into a trap. The TNI soldiers were then pinned down by the GAM troops above them. According to *Tempo*, the fighting went on late into the night when the GAM troops under Darwis melted away into the surrounding jungle-covered mountains, leaving five dead TNI soldiers in their wake.

What the clash showed was that the fighting capacity of the GAM units was still high and, in certain circumstances, they were more than a match for the TNI.

The Indonesian military continued to direct their campaign at the civilian population.

By May 30, the gap between what the Indonesian military said they were doing in their 'integrated operation' and what was being reported was acknowledged by a statement from UN Secretary General Kofi Annan. His spokeswoman at the UN delivered the message that Kofi Annan was 'deeply concerned' by the impact on Aceh's civilian population of the renewed hostilities. 'In particular he is disturbed by reports of extra-judicial killings and widespread burning of schools,' she said. He urged all parties to uphold their obligations to protect civilians and called on the Indonesian government to 'ensure the necessary security conditions to allow international aid organisations safe and unhindered access to affected populations'.

The Indonesian government, meanwhile, continued with its efforts to order the foreign aid workers still in Banda Aceh out of the province. Statements were made regarding the desire of the government to eject the remaining organisations on the grounds that their safety could not be assured. Foreign ministry spokesman Marty Natalegawa said that the local government and PMI (Indonesian Red Cross) would be responsible for distributing all humanitarian assistance. He also said that the foreign aid workers should be aware of this policy and leave Aceh.

The security situation meant that none of the foreign NGO workers had been out of the capital since the start of the operation, but they declined repeated requests from the authorities to leave Banda Aceh, knowing they would not be allowed back in to the province once they had gone.

By the end of May, the PMI was reporting serious shortages of blood and medicine. Its head in Aceh said the humanitarian crisis was likely to increase with food shortages in most areas due to the lack of transport. The government's own health officials had already registered 21,252 internally displaced people, although the number was believed to be much higher. Humanitarian aid organisations were told that any assistance would have to be given through the Indonesian government and at the same time it was announced that 40 subdistrict heads were to be replaced with retired military officers.

The government claimed that at least 84 GAM rebels had been killed in the first 11 days of the operation, along with 14 civilians, seven soldiers and three policemen. GAM claimed that about twice as many civilians and Indonesian military had died.

A few days later, Amnesty International issued a report stating that the situation was dire and that no normal economic activity was taking place. 'Grave human rights violations have been reported,' it said. 'The population of internally displaced persons, forced from their homes because of the conflict, is estimated to be several tens of thousands.' It also suggested that, rather than attempting to 'drive out' professionals who could help the government prevent rights violations and deliver aid, authorities should be making every effort to work with them and protect them.

The Indonesian government ignored that and similar pleas from humanitarian agencies around the world. Foreign governments held to their positions that the matter was an internal one for Indonesia. Australia's prime minister, John Howard, when asked by high school students to explain his government's position on ABC talkback radio, said it was difficult to make a judgement about describing the events as atrocities without having people on the ground monitoring the situation. When asked why the situation was different from East Timor, he simply said, 'I thought you might say that and the two places are historically different.'

On June 3, the *Jakarta Post* ran a story in which Indonesian foreign ministry official Wahid Supriadi admitted that the visa applications of ten foreign journalists to cover the conflict in Aceh had been rejected. The responsibility for issuing visas for Aceh now rested with the martial law authorities in Aceh under Major General Endang Suwarja, who told the newspaper that he did not need 'foreign observers' in the province. 'We are capable of overcoming by ourselves the problem here,' he said.

It was something I didn't really need to be told. After two weeks of daily phone calls to Supriadi's staff in Jakarta and visits to the consulate in Melbourne, the staff finally admitted that my application was one of the ten that had been rejected.

The high-profile commencement of the military operation had backfired on the Indonesians with the subsequent reports of Indonesian military abuse. They had wanted to legitimise their actions by behaving as though they had nothing to hide, but then panicked when the media didn't follow their script. They reacted like they always had in the past – by trying to shut down the coverage and seal off the province. This only whetted the appetite of some media organisations, who wanted to know what they were trying to hide. The *Bulletin* magazine in Australia had advanced me some funds to get to Aceh so I travelled to a third country to get an entry visa.

▷─◁─○─▷─◁

As I walked through the airport terminal in Jakarta, I saw a headline on a news stand: 'German tourist killed in Aceh'. Below the words was a photo of the dead man's wounded wife being wheeled on a hospital stretcher. She was staring at the photographer with a shocked and suspicious look. It was clear to me exactly what had happened. It was a warning to all NGOs, journalists and foreign activists in Aceh, or those considering going there. The TNI was in no mood to play around.

The incident had apparently taken place on June 4 some time after 9 pm, on the west coast of Aceh near Meulaboh. The military's story was that the two German tourists, Luther Hendrik Albert, 53, and Elisabeth Engel, 49, had been camping on a beach, and a local villager had reported their suspicious flashlight beams to the local TNI. The soldiers went to investigate and, after firing warning shots and shouting for the couple to identify themselves, opened fire when the light was extinguished.

The military and the government had moved quickly to get their story about the incident straight, and the wounded woman was made to write a declaration in English that the incident was a 'misunderstanding'. Signed the day after the shooting while Engel was in Banda Aceh under the care of the military, the letter said in bad English that Engel and her husband knew it was dangerous to camp on the beach. Susilo Bambang Yudhoyono, minister for political and security affairs, moved quickly to hose down any criticism from the international community over what was in effect the murder of an unarmed man. 'I asked for an immediate, honest and objective investigation,' he told the *Jakarta Post* in the initial report of the shooting on June 6. 'This is an undesired incident and this issue could trigger the wrong perception among the international community about what we are doing now in Aceh.'

In my opinion, however, the shooting of the Germans was a convenient pretext to remove all foreigners from Aceh. The government had been trying to move the NGOs out for weeks with the argument that Aceh was too dangerous for foreigners, and it was also the standard reason for preventing journalists from accessing areas where the military had been active. Now they had their proof that it was indeed dangerous, even though they had to shoot unarmed German tourists to make their point.

⊢┈✦┈O┈✦┈⊣

SPEEDING ALONG the freeway into Jakarta with the report of the shootings of the foreigners in front of me, I had to make a decision. Either I would try to go to Aceh immediately without any accreditation, or I would try to get a press card from the same Foreign Affairs office that had rejected my visa application. I knew the ministry would not be aware of the fact that I was in the country with a valid journalist's visa, issued by a country that hadn't bothered to follow procedure and clear the visa with the Indonesians first. However, without the press card the visa would be useless, especially in Aceh. Being a Friday, I had about a two-hour window of opportunity to get it done. I decided to give it a try and told the taxi driver to take me straight to the ministry.

In the past, I had never bothered to tell the foreign ministry where or what I was intending to report. The less I told them, the less they could be held responsible, and that arrangement had seemed to work fine. Despite the fact that for the last three years I had been regularly reporting from Aceh and West Papua, every time I entered Indonesia I would write down something like 'general news' when I had to fill out the accreditation forms. Supriadi, the man responsible for foreign journalists at the ministry, had served with the Indonesian embassy in Melbourne and our conversations never went beyond the tennis tournaments being held in Melbourne and the miserable weather. On this occasion, however, when the staff took my passport into his office, I heard yelling and reprimands. This wasn't good. I knew they'd be surprised to see me, having rejected my application from Australia the previous Friday, but I had thought somehow that I could just get the card and get out of there. I had hoped that the visa issued to me by their foreign consul meant that I had a legal right to work.

I sat and browsed through the printouts of Internet web pages about Chinese fighter planes that for some reason were the only reading matter in the waiting area. I was trying to look nonchalant as the assistant came back in. 'Are you intending to go to

Aceh?' he asked. No, I really didn't want to go there, I said. I tried to work around the issue. I said that my organisation had wanted me to cover the opening of the Bali bombing trial in Denpassar that was starting that week but, owing to the situation in Aceh, my editor requested that I go to Aceh, even though I'd made it clear I didn't want to.

It was ridiculous. The Indonesian government was trying to ban journalists from Aceh without having to publicly admit that they were doing so. They were rejecting or obstructing the applications of journalists outside of the country and intimidating those who were resident in Indonesia by either shooting at them when they were in Aceh or making vague legal threats against them in Jakarta or, in the case of one correspondent, threatening tax investigations that would keep them in the capital.

I was trying to choose my words carefully, trying to extract from them some official recognition that I had a legal right to work in the country. They knew the game I was playing and, being bureaucrats, were a lot better at it than I was. They smiled and told me to wait and said there would be no problem. I heard laughter coming from behind the office partitions. I thought that perhaps my reference to the Bali trials would win me a press card to cover the politically acceptable spectacle of Indonesia punishing Islamic terrorists apparently connected to al-Qaeda – as opposed to their own military conducting terror in Aceh.

'If you could just sign here and here, Mr Martininikus,' said the assistant, glancing at my name again as he mispronounced it, and proffered me a form. I signed and he handed me the coveted press card.

'What is this?' I asked, handing it back to him. Stamped

across the front in bold black type were the words, 'Not for visits to Aceh, Papua and Maluku.' And I had just signed a form acknowledging that I understood those conditions applied.

My visa difficulties were a source of great amusement to my colleagues in Jakarta. That night I was sitting in a bar with a friend who had returned from Aceh the week before. He was one of the sources for the report on the bodies in Cot Batee and he was telling me the story of how he had been shot at very soon after passing a Brimob checkpoint on the highway where they told him not to proceed for his own safety. In all likelihood, based on our past experiences in East Timor, the very same troops who had warned him were the ones who had shot at him. But he didn't know for sure and certainly couldn't print it.

On the television they were playing footage from some of the Indonesian-embedded journalists. It was the interior of a Brimob armoured truck under attack and there were bullets pinging off the sides and the troops were returning fire and yelling. The piece had been running for what seemed like over five minutes with no commentary. It was typical of the wave of patriotic coverage of the conflict on Indonesian television and was like nothing I had ever seen before.

The Indonesian public were bombarded day in and day out with footage that was very sympathetic to the military and actually seemed to be getting behind the war. It was a kind of collective nostalgia for the stability of the Suharto era coupled with resentment over the so-called 'loss' of East Timor and the humiliation of their military.

My colleague was telling me that it might be just as well that I couldn't get up to Aceh as the situation for reporters had become worse and worse until the point when he felt they were literally fleeing Aceh with more than a little fear for their lives. He had left by the road down to North Sumatra, as had many others. The situation along the highway between Lhokseum-ahwe and Banda Aceh was very unpredictable and there was no traffic on the roads.

Many of the reporters based in Jakarta were at a party that night. Because journalists were not being allowed into the country, or if they had somehow managed to get a visa like I had, their movements were restricted, the resident correspon-dents – numbering no more than 20 – were the only ones who could officially get into Aceh. Many of the journalists at the party had just come back from Aceh – they had done their features on the start of the operation and their organisations didn't want any more material. Others had just come back after months in Iraq and wanted a rest. Others had been ordered to cover the Bali bombing trials. Some just didn't think the Aceh story was worth it. And that was the real reason why the coverage on Indonesia's latest war had petered out. There just wasn't the demand from news organisations for daily stories about the killings of Acehnese civilians for what looked like a long time to come. The violence would have to be reported at extreme risk to the journalists, and the organisations they worked for made decisions based on the demand for news.

At that stage, just over two weeks after the operation began, Billy Nessen, as far as we knew, was the only foreign reporter in Aceh, and he was known to be with GAM but had been unable to file anything but the shortest radio report. For the Indonesian authorities, this meant they could slowly implement a ban on media coverage without the embarrassment of having to round up the journalists. Reporters were obstructed coming into the country and restricted if they'd already arrived, and the resident journalists were harassed and pressured to leave Aceh and to stay out. The Indonesian government knew media interest would taper off if nothing sensational was reported, and they knew that eyewitnesses such as foreign tourists and NGOs had to be removed to dry up the information sources.

The next morning, Saturday, June 7, 2003, at the Gatot Subroto military hospital, the TNI doctor who had operated on Elisabeth Engel, the German tourist, recognised me from Dili in East Timor. Dr Robert Hutaruak had been in charge of the Wirahusada military hospital in East Timor in 1998 when I had walked in there one day to try and verify accounts that pro-independence East Timorese who had been taken there for treatment had been killed and tortured by the military instead.

After I and two other reporters had interviewed him about the German woman's injuries – she had been flown to Jakarta following the incident for treatment of the bullet wound to her leg – the doctor asked if I remembered him. I had not believed a word of his denials back in 1998 that any of the Timorese taken to the military hospital in Dili had been harmed. I was equally suspicious now. Back then I had lists of names of Timorese people who had disappeared from his hospital and had never been seen again and he had blithely denied any knowledge of them. I could only think that if the military were trying to cover up the circumstances of the current shooting, Dr Hutaruak was very well-qualified to handle the inevitable inquiries.

He was very personable and told us in a mixture of English and Indonesian how Elisabeth Engel was in good condition. He said a bullet had entered her leg and split apart as it struck her knee. He had extracted two fragments of the bullet, which appeared to come from an M-16, and estimated she had been shot from more than 100 metres away because a bullet fired any closer would have destroyed her knee. Describing Engel as 'conscious but confused' after the shooting, he said the following day they would start to get her walking with the aid of crutches so she could leave for Germany as soon as possible. We weren't allowed to see her because she was feeling very tired. There were armed guards outside her room to ensure she wasn't disturbed. He invited us to see the body of Luther Hendrik Albert, her dead husband, which they had prepared so Engel could view him.

Outside the hospital morgue there was a gigantic wreath and condolences from General Endriartono Sutarto. Two soldiers dressed for the parade ground wearing white gloves and leggings stood guard. Inside, Luther Hendrik Albert lay on a low platform dressed in a cheap, black, single-breasted suit. The top of his head looked like it had been blown off and then taped back on with the sticking plaster that criss-crossed it. Stitches under his chin marked what looked like a small entry wound; if you looked closely, it appeared he would have been lying on his back when he was shot. There was also a small wound on his left temple that looked like a neat bullet-entry wound. The shirt and tie the man wore covered a rough, unnatural patch where they had plugged the three bullet wounds in his chest with sticking plaster.

The smell of disinfectant filled the room and I felt sick

looking at the body. To me, the head and chest wounds were those of someone who had been assassinated, not someone shot randomly from a long distance on a dark night.

Maybe it was my personal dread of my imminent departure for Aceh. Or maybe it was the memories brought back by seeing that particular doctor and knowing what he had overseen in Dili. Or maybe it was just the hangover and the sweet, disinfected air of the morgue. But Dr Hutaruak's readiness to show us the German tourist's body made me feel like it was some kind of trophy for the Indonesians, or a warning to foreigners in general. The waxy grey face of the dead German with the plastered-up hole in the top of his head and the ill-fitting black suit made me scared of the impunity with which the military acted in Aceh and how they were never held accountable. I wasn't scared for him – he was already dead – but for myself. I left the room before the others. One of my colleagues pointed to the wreath from Endriartono Sutarto when they came out and joked, 'I bet they don't give you one of them.' I went off into the stifling heat feeling sick and looking for some water.

⊱─◆─○─◆─⊰

IT EMERGED that the German couple had been touring Aceh as part of a six-year world cycling trip and were on their way back to North Sumatra. Fairfax correspondent Matthew Moore reported that he had seen and spoken to them in Aceh on May 18, and that Engel did not speak English.

The nine soldiers responsible for the shooting were given leave until the investigation was completed but it was found there was no wrongdoing on their part and they were not charged. They claimed to have fired warning shots and shouted, 'Who's there?' before opening fire on the pair. Elisabeth Engel told the German newspaper *Frankfurter Rundschau*, 'They told me [later] they had shouted, but I heard nothing but one or two warning shots.' She said that she and her husband had no time to react after hearing the warning shots and that the soldiers had to bear some guilt for firing so quickly. The Laksamana news service quoted the army chief of staff, Ryamizard Ryacudu, as saying that the two German tourists were 'stupid' for taking a holiday in a war zone.

'Only stupid people and idiots have a picnic in such an area,' he was also quoted as saying by the German news agency DPA. He also tried to raise suspicions as to their motives for being in Aceh: 'The important thing, what this nation has to know, is why they were in Aceh. Don't look into why they were shot and so forth.'

There was no real need for the military to slander the two Germans. It became quickly apparent that there would be no real repercussions from the incident. The German ambassador to Indonesia, Gerhard Fulda, simply told the *Jakarta Post* that he was 'a bit astonished' that unarmed tourists could be shot. 'And I assume they were shot simply because there was no real communication. They didn't understand,' he was quoted as saying.

Within four days of the incident it was announced that all tourists would be banned from Aceh; the TNI had successfully created a pretext to ban foreigners from the province. Security minister Susilo Bambang Yudhoyono, speaking in the northern

Aceh town of Lhokseumahwe, said the ban would be put in place within two days and would keep foreigners away from areas where there were military strikes on rebels, Media Indonesia reported on June 8. Yudhoyono also told Indonesia's Antara news agency that the government would review the presence and activities of nongovernmental organisations and foreign journalists in Aceh 'for their safety'.

After seeing the dead German man at the hospital, I dropped into a colleague's office who handed me the latest report from Aceh. That afternoon, Saturday, June 7, I learned that two Malaysian journalists were being detained and questioned by police in Banda Aceh. It appeared from the report that they had the same class of short-term visa as I did but they had managed to get hold of press cards without 'Not for Aceh' emblazoned across the front. Still, it didn't look good for them. The wire report said they had already been detained for six hours and the Aceh police spokesman said it was still being determined whether the pair had misused their visas – even though they appeared to have had permission to be there from the Department of Foreign Affairs, namely a visa.

'Did they have permission to carry out journalistic activities?' the police spokesman, Sayed Husaini, asked the local reporters.

'Well, they had fucking journalists' visas didn't they?' was how I responded. But I could imagine how ridiculous and repetitive the questioning would be for the two Malaysians – just as I had seen the same Aceh police in action with their twisted logic at Lesley McCulloch's trial. There would be searches of all their belongings, accusations, checks on their computers, detailed reading of their notebooks. The police would be trying to come up with something, anything, with which to charge them and then, of course, would ask for money.

It seemed the Malaysians who were being questioned, and Billy Nessen in the hills with GAM, were the last foreign journalists left in Aceh.

I left Jakarta for Medan in North Sumatra early the next day. At Polonia airport in Medan I was told that the morning flights to Banda Aceh were full but if I waited there might be a seat on the afternoon flight. At the arrivals hall it was easy to spot the two Malaysian journalists in the crowd of military and jilbab-wearing Acehnese women and men with their embroidered Muslim caps. The two journalists were carrying camera bags and looked like they were being escorted by plain-clothes policemen. And they were clearly ecstatic to be out of Aceh and on their way out of the country.

One of the two, Shamsul Akmar, told me excitedly how the police in Aceh had come to let them go. When they had returned from Lhokseumahwe to Banda Aceh, they had been picked up by the police in their hotel as they were having breakfast. But because they already had their tickets organised for a flight out the next day, the authorities had eventually let them leave. Only just, however, which was why they were so relieved to be out of there. 'They showed us a list of all the journalists who had registered in Aceh and they were asking us where they all were,' said Shamsul. 'They told us they are going to round them all up and throw them in jail.'

The police had kept them from 9.30 am until after 10 o'clock that night at the headquarters in Banda Aceh, where at least four different officers had questioned them about everything they had done in Aceh.

The police had held their passports until that morning and, until they got on the plane, they weren't sure whether they were going to be called back in for another round of questioning, or even if they were going to be detained and charged. The police were still escorting them to ensure they flew directly to Jakarta.

'Just don't go there,' said Shamsul, with a glance at his minders. 'They are all over the place. Or at least don't go to Banda Aceh. We were fine until we got there. But then they told us they had been looking for us.'

This whole conversation had taken place in a few minutes while Shamsul's colleague spoke to the police and collected their bags. Then they were hustled away into the surrounding crowd to get the flight to Jakarta and then another one out of the country.

⊢•⊹•O•⊹•⊣

SINCE THERE were no seats on the Banda Aceh flight for that afternoon, I went into town. From what the Malaysians had told me, as soon as I checked into a hotel in Aceh the police would be looking for me – Shamsul and his colleague had been found through their hotel register form in Banda Aceh and the police had been waiting for them when they had returned from a few days down in Lhokseumahwe. Although I knew all of this, I wondered whether there was some way to get around it.

Completing the hotel register in Medan filled me with dread, however. Along with having to list my occupation and visa type, they also demanded copies of my passport and visa, and even asked for my incriminating press card. I often used to fill in these forms with confusing misspellings of my name, just to annoy the INTEL officials they were passed on to. This time, even here in Medan, things were being taken much more seriously; the hotel staff scrutinised every entry and were on the phone to the police with the details before they had even given me my room key.

When I got to my room I called Dave Gorman from the HDC in Banda Aceh and, to my great surprise, he answered. Yes, they were still there, and the HDC office was still open at the Kuala Tripa he told me, almost defiantly.

'Everything is fine. We are staying put. No-one has asked us to leave. When are you coming up?' he asked reassuringly.

On further questioning it transpired he was the only foreign HDC staff member left – one of the 12 foreign NGO personnel left in the province. They were facing pressure from the authorities to leave but as yet no action had been taken.

Gorman told me that none of the foreigners in Banda Aceh had left the capital since the start of the operation on May 19, and that he didn't think any transport was running outside of the capital. I asked what the situation was like considering the reports we'd received of food shortages, several bomb explosions, refugees from the countryside camping in the sports stadium and power blackouts.

'Oh, you know, it's pretty normal, pretty quiet,' he said. 'Prices have gone up but things have settled down.' But Gorman had been living in Banda Aceh for more than two years and perhaps his perception of normal had become a little skewed. Off the record he didn't think the operation had really affected GAM. 'They have not captured or killed any of the even mid-level commanders so far,' he said.

Despite the declaration of martial law and the highly publicised commitment of more than 50,000 troops, I believed Gorman's assertion that GAM had not really been militarily affected by the offensive. They were still in regular contact with the outside world and my girlfriend, Meredyth, in Australia was still receiving messages and emails from the leadership on a regular basis, which she was forwarding to me. I had begun receiving text message updates from GAM in the field on my new Indonesian mobile phone as soon as I gave them my new number, and some of the commanders could still be reached for comment by colleagues in Jakarta.

But walking down the street in Medan, the signs of the nearby conflict were everywhere. Armoured cars and black Brimob trucks with metal panels welded to the sides were forming a convoy outside the main mosque in the centre of town. The black-uniformed Brimob troops were snapping magazines into their weapons and mounting light machine guns on top of their vehicles. Indonesian air force F-16s and Hawk fighters screamed overhead on their approach to Polonia airport, which is situated almost in the middle of Medan. The ear-splitting sound of the fighter jets, I later learnt, became a constant reminder of the nearby operation.

Back at the hotel, the desk clerk nodded to several men sitting in the foyer and pointed in my direction when I walked in. As I waited in the dining room for the beer I'd ordered, they sat down at the next table.

'So you are a journalist that wants to go to Aceh,' one of them said. 'Better luck next time.' They all laughed. They were the local INTEL guys just making their presence felt.

It was annoying that they had turned up so soon and it only confirmed what I already knew about how they worked and how Medan, as the closest large city to Aceh and a transport hub both to the rest of Indonesia and across to Malaysia and Singapore, was always heavily monitored by the security forces. But Medan wasn't listed as a restricted area on my visa, so I just laughed along with them and drank my beer.

Upstairs in my room, the local television station was playing the nightly combat footage highlights from Aceh – synchronised shots of TNI troops landing by parachute and shimmying down ropes from helicopters to the sound of the Rolling Stones song, 'Paint it Black'. Raised on a diet of US television series reruns like *Tour of Duty* and *China Beach*, the Indonesian producers were excelling themselves in producing the patriotic images the TNI generals kept asking of the media. With their ageing Vietnam-era Bell helicopters and M-16s, the TNI troops almost looked like the US soldiers of 30 years ago, and in many ways the war they were fighting against their country's own citizens in Aceh was similar to that of the Americans in Vietnam trying to fight a guerrilla war with a conventional army. They were even using many of the same tactics. There were lots of close-ups of soldiers' tense faces and shots of their hands gripping their rifles and their boots sloshing ashore from landing craft.

It was like another war entirely, however, from the one of roadblocks, mutilated civilian bodies dumped by the road, cleared villages, random reprisal killings and petty extortion that I and many others had been reporting from Aceh for the previous three years. Still, I have to admit it was good television compared to the game shows or music videos on the other stations, and I watched it until I finally went to sleep.

><+<>-<><><>+<

As WELL as making life difficult for journalists, the police in Aceh were arresting anybody they thought had the slightest connection to GAM. They were also targeting human rights activists and people employed by the NGOs and accusing them of being associated with GAM. On June 6, security forces had arrested a volunteer working for the Red Cross in the East Aceh regional capital of Langsa; the day before, another Red Cross volunteer had been kidnapped there by unidentified men. The PBHAM legal aid post in Langsa was raided by security forces and six employees, including the director, were taken away for questioning by the police while the office was ransacked and smashed.

An activist from Forum Rakyat Aceh, a human rights NGO also in Langsa, narrowly evaded arrest by fleeing via the back door when four INTEL operatives raided his house. He was later arrested, however, as were two female activists from the

Acehnese women's organisation PHIA (Empowerment for Acehnese Women) in Langsa. The People's Crisis Centre in Langsa was surrounded by intelligence operatives on the same day, but the people they were looking for were not there at the time.

The following day, an activist from Kontras, Saiful Bachri, was shot dead in East Aceh and the military, who would not allow Kontras investigators into the area to investigate his death, claimed he had been killed by GAM. Another activist was killed by unidentified gunmen near Banda Aceh on June 8.

On Monday, June 9, the TNI announced it had arrested 186 GAM members, 'including sympathisers from local NGOs'. It seemed as though the authorities had waited until the journalists had left and then started picking up the people they knew to be among their sources of information.

Most of those arrested were charged under the martial law provision for subversion through assisting GAM. It was a charge that carried a maximum of life imprisonment. Martial law admin-istrator Major General Endang Suwarja widened the scope of those affected when he threatened to arrest all activists from the pro-referendum group SIRA – whose chairman, Nazar, was still in jail for organising rallies – and the Student Solidarity for the Peoples movement, SMUR, if they did not stop supporting the separatist movement. Both groups had campaigned for a peaceful solution to the conflict in Aceh. Suwarja even formally requested the HDC to leave Aceh on Monday, June 9, on the grounds that they were no longer mediating the peace process. Despite Dave Gorman's cheery reassurances the night before, unknown to me, he was on the plane out of Aceh the next morning.

Some groups kept working regardless of the danger. The Indonesian Red Cross, PMI, was able to report that it had removed 151 bodies from the conflict zone by June 11. But they were being severely restricted as to where they could go and when. Given that their job involved corpse removal, they provided a necessary service to the TNI. The secretary general of the Indonesian Red Cross told AFP that, 'their identities [the dead] were not clear, all of them wore civilian clothing. But if I have to say they were civilians, I am not sure'. He was referring to the military claims that almost all the dead were GAM.

After filing what details I could for the *Bulletin* in the morning, I went to a travel agency to get a plane ticket to Banda Aceh. I'd promised them copy from Aceh and they had extended me the money, so I was obligated to at least try. From what I could figure, if I flew in and got out of the airport without being arrested, I could get out of town before the Indonesian officials realised. At least I would be in Banda Aceh before I had to deal with any roadblocks where, if questioned too thoroughly, I knew I would be arrested.

There were now only two flights a day from Medan to Banda Aceh, and they were booked solid for three days. I was waitlisted on all flights and the travel agent assured me it wouldn't be a problem getting there. As I left the office, I saw two of the guys who'd talked to me at the hotel walk into the travel agent.

When I went back to the travel agent the next day, the same staff who had helped me previously looked at me coldly. The boss was summoned to tell me they couldn't get me a flight. I asked about the next day and he said I could come and ask again, but he thought the answer would probably be no. They were all booked. It did seem a bit strange and I suspected it wasn't really the case. Even half-disguised offers to bribe him didn't seem to have any effect. I checked with other travel agents, but the situation was the same. Even the Pelni passenger ferry that ran between Medan and Banda Aceh had been cancelled, and I was told the intercity buses to Aceh weren't running either.

Outside one of the travel agents I saw a Westerner, whose sloppy attire in the middle of the business district – dirty shorts and a T-shirt – told me he must be an Australian. He was a devout Islamic scholar who had just come from a small village outside of Sigli, where he lived with his Acehnese wife. About four days earlier the military had stopped by his house and told him he had better leave Aceh for a while as things were going to get very bad.

'Well, when they tell you to go, you go,' he said, laughing. They had never asked him to leave before even though there had always been problems. He had lived there for several years studying Islamic teachings. He told me how he lived with no television or radio and had a chair at the back of his house where he sat looking over the mountains.

He was waiting for his ATM card to arrive from Australia before travelling on to Malaysia. I wondered what the straight-laced Acehnese clerics thought of the long-haired, bearded Australian with missing teeth who had landed in their village and begun quoting the Koran.

We went for a coffee and – in between telling me that the problem with Acehnese Islam was that somewhere along the line it had got mixed between the real teachings of the Koran (which he knew and adhered to) and the local traditions passed down in the villages – he gave me a rundown on conditions in the countryside. The only transport still moving, he said, were the small public minibuses that went from town to town – that was how he had come from Sigli to Banda Aceh. I asked him if you could get all the way from Medan to Banda Aceh by jumping from one local bus to the next. 'Well, it could be possible, but mind they don't shoot you for being a spy,' he said.

The perceptive Australian Muslim had a good understanding of the mood of the TNI at that time. By the following day, Billy Nessen would be accused of exactly that – spying – and just about everything else the TNI could think of. On June 10, the Committee to Protect Journalists (CPJ) issued an urgent open letter to President Megawati, urging her to take 'immediate action to ensure the safety of American freelance journalist William Nessen, who has come under fire from the Indonesian military while reporting on the civil war in the restive province of Aceh'. As the report explained, Billy had been talking on a satellite phone to his wife, Shadia Marhadan, who had left Indonesia for her own safety a few weeks earlier. He had told her he was with some GAM fighters who were surrounded by TNI. Then, she was reported by the CPJ to have said, 'I could hear gunfire then the line went dead.' The report said Nessen had tried to give himself up but had been shot at by TNI troops.

The CPJ report went to great lengths to confirm that Nessen had been in the country on a valid journalist's visa and that he was legally permitted to be reporting in Aceh. Wahid Supriadi, the man in charge of issuing visas to the foreign press, would have had Nessen's details on file, but showed his true colours by telling the CPJ, 'As far as we are concerned he is a tourist. He has no right to be there.' The statement was a treacherous rewriting of the rules. The foreign ministry was washing its hands of Nessen by denying his position any legality. Similarly, Major General Endang Suwarja had told a press conference the day before that he was aware an American journalist was trapped in GAM territory but that the Indonesian military 'cannot guarantee the safety of foreign journalists in Aceh'.

What had basically happened was that Nessen's equipment, including digital stills and video cameras, had been captured by the Indonesian military in a raid against GAM in which two of the GAM members with Nessen were killed. Nessen had barely escaped with his life. It had been such a close call that Nessen, after losing all his gear, had decided to leave, figuring he couldn't report any more. The situation was so dire that his wife Shadia had decided to go public with his story to try to pressure the Indonesian government to protect Nessen from being killed on the spot by the TNI, who were very close to catching him. Shadia was a very well-respected Acehnese woman who often worked as a fixer for foreign media in Aceh and Indonesia. She was also well known by the authorities for organising interviews between the foreign press and officials.

If Shadia Marhadan had made the decision to go public with Nessen's plight, the situation he was in must have been extremely dangerous, and I think most journalists who had worked in Aceh with her knew that. It was also well known among both foreign and local journalists that Nessen was with GAM, and it was not inconceivable that the TNI were trying to kill him as an example. The TNI had already forbidden the press to carry any statements from GAM, and here was a reporter travelling with them. It was a major affront and the TNI did not want Nessen's version of their operation getting out.

The CPJ appeal for Nessen had come on the same day the military announced it had lost seven men in the fight at Bukit Sudan.

The press in Indonesia jumped on the Nessen story from various angles. They implied he was a spy and made derogatory references to Shadia Marhadan for marrying a foreigner. His house in Jakarta was raided by police and the other people living there were interrogated.

The attention and pressure the Indonesian authorities were receiving from the US embassy in particular seemed to be working – Security Minister Susilo Bambang Yudhoyono in Jakarta announced that although the offensive could not be halted because Nessen was travelling with GAM, he could surrender. 'So it is up to the reporter concerned if he wants to leave [GAM] properly and try to communicate with the military authorities . . . surely he will be saved and protected,' the minister said. But the authorities refused to agree they would not arrest and detain Nessen. Darmono in Lhokseumahwe showed some of Nessen's footage to the press and gave him a deadline to hand himself in. But the deadline passed and the story kept dominating Aceh coverage for the next week. The story did, however, bring into focus the issue of the legality of journalists' presence in Aceh, and Yudhoyono announced that the issue was being 'reviewed'. By then, however, there were no foreign journalists left anyway, except for Nessen.

The next morning I checked out of my hotel and went to the airport, determined to get a flight to Banda Aceh. There were no seats on the morning flight but it seemed I might be able to get one on the early afternoon flight if I waited around. The newspapers were full of reports on Nessen and as I was waiting, a colleague called me from Jakarta. He told me Yudhoyono had made a statement saying that all journalists were to be banned from Aceh and that new regulations were being prepared regarding access for all NGOs and journalists. I called Dave Gorman on his mobile phone – who I thought to be in Banda Aceh – and he said he hadn't heard anything. As far as he knew, everything was the same. I said I might see him that night in Banda Aceh. 'Oh, I am actually driving down an autobahn near Geneva,' he said.

Finally, it was time to check in and I lined up for my ticket. Standing in a queue leading to a desk underneath a large sign saying 'Banda Aceh', a man approached me and asked if I was going to Banda Aceh. I thought it was a stupid question and told him to read the sign. But he wouldn't go away. I tried to ignore him but he asked again whether I was going to Banda Aceh and I said yes, that was where I was going. 'Ah, well, then I have to inform you that I will contact my colleagues in Banda Aceh and you will be arrested when you arrive. The penalty for this kind of visa violation is five years in jail,' he said politely. I thought it was a joke and I asked him who he was and whether I could see his ID. He pulled out a police identification badge and handed it to me, smiling.

The same colleague who had called me at the airport called me again that night as I sat drinking beer back in Medan. There had been confirmation of a reported mass grave containing the bodies of around 50 civilians who had been killed in the violence near the town of Bireuen. The confirmation had come from the Indonesian National Commission of Human Rights, *Komnas Ham*. M. Billah, the chairman of the Ad Hoc human rights commission for Aceh, said that the existence of the grave had been confirmed but the number of victims in the grave had not and he was hoping to send a *Komnas Ham* team to investigate the following week. They had collected evidence on a recent investigation in Aceh, for four days from June 5, when they visited Banda Aceh and Bireuen.

The military immediately ridiculed the claim. Army Chief of Staff Ryamizard Ryacudu told Associated Press in Aceh, 'Ask them to come here. I will knock their heads off, if they are just talking.'

The military said they would take legal action against the commission if the claims proved incorrect. *Komnas Ham* responded with a press conference in which Billah sealed his mouth with black cloth to symbolise the government's gagging of criticism. A member of the investigative team, Zoemrotin, said they had interviewed five people who were relatives and neighbours of seven people who were shot near Alue Glumpang, Matang Mamplam and Cot Rabo Tunong.

'One woman testified that her husband had been killed in the forecourt of their home,' he said. 'All this evidence points to the occurrence of extrajudicial killings.' Zoemrotin also said they had received testimony about sexual harassment: 'The perpetrators were dressed in black shirts and brown jackets, with the word Brimob written on the back.'

In regards to the mass grave, Billah said all the evidence had been taken from witnesses. He said his team had not picked out their information from the dustbin.

Bireuen was along the main Banda Aceh to Medan highway. I was starting to think the only way to get to Aceh would be to follow the Australian Muslim's advice and take my chances with the minibuses. Then I'd pass through the area where the mass grave was supposed to be, if I got that far. I got a call from SBS *Dateline* journalist David O'Shea, who was leaving for Aceh in the morning. He had attached himself to a group of embedded Indonesian journalists and was using his resident's visa to get in before they closed access to everybody. I was surprised that more of the 20 or so resident journalists were not doing the same, as it was obvious the province would be completely closed soon. But most of them were down in Bali covering the bombing trials.

As I got to the border the next day, a convoy of 25 military trucks was heading into Aceh. The drivers had draped their bullet-proof vests at head height from the side windows as protection from snipers. The minibus I was travelling in followed them across the border without being stopped. Lines of vehicles stretched back along the outgoing side of the highway, and soldiers prevented anyone leaving their vehicles before they had been searched. Some ordered people out of the vehicles to check their identity cards while others emptied the contents of the minibuses and cars onto the road.

I knew that it was just chance the convoy had been going past. That, together with a minibus driver who didn't stop where he was supposed to, and just kept driving, meant that we had avoided a search and the inevitable questions at the border as we were going into Aceh. In that kind of situation, it only takes one shout from an overzealous soldier to transform an otherwise apathetic group of troops into a hostile one and you find yourself being interrogated. And sure enough, there he was – a stocky Javanese sergeant standing at the side of the road, peering into the passing vehicles. Luckily, as he scanned the vehicles in front of us, the convoy of military vehicles accelerated. I just glimpsed the shock on his face as he saw what he thought might have been a foreigner go by in the back of a minibus, and then we were gone as the driver sped away.

After passing through the border town of Kuala Simpang, the back of the bus was empty except for me. The driver seemed practised at avoiding searches and we passed two more groups of soldiers who were stopping vehicles without being pulled over ourselves. Approaching Langsa, there was a traffic jam as the military convoy banked up in front of us because two empty Indonesian tank transporters were parked on the highway in the opposite direction. It was hot and dusty, and police were yelling at soldiers to get the trucks moved out of the way. We had pulled up outside a Brimob base and the minidriver glanced back at me so I slid down lower in my seat. He wanted to drop me off there but because there were soldiers outside the bus, I asked him to take me off the main street and around behind the market.

Although it was only about 3 pm, the buses that went further north had already stopped for the day. So I had to spend the night in Langsa, the regional capital of East Aceh and only 38 kilometres inside Aceh.

From an upstairs room in a rundown guesthouse in the middle of town, the view through the broken louvres was of an empty street with Indonesian flags on poles outside every closed shop. Strung across the street were banners declaring the support of the local authorities for the 'integrated operation' and exhorting the local population to be vigilant against GAM.

The flags were something I'd seen before in other parts of Indonesia – in East Timor before independence, in Papuan towns near military bases and outside the shabby lean-tos of East Timorese refugees in the militia-controlled camps of West Timor. It was just one of those things the Indonesian military did when they had an operation in a separatist area. They came around in trucks loaded with flags and told the residents to fly them or they would be considered suspect and maybe beaten, arrested, raped or, in some cases, killed. Everybody always did what they were told and flew the flags. It was such a small, meaningless thing to have a flag flying outside your shop or house, especially when they gave you the flag anyway. But to the Indonesian military, with their twisted logic, the sight of all these flags in areas where the population despised them, and was inclined to kill them if given a chance, meant they had some kind of control.

Downstairs in the coffee shop, a group of men talked freely about the situation. They were all Acehnese and there were no Indonesians present. They told me in a mixture of Indonesian and English that the road further north was blocked. They disagreed with each other and argued about how many road-blocks there were between Langsa and Lhokseumahwe. Some said four, some said six. Someone else said he knew of a man who had come through and hadn't been stopped. The others laughed and talked about how that wasn't possible for this one, pointing at me, an obvious foreigner trying to get into Aceh when the Indonesian government was changing the law to keep foreigners out. It was almost relaxed, almost like any gathering of men anywhere else in the world. Only here they argued over roadblocks not football and they drank coffee instead of beer or wine. They talked openly about how the Indonesians in Langsa were scared of GAM and wouldn't go out at night; about how the operation would not destroy the rebels.

'We have been living like this, with the military here, for years. This is no different from DOM,' said one. One of the younger men made a great show of running outside and coming back with the Indonesian flag on its white pole from out the front. Everybody laughed. But none of the men would give me their names and none of them stayed very long. I noticed before I left that the young man had gone and put the flag back in front of the guesthouse.

Most of the shops were closed and as it got dark there were few people on the street. I had wanted to go to the hospital to get a sense of the situation, but my attempt had been aborted because a Brimob truck was parked across the road and soldiers were lounging out the front. I knew there was no point in going to see the legal aid office, which would normally have a good idea of what was going on, as it had been destroyed and the staff arrested. Even the Indonesian Red Cross volunteers had been arrested and as the light faded I found myself ducking into shadows at every passing vehicle, afraid I would be picked up by the police.

By removing my legal right to be there, the authorities had made me feel like a criminal and I quickly realised that in such a heavily militarised place, there was virtually nothing I could do to avoid making contact with either the military or the police. In the marketplace the man who sold me some food was shaking like a leaf as he handed it to me, and glanced up furtively behind my shoulder. A truckful of soldiers had stopped. I quickly walked the other way out of the light as they started jumping onto the ground from the tailgate.

I sat in my cockroach-infested room watching the street through the broken louvres while flicking the huge insects off me. At 10 pm the power went off and the heat became oppressive. At 11 pm an insistent knocking at the door let me know the police had found me. I hadn't filled out a registration form and they had heard there was a foreigner in the guesthouse. When I opened the door, they walked past me into the room waving the form. I pretended not to understand them and mentioned Sabang, the tourist destination, and Medan. They looked tired and disinterested, and I told them I would complete the registration form first thing in the morning and gave them cigarettes. No, not now, I told them. I couldn't get my passport out, I wanted to sleep. There was no power and only a candle for light. So they went back into the corridor, where the manager was standing with another candle. They said they would come back at seven in the morning. I thanked them, perhaps a little too profusely, and shut the door while they were still asking for my passport. I could still hear them talking in the corridor as I bolted the door.

My passport had a journalist visa, which meant I needed a press card, which said 'Not for Aceh', which meant questions and searches. Which meant I couldn't show them anything. I lay awake most of the night listening for sounds in the corridor and thinking about Lesley McCulloch's trial, prison and the dead German. Which is precisely what the Indonesian authorities in Aceh would have wanted me to be thinking about. I got up early and headed off to the bus station before six.

The bus to Lhokseumahwe was waiting to leave and I squeezed into the back. The other passengers were women, children and old men. Only a few kilometres outside of town, the bus joined a long line of stationary traffic. Military vehicles were parked on either side of the road, and soldiers were putting on body armour and pulling down the metal shutters welded over the windows of their trucks. Getting out of the bus, I could see an armoured car and a tank with its guns pointed directly at the line of stationary traffic, and people being lined up on the side of the road. The other passengers looked very scared and told me there were at least four complete checks like this before Lhokseumahwe. After that, the road to Banda Aceh was more or less closed to traffic. I grabbed my bag and jumped into another bus heading back to Langsa. Without the right papers, I didn't think I'd be lucky enough to get through all the checks without being arrested.

What was happening at that time beyond those roadblocks was only filtering through in bits and pieces from a few GAM reports. The power to the whole region, from Langsa through to Lhokseumahwe and up past Sigli to just below Banda Aceh, had been cut for the previous two weeks. As with the destroyed schools, the TNI blamed GAM for sabotaging the power lines and GAM blamed the TNI. The fact was, the military could rely on generators and the black-out seriously affected the guerrillas' ability to communicate with each other and the outside world.

It was precisely in that area where the military offensive was being conducted.

⊷○⊷

ON JUNE 16, GAM reported they were being attacked by British-made Hawk fighter aircraft and US-supplied OV-10 Bronco ground-attack aircraft. The details were specific. Ten bombs were dropped at 2.36 pm in the Jambo Aye and Baktiy districts by two Hawks and two Broncos. It was in that area, 90 kilometres east of Lhokseumahwe, that the TNI claimed that the GAM leadership was based.

The GAM report of Indonesia bombing villages was in the first few days of the operation, but it wasn't the first and the reports kept coming. GAM was issuing field reports that listed the daily firefights which at that time were averaging three clashes a day. The picture that emerged from these reports was of the civilian population being treated as brutally as if they were combatants, with beatings and disappearances common.

Until June 13, GAM had named 68 civilians who had been executed by the military and more than 32 who had been beaten and arrested. In one incident, a 37-year-old woman was reportedly held by the military for two days and gang-raped. But the area covered in the reports had shrunk dramatically to just a section of North Aceh, demonstrating how GAM's communications had broken down. This was due in part to the power cuts and also to their positions being moved beyond the range of the mobile phone system – something Brigadier General Bambang Darmono had told the Detik news service was one of his objectives the previous week.

On June 10, GAM had reported that 40 villagers had been taken away from the village of Gampong M4 in northern Aceh. The report stated that on June 8, four of those people were found dead in nearby villages with their heads removed. Six more headless corpses from the same group were found on June 10, and the other 30 people were still missing. On the same day, GAM reported that another two men had been arrested and their headless bodies had been found in the same area.

As demonstrated previously in counterinsurgency campaigns in East Timor and West Papua, the dumping of victims' bodies in public places was a common army tactic, used to instil fear in the civilian populations in rebel areas and to force them to flee to government-controlled areas, ending their support for the guerrillas.

>-·+◆-·0·-◆+·-<

BY MID-JUNE, with the foreign journalists out of the way and the Indonesian journalists firmly under the authorities' control, the military was moving ahead with its textbook counterinsurgency program. GAM admitted in its reports to attacking a Brimob post near the village of Aleu le Mirah on June 11. The road to the area was blocked by the military, leaving the civilians with the choice of going over to the Indonesian side, to be rounded up and taken to the TNI-run refugee camp in Bireuen, or to flee to the countryside and face air attacks. It was another example of replication of the strategic hamlets tactics the US employed in the Vietnam War, which was also copied by the Indonesians in East Timor in 1978 and 1979 – in that conflict they encircled Falintil guerrillas in the mountains and drove the population to relocation camps on the coast using the same Hawk and Bronco aircraft. The result in East Timor was a widespread famine and a significant decrease in guerrilla activity in the short term.

In Aceh, the Indonesians followed the same pattern by attacking the Aleu le Mirah area with aircraft the following day, killing six GAM fighters and ten civilians. On June 13, according to GAM, they continued with two sorties over the area of Gandapura in northern Aceh, strafing and bombing civilians.

On June 15, the program continued with residents of the Juli subdistrict facing air attacks after 17,000 of them had already fled to the Cot Gapu football field in Bireuen. Images of the refugees in tents on the open field were widely screened in Indonesia, but they were portrayed as victims fleeing the violence of GAM. The fact that the camp had been set up before the people had become refugees and that the roads back to their villages had been blocked to prevent their return were not included in most of the coverage from the Indonesian-embedded journalists.

According to GAM reports, the villages they were forced to vacate were looted and sometimes burned down by the military. Sofyan Dawood claimed that about 400 civilians had been killed in the operation to date.

><+>-0-<+><

THERE WERE no more roadblocks until the border, where all the passengers had to get out and line up by the side of the road. I was told to report to the police and military under a small roadside shelter. The other passengers were lined up with their hands on their heads and told to identify their luggage, which was then emptied onto the ground in front of them by one soldier as two others covered him and the passenger with their weapons.

The officer looking through my passport couldn't find the visa, and paid more attention to the UN stamps from independent East Timor. He mentioned Sabang and I nodded. It was obvious he just thought I was the last of the tourists leaving. One of the policemen seemed a bit too interested, however, so I started talking to the soldier who was waving my passport around and saying, as much for the amusement of those around him as for me, 'As long as you are not American. If you are American, I kill you.'

He handed my passport back. It was a bad joke; he was referring to Billy Nessen.

Back at the bus, a soldier was pulling my computer out of my backpack. I grabbed it and stuffed it back in as he asked what it was. 'A computer,' I replied, and watched him hesitate as if he should stop me as I got back on the bus, which sat still for what seemed like a very long time.

Finally, all of the passengers got themselves and their possessions back on the bus and we moved on. Relieved, I wound down the window to get some air. Travelling back into North Sumatra, I saw groups of armed men wearing civilian clothes checking houses. Military and police trucks were stopped on either side of the road at one point and soldiers in uniform were searching through the scrub and the trees for the next two kilometres. They were obviously looking for people who had tried to evade the final checkpoint. This wasn't an international border and the search went on well into Indonesia.

As well as catching people who had tried to flee across the border, at least eight GAM members had been arrested in Medan since the operation in May and many more would be picked up. Arrests had also already been made in Palembang and Bengkulu in Sumatra, in Jakarta, in West Java and on Riau near Singapore.

Just past the border, my phone rang. It was John Aglionby in Jakarta from the *Guardian*. He was letting me know that the journalists in Jakarta were planning to protest the now official closure of Aceh to the foreign press. I could only say that, as far as I could tell, it was already well and truly closed.

Two days after I had arrived back in Medan, on Monday, June 16, the presidential decree was signed by President Megawati that effectively banned all foreigners from Aceh. The document banned all tourists and placed restrictions so severe and conditions so impossible on humanitarian workers and journalists, that none could be met by anyone seeking access to the province. Journalists needed permission from the foreign ministry and the martial law authority, and it was months until any foreign journalists satisfied this requirement with most applications being shuffled between the military in Aceh and the foreign ministry in Jakarta. The decree stated 'journalistic activities undertaken by foreign journalists and correspondents in Aceh for the foreign media shall be carried out selectively'; in other words, only permitted if the military's view of the operation was presented and the journalist strictly controlled. Journalists were not allowed to enter the province through anywhere but the airport in Banda Aceh, and they were not allowed to work outside any main town. In other words, they were not to be anywhere where they might come in to contact with the victims of the military operation.

The previous week, on June 13, Indonesia's coordinating minister for political and security affairs, Susilo Bambang Yudhoyono, announced the government had already made certain arrangements to enable foreigners to work or be in war-torn Aceh. The arrangements were yet to be made public, 'but, in principle, they are already in effect in the field,' he had told reporters. I had already seen what that meant – reporting independently in Aceh was now impossible without being arrested and, at the very least, being thrown out. Basically, the decree was just a formalisation of a ban that had been implemented as soon as the negative reporting became apparent in the first few days of the operation.

The same day, Australia's foreign minister, Alexander Downer, told CNN, 'Actually, there is more access in Aceh now for human rights groups and others – for example, the media – than traditionally has been the case.'

The Indonesians had just announced the barring of all foreign journalists and humanitarian workers from the province. But, of course, not in so many words.

Alexander Downer also said, 'There is a lot of focus in the Western media on the Indonesian military and there's some history to that, no doubt. But it also has to be remembered that GAM have been perpetrating some terrible acts of violence and the pressure should also be maintained on them and they should not be seen as some sort of honest and honourable victims.'

It was obvious that not only would Australia ignore the human rights abuses being carried out by the Indonesian military in Aceh, it would actively lie and misrepresent the facts to curry favour with Indonesia. As for the statement that the Indonesian military got a lot of attention in Western media, that may have had something to do with it having been responsible for two of the 20th century's lesser-reported acts of genocide – the 1965 slaughter of communists and the deaths of almost a third of the population of East Timor during their 24-year occupation of the territory that began in 1975. Now the Indonesian military looked as though it was carrying out a third act in its bloody history in Aceh. As for highlighting GAM's record, it had to be acknowledged that GAM was fighting a war of survival and that they had killed people in the process.

Alexander Downer was attending the ASEAN meeting of foreign ministers in Cambodia, and the Indonesians, assisted by Downer, had pressured the whole of ASEAN to support their campaign in Aceh. They had secured a joint communique from the ASEAN foreign ministers: 'We . . . pledge our support to deny the separatist movement access to means of violence through . . . preventing arms smuggling into the Aceh province.' This was directed mainly against Thailand, Cambodia and Sri Lanka, who the Indonesians had accused of supplying GAM's weapons.

Downer's claim about the access enjoyed by journalists was laughable, but to say that NGOs had more access than previously was obscene when their personnel were being arrested, beaten and, in more than one case, killed by the security forces the Australian foreign minister was defending.

Back in Medan, I had tried to call anyone I knew in Banda Aceh. One of the few people I got through to was Feisal Hamdi from the Aceh Coalition for Human Rights. 'My office was raided by the police on May 27,' he told me. 'They suspected GAM members were hiding here so they came three times in one day and took away three staff and the office boy and interrogated them for 12 hours.' He said the situation was now so bad that he could not carry out any investigations outside of Banda Aceh. 'I cannot send my people out, it is too dangerous for them,' he said. Most of the six regional offices in his organisation were out of contact due to the power cuts. 'They can't send a fax, they can't use computers. I ordered them not to leave the regional centres but I haven't heard from them for almost two weeks,' he said. All he could do at that time was to try and help the people who came to his office with details of relatives who had been arrested or had disappeared by making inquiries to the authorities. 'So far in Banda Aceh we have received information of 29 civilians killed, seven arrested and 24 missing. But that is mostly in Banda Aceh, not from the countryside where the operation is,' he said.

Similarly, Abdi Dalem, director of Indonesian legal aid service, Lembaga Bantuan Hukum (LBH) in Banda Aceh, said, 'So far our clients are only 20 people. There is not too much space for us to work under martial law. Before we used to work in the whole of Aceh but now we cannot travel outside of the capital. It is not safe.

'I am a lawyer who used to defend GAM clients. Now they are arresting everybody with connections to GAM. I am occupying a very thin space here, if you understand what I mean.'

They had already arrested 108 GAM members in Banda Aceh alone. Just about everybody else I had in my contacts list was now arrested or had gone bush. Kamaruzzaman and the other GAM negotiators were still in prison, where they had been since martial law was declared. Nazar was in jail on charges relating to free speech. The Kontras office was closed and had been for some time, with one of their workers dead and the others in hiding. The HDC personnel had now all left and the 12 foreign workers who were left in Banda Aceh would not even speak to a journalist, fearing that their phones were tapped and that they would be thrown out immediately if they did.

At the same time as Downer's statement was reported, the military claimed it had so far killed 204 GAM members and lost 28 of its own people, with 63 wounded. By June 18, the Indonesian Red Cross, PMI, announced it had removed 194 'bodies in civilian clothes' from the areas where there had been fighting, mostly along the main Banda Aceh to Medan highway. According to the AFP news agency, at least 41,000 Acehnese had become refugees in their own country by June 18.

Indonesia's military chief, General Endriartono Sutarto, told reporters in Jakarta that, 'The jet fighter deployment was merely aimed to show the community that TNI is more powerful than GAM rebels.' He had no objection to their use, he said, as long as it was not against civilians. The military also admitted they had begun using F-16s – the most sophisticated weapon they possessed.

On May 18, I received a final message from the GAM spokesman in North Aceh. 'The escalation of violence here is getting worse by the hour,' he reported from the area where the air attacks were continuing. 'Many civilians killed by TNI in the last three days. TNI force civil society to become refugees. It is difficult for me to update you like usually.'

⊢•⊶•○•⊷•⊣

THE INDONESIANS had been challenged by the British government over the use of the Hawk fighters, which had been sold to them in 1996 with an agreement that they were not to be used for internal operations – essentially those involving attacks on civilians. The stipulation had been meant to prevent them from using the planes in East Timor and had been a concession to human rights lobbyists in England such as TAPOL and Amnesty International. The agreement was also part of the Blair government's claim to be implementing a moral foreign policy in relation to arms sales.

Indonesia's military chief, Major General Endriartono Sutarto, simply responded to the press with: 'I am going to use what I have. After all, I have paid already.' Indonesia's former defence minister, Juwano Sudarsono, who had been responsible for the purchase of the jet fighters, reiterated the same point with the Antara news agency: 'As I see it, once the weapons have been sold, Indonesia should not be expected to abide by restrictive conditions on their use. Please, be reasonable. If they have been sold, they have been sold.'

Mike O'Brien, the British trade minister, had visited Jakarta in early June and had told President Megawati that further deliveries of spare parts for the British-made Hawk jets and Scorpion armoured cars could be in jeopardy if the

British equipment was used against civilians. 'I reminded them of the assurances about the use of British-supplied military equipment in Aceh,' he told the British parliament on his return. 'And warned of the possible consequences for defence sales and defence relationships if there was a breach of the assurances. I also stressed that Indonesian military action in Aceh should be proportionate and in accordance with international standards on human rights.' No further action was taken and deliveries continued regardless of what had happened in Aceh.

THE *JAKARTA POST* reported that the area around Jambo Aye was being attacked by F-16s and that the rebel leadership, and in particular Sofyan Dawood, was supposed to be there. The newspaper quoted Captain Mohamad Fajar from the first air force detachment which carried out the mission as saying that two F-16s from Medan in North Sumatra had dropped four bombs in the area. Another two OV-10 Bronco planes, also from Medan, had fired 16 rockets and 500 rounds from large-calibre cannons at positions believed to be occupied by rebel units.

This was later denied by Major General Endriartono Sutarto, who said the aircraft were only being used to make a sonic boom to scare the rebels and the population. But one person who did know the reality of what was going on told a very different story of how the Indonesians were using their aircraft. Billy Nessen told ABC Radio, by mobile phone on June 17, that he had witnessed air attacks on unarmed civilians: 'People, from many accounts that I've heard, were in a field sleeping, it was about nine in the morning, and they saw these planes come over, three planes, and they saw them circle over. And people stood up – these are unarmed civilians, these refugees who've rarely seen planes – and they saw them circle. And then, all of a sudden, one seemed to fall, and someone said to me, "We all thought, oh god, the Indonesians can't even fly a plane." But, no, that was coming in to bomb, and it dropped a bomb.

'They did not have guns, they were not shooting at them, this was not cover fire from the Indonesians, which they're claiming that they bring in the planes when they're fighting the guerrillas. These were hundreds of unarmed people looking up at the planes, and they dropped the bombs on them, and I do not know to this day how many people were killed.'

Nessen was still in the field with GAM when he made that report. He did not surrender to the Indonesians until June 24, when they immediately locked him up in Banda Aceh for 40 days.

THE US, for their part, had no complaints about the use of the F-16s and Bronco aircraft they had supplied to Indonesia. Their response to the Aceh operation was summed up by Deputy Secretary of Defence Paul Wolfowitz, who was acknowledged to be the Bush administration's expert on Indonesia: 'It would be helpful if Indonesia would make sure that the actions of its forces are transparent. It will help encourage the world that Indonesia is behaving professionally and carefully.'

And that was more or less the extent of international pressure on Indonesia over the conduct of the operation until mid-June.

The Indonesian military had reacted quickly to the accusations against them in the first highly publicised days of the operation, before they had removed the journalists from the equation. On June 11, a military tribunal found three soldiers guilty of beating three civilians unconscious in the village of Lawang on May 27 after they denied knowledge of GAM's whereabouts. The soldiers were given sentences between two months and 20 days and four months and 20 days. However, a charge against them for killing a 35-year-old farmer in the same incident was dismissed on the grounds that the man was a member of GAM. Associated Press reported at the time that villagers had told them the murdered man had no connection to GAM. The case had come to trial because the incident had been reported, but the number of cases of abuse being tried by the Indonesian military declined dramatically, along with the critical reporting.

Another sign of the pressure the military was putting on the Indonesian media came with the dismissal of an SCTV producer from his job as a television reporter for the Indonesian network after he interviewed an Acehnese poet who promoted peace. Dandhy Dwi Leksono was sacked after a high-ranking TNI officer complained about the interview.

A harsher message to the Indonesian media from the military in Aceh was driven home on June 17 with the discovery of the body of cameraman Mohamad Jamaluddin of the state-run TV station TVRI. To make the point clear to local journalists that they must see and say nothing, adhesive tape was plastered over his mouth and eyes, and his hands were tied. His body was found in a river near Banda Aceh; he had a stone tied around his neck. He had been missing since the first day of the operation, and it was common knowledge he had been kidnapped, tortured and killed by the authorities.

After filing a long piece from Medan for the *Bulletin*, I was free to leave. It was obvious that going back to Aceh now would just invite arrest, and I was attracting a lot of attention in Medan where the INTEL officials were still sitting in the hotel foyer noting my comings and goings.

I'd had ideas of somehow getting back into Aceh by road through another point, maybe over the hills through the central road to Takengon or further south along the coast near Tapaktuan. The militia who had chased out the HDC were based in Takengon, and whenever I inquired about the road through central Aceh, I was told there was no road.

It was near Tapaktuan in South Aceh where Lesley McCulloch had been arrested, and the stories I heard from local reporters in Banda Aceh about the police down there, who were unaccountable due to the remoteness and bad communications, made me reluctant to try that route. So those plans remained ideas and I knew this time I would have to accept defeat.

Everywhere I could have gone would have been full of soldiers who would have demanded documents, and it would have only been a matter of time before they got me. I was thinking like a criminal, thanks to the Indonesian government and military. They had removed the legal basis for anyone – journalists, humanitarian workers, human rights workers, locals as well as foreigners – to carry out any kind of work that monitored what the military was doing. They had done all this openly and nobody, except the Acehnese, really seemed to care. Quite suddenly, there was no-one left to listen to the Acehnese and whoever did know what was happening, such as the local media and the population, were rapidly becoming too scared to talk about it.

From the Indonesian military's perspective they had done a remarkable job silencing the details of their operations – and that was just what the international community required of them. As far as the governments of the US, Australia and the UK were concerned, the less information coming from Aceh the less problems they would have in continuing to deal with Indonesia on a variety of levels. They protested the regrettable loss of human life, but not too loudly, and without any implication that there was anything wrong in what the Indonesian military were doing.

The whole of what is called 'civil society' that had sprung up in Aceh after the downfall of Suharto was being dismantled. The only period in which the Acehnese people had been able to speak about what had happened to them was over. Nothing had been resolved, no-one had been punished for the crimes of the Suharto era, there had been no serious attempts to redress the economic drain by Jakarta that had fuelled the rebellion. Nothing had changed and the calls for democracy and a referendum by the Acehnese people had just been met with intensified repression.

It was hard to believe that less than four years earlier, a million people had marched for a referendum in Banda Aceh. Almost one in four of the entire population of Aceh had marched. Some were GAM people who wanted a sultanate, some were students and intellectuals who wanted a democratic country, but most were simply Acehnese people who wanted an end to the violence and economic exploitation of what they called Javanese colonialist rule.

Then, by degrees, the freedom of expression and action had been removed. It had come full circle back to the DOM era, when, as now, to speak against the military either landed you in jail or ended your life. And most foreign governments, at least publicly, seemed comfortable with that.

━━◆━○━◆━━

I CAUGHT a ferry from Medan to Penang in Malaysia. The trip, which takes you directly across the Malacca Straits, is only about three or four hours, depending on the weather. These waterways are some of the busiest in the world, linking the Pacific to the Indian Ocean and running past Singapore, Malaysia and Thailand. The Strait is also where GAM takes advantage of the closeness of Sumatra to the Malay Peninsula, and runs small boats with weapons, ammunition and personnel to augment the supplies they bought directly from the Indonesians themselves.

It was common knowledge that GAM used these waters for this purpose, but it wasn't something the Indonesians could easily stop. They'd enforced a 19-kilometre coastal exclusion zone from Acehnese waters since the declaration of martial law, and 15 warships had been stationed off Aceh. There were always reports of boats being intercepted.

On the ferry, a man who said he was from Lhokseumahwe began talking to me. After I told him I was a journalist he wanted to talk about Billy Nessen. The coverage Nessen was getting in the Indonesian press had made him a hero to people like this man. He told me he was with GAM. That he was involved in logistics. That they had boats and he could get me across but, as he repeated many times, it was 'life or death'.

Our conversation was taking place in a doorway on the ferry and every time someone passed, he'd look at the sea or at the deck. He said the trip would be at night and that they often lost boats. There would be nothing they could do if the boat was lost, he said. It was 'life or death', he repeated.

By the look of him, nervous and furtive, I could tell he knew what he was talking about. It was logical, when you thought about it. Anywhere along the length of the entire northern coastline of Aceh, the trip across the Strait would be similar to the one we were now taking.

We talked for a while longer and he gave me a phone number. For the rest of the trip I thought about the possibility. There would have to be no contact with any villagers who were sympathetic to the Indonesians once there. There was no way I could really control that, nor whether the boat I was on would be attacked from the air or by another boat, or when I came in to land. I would not be able to go to any towns, travel on any main roads or even exit the province by any but the most secret bush trails into North Sumatra. The knowledge that there was a white reporter with the guerrillas could be the pretext for an operation by the Indonesians to find me, in which case god knows how many Acehnese would be tortured or killed by the military and police. And if I was caught, I would either be killed soon after, and my death presented as some kind of accident, or I would face at the very least a five-year sentence for immigration charges, or much worse, espionage or subversion charges that carried 25 years to life. This was what it had come to. This was the only way I could cover the conflict in Aceh and, not surprisingly, given the risks, neither I nor anyone else wanted to.

Strangely, I didn't see the man pass through immigration with the other passengers when we arrived in Penang. I didn't call him later in Malaysia. I felt like I had been put on the spot. I had been presented with a clear-cut choice – should I pursue my ideals about what I thought should be reported, for which I had to be prepared to pay with my life?

I have to say that the presence of a Malaysian police officer who also engaged me in conversation influenced my thinking, too. As did some suspicious-looking passengers who I felt were watching my movements. But can you blame me for my rampant paranoia in that situation? The thought did enter my head that it was all some kind of elaborate counter-intelligence set up.

But I couldn't stop thinking about how my reports from

inside Aceh – of the still unconfirmed mass graves, the executions, the air attacks against civilians – could turn around the situation. Like how Max Stahl's footage of the 1991 Santa Cruz massacre in East Timor had turned international attention back to an occupation that many in the Australian, US and UK governments said was irreversible, and created the international support for an independent East Timor. But, you had to ask, could that happen Aceh in 2003?

Had our world changed so much with the terrorist strikes on New York and the bombing in Bali that human lives in places such as Aceh no longer grabbed our attention? Were things so different now that the abuses being carried out in Aceh by the Indonesian military were acceptable? When only four years earlier the same acts being carried out by the same military caused enough concern for international peacekeepers to be sent in? Maybe the answers lie in the way governments and institutions have learned to handle these situations – burying them before they have the potential to cause the kind of public emotion that forced world leaders to act against the Indonesian military back in September 1999. And one of the lessons the Indonesian military learned from East Timor was to keep the reality of what they were doing hidden – as they were doing now in Aceh.

By mid-June the press had been silenced and the people were too terrified to talk. But how long before someone got in again with a camera or a story came out? The answer: long enough for the international community not to care about it. Which at this moment in history doesn't seem to be very long at all.

PART IV

Institutionalised Impunity from Sabang to Merauke: The Legacy of East Timor and the Reality of Papua

In mid-January 2003 I was in East Timor, now known offi-cially as Timor Leste, the world's newest nation. The events in Aceh were still running their course towards the violent re-imposition of Indonesian military control, and I had just travelled from there through Indonesia to the one part of the archipelago that was now no longer under the rule of the Indonesian military. It was a relief to be away from the constant surveillance and implied threats that accompanied working as a journalist in Aceh, but in independent East Timor the problems caused by the 24-year occupation by the Indonesian military were still playing themselves out.

Five people had been killed near the mountain town of Atsabe by what the local people were saying was a group of former pro-Indonesian militia who had infiltrated the border with Indonesian West Timor, which was being guarded by

Australian peacekeeping troops. I went up there to have a look. I hadn't been up in that area since January 1997 when I had spent the night with a local priest who had told me how the Indonesian Kopassus troops were impersonating Falintil guerrillas and operating in small groups. Back then, in the remote villages, they would knock on people's doors in the middle of the night and ask for assistance. Any villagers who helped them would be arrested the following day for supporting the pro-independence guerrillas.

In the six intervening years, of course, a lot had changed. The area, only 30 kilometres from the border with West Timor, had seen a lot of violence in late 1998 with the emergence of militia groups made up of West Timorese and paid East Timorese men who terrorised the local people at the instruction of the Indonesian military. I remembered stories of Indonesian units in civilian clothes coming through the area from West Timor in mid-1998 and in mid-1999, I'd had a nasty encounter at gunpoint with some of these men at a mountain roadblack as I had tried to enter the area to investigate the killings of pro-independence supporters. Running into armed, long-haired Javanese men in the middle of the mountains who cocked their weapons and ordered us out confirmed a lot of the rumours we had been hearing about covert Indonesian operations in the area at that time.

As in the rest of East Timor, the Indonesian military had thoroughly destroyed all the buildings in September 1999 as they withdrew following the independence result in the UN-sponsored ballot. Flying over the mountains a few weeks later in an Australian Army Blackhawk helicopter as the troops deployed on the border, I could see the clusters of black piles of ashes on the ground that were once villages. Even the most remote hamlets of only three or four huts hadn't escaped the Indonesian military, whose men had even removed the electric wiring and plumbing from the buildings in the towns near the border before they burned them to the ground.

There had been very few people left here as the troops moved into those areas. Almost the entire population had joined the 280,000 people forced across the border, or they had fled further into the hills. The remains of the people who had been killed for refusing to leave with the departing Indonesians were still rotting in the destroyed houses and fields when the peace-keepers arrived.

Slowly, the people had come back from West Timor and begun rebuilding. The road up through the mountains from Dili was still as bad as it had been in 1997, but the gardens were thriving and there was livestock in fields where there had not been before. People walked beside the road and there were small shops in the villages. The fear that had kept people indoors for years had dissipated with the departure of the Indonesian military. The villagers were actually sitting outside their houses and carrying out their normal day-to-day tasks in a way that would have been unthinkable only a few years earlier.

It was like that in all of East Timor once the UN mission had wound down. People were now concerned with the necessities of existence. They were getting on with their lives which had been disrupted by the 24 years of Indonesian occupation and its final destructive frenzy in 1999. In other words, although East Timor was poor, in the mountains the people had reverted to a relatively normal peaceful rural life after the Indonesians left. Coming as I had from Aceh, I was struck by the relaxed atmosphere as I rode up to Atsabe on a small motorcycle.

On the Saturday night of January 4, volleys of gunfire rang out in three villages near Atsabe. Men surrounded the house of a local leader and one man went inside and killed the only occupant, the leader's nephew. The attackers fled, taking four other men with them. The East Timorese police in Atsabe then found the bodies of three of those men about four kilometres away, surrounded by the shell casings from Indonesian military weapons. The fourth had escaped and told police he recognised five of the men who had captured him as former militia from the area who had fled to West Timor in 1999.

'The people who came to do this were exactly the same people who committed the trouble in 1999. They came back to kill these people,' said Major João Pedro da Silva, the police officer based in Atsabe. He said they had information that the man who had killed the village chief's nephew had been seen in Atambua, the town on the other side of the Indonesian border. They presumed all the attackers were back there safely in Indonesia. They said it was only a six-hour walk to the border across the mountains if you moved quickly.

This had been the worst militia incursion since 1999, and the local people were rattled by it. They were worried that it might be the start of more activity by the militia, who they knew were still just across the border and still protected from prosecution and supported by their former bosses in the Indonesian military.

The fact that both Eurico Guterres, the high-profile former militia leader in Dili, and Abilio Soares, the former Indonesian-appointed governor, were still at large and had returned to West Timor for Christmas despite having just been given ten- and three-year sentences respectively at the Ad-Hoc Human Rights Court on East Timor in Jakarta, was not lost on anyone in East Timor. Most people regarded the trials and convictions as a sham.

In Maliana, an old contact I knew from before the ballot, Paulo Maia, had more information. He had worked for the Australian peacekeepers based there, passing on information about the movements of militia and Indonesian troops across the border. But, he told me, he had stopped because they didn't seem interested in the information any more. He said that despite warnings from the local population that militia incursions had been planned for December and January, the Australian troops had abandoned their long-held platoon-sized border post at a village called Nunura. According to Maia, the removal of the post left a gap in the border that gave access to the Nunura River valley, which the militia used to trek deeper into East Timorese territory.

On January 8 three militia were seen filling their Indonesian military issue canteens in the Nunura River. More than 100 local East Timorese gave chase and threw rocks at them. The militia responded by emptying a magazine from an automatic rifle into the air, scattering the people. The militia then fled towards the border as the locals yelled that the PKF, the UN Peacekeeping Force, were on the way. According to Maia, who was present, the militia left behind balaclavas and Indonesian military equipment such as waterproof capes, empty magazines, canteens and uniform pants.

The Australian troops five kilometres away in their new base at Mouliana were unaware of the incident. 'The Australians and the Indonesians have very good relations, but still the militia come across and the border is still a very dangerous place,' Maia said. He told me with incredulity how the troops on either side of the border had barbecues together.

Australian policy allowed no room for the troops on the border to comment on who they thought was behind the attack, but off the record they dismissed the incident as criminal elements engaged in a dispute over money. Even after all the violence of 1999 and the eventual destruction of East Timor by the Indonesian military, the Australian government could not bring itself to directly blame Indonesia for its orchestration of the violence.

The infiltration of four groups of armed militia back into East Timor through Nunura had begun in December, according to Maia, and according to information from the East Timorese people in the border town of Atambua, the groups were armed and controlled by former pro-Jakarta militia head Joao Tavares, who was still living in Atambua. The plan was to infiltrate four groups of 11 men and send them to the towns of Hatolia, Atsabe and Maubara, all in the western part of East Timor, where they were to assassinate local leaders who had fought for independence. Only the group that reached Atsabe seemed to have been successful, but the information was well known locally beforehand – and ignored by the PKF. Similar warnings were passed through President Xanana Gusmão regarding the withdrawal of Portuguese troops from their base in the hill town of Ermera in the vicinity of where the attacks took place to a base in the coastal town of Liquiça, leaving the area undefended on January 4, save for a few East Timorese police with handguns.

The morning after the incident, President Xanana Gusmão and the heads of the East Timor defence force and police met with UN officials in Dili and requested they be allowed to undertake an operation to secure the area. Permission was granted and despite protests from some NGOs in Dili that the army was acting outside of the constitution, they moved into the area and arrested 130 people, most of whom were released the following day. However, eight were detained and one of the militia suspects in custody told the media that he had been briefed by junior Indonesian military officers before crossing the border into East Timor. Brigadier General Taur Matan Ruak of East Timor's armed forces (FDTL) was reported in the local press as blaming the Indonesian military for the incursions.

Australian Brigadier General Justin Kelly, the second in command of the 3800 UN Peacekeeping Force in East Timor, simply said the border was difficult to seal: 'There are 142 kilometres of very rough terrain. Anybody who wants to sneak through has a reasonable chance of getting through. I could infiltrate through if I wanted to.' He added there was no evidence that Indonesia was involved, although he did admit that his troops had found evidence of a militia camp in the area and that he believed they had left East Timor through the Australian zone of operations. In other words, they had gone back across the border to Indonesia.

I had to laugh as I hung up the phone after having this conversation with the brigadier general. The Australians were still trying to keep things quiet and playing down any activity that could be related back to the Indonesian military.

It was a game being played not just by the Australians but by the East Timorese leadership as well. When I spoke to President Xanana Gusmão back in Dili, he explained, 'Now that we are independent we do not want to see small problems there [the border] reach the level of diplomatic problems.' He said that he couldn't accuse former militia men like João Tavares of being involved in the latest incidents without evidence. 'People that are still there [in West Timor] feel themselves in one or another way involved in September [1999]. We have gone through the last stage of repatriation and those who have felt they have nothing to do with the militia have come back. The other people are influenced by family links or knowledge. They are still there and essentially those that committed the crimes are still there.'

It was the closest President Gusmão had ever come to admitting what everyone knew – those 30,000 East Timorese were still in West Timor because they had a reason not to come back, and among them were people who had been responsible for the deaths of thousands of other East Timorese.

'I would like to believe that João Tavares had nothing to do with this,' said President Gusmão, 'because we are involved with more contacts with him. But if people say we know that those people coming across the border are from Bobonaro district, of course they know them.'

The involvement of elements of Kopassus and the Indonesian military in the incursions was also something President Gusmão was wary of pushing: 'What we need is evidence. Until now what we know is people discuss this, people talk about this possibility, but like with Tavares, if there is evidence I can contact him and say what is this?'

'What I do know is that before there is some clashes and I ask UNTAET [United Nations Transitional Authority in East Timor] to allow me to go to the border and to start talking to the commanders of the militia, and I ask to them please, if you do something we don't talk anymore. We stop these meetings and to my knowledge was after the first meeting in Salele the militia start to calm down.'

I had been at that meeting in Salele, the southern border crossing, but at the time the press was being kept at arm's length by the UN; we just stood around and watched Xanana Gusmão and militia leaders Cançio Carvalho and his brother Nemezio embracing. Back then the primary concerns when dealing with the militia leaders were to prevent incursions and get them to allow the East Timorese people still under their control in West Timor to return.

There had been a long series of negotiations and meetings to try and convince the militia leaders to come back. Cançio Carvalho, in particular, had entered into negotiations to be allowed to return to East Timor in exchange for some kind of amnesty. The offer was made on the grounds that he would testify for the UN serious crimes unit, who were building cases to prosecute those involved in the violence. The main suspects were, of course, senior Indonesian military officers, and militia leaders like Cançio Carvalho were the ones who could link the crimes carried out by their men to the orders they had received from above. But after many negotiations, some questionable offers of protection and even the provision of a lawyer for Carvalho paid for by the UN, the whole deal fell through on the eve of East Timor's independence in May 2002. Carvalho had decided not to come across and the indictments built up around his testimony were not issued.

This exercise was supposed to be the final success of the UN administrator Sergio Viera de Mello before he left East Timor to become UN High Commissioner for Human Rights, but it had backfired and resulted in an internal UN investigation.

But in 2003, with the UN disengaging from East Timor, it seemed more likely that the international community would leave this problem with the East Timorese. President Gusmão was emphatic that no more deals were to be offered: 'We are now entering a difficult phase of reconciliation. Before it was only repatriation. Now we are entering into dealing with the criminals. Now is the time of decisions. We can give them assurances justice will be fair. They ask for amnesty and we say we don't give this.'

The whole issue of what to do about justice for the East Timorese who had died, punishment of the East Timorese who had been involved in their deaths and, more importantly, their Indonesian bosses, had hung like a dark cloud over the birth of the East Timorese nation in May 2002. The scenario presented to the international community was that the Indonesians would be given the opportunity to conduct the trials themselves, and that those responsible in East Timor itself would be prosecuted through the East Timorese courts by the UN Serious Crimes Unit. In theory, if this proved inadequate, an international tribunal would be formed to deal with the issue. This solution was formulated to avoid criticism that the perpetrators of the crimes in East Timor, principally the Indonesian military, were going to get off scott free. Which in the end is pretty much what happened.

At the time of East Timor's independence celebrations I spoke to Nobel Laureate and East Timorese Foreign Minister José Ramos Horta about the issue. 'We are the victims. We cannot be at the same time the prosecutors,' he said. 'The crimes and the violence that happened in 1999 are a matter for the international community, so I hope the UN does not even entertain the idea that the East Timorese will be gullible enough to accept the responsibility.' He also said that he thought sceptics like me would be surprised by the results that would come out of the tribunal in Jakarta.

At the same time, in May 2002, I spoke to the deputy head of the UN mission in East Timor, Robert MacNamara, who had been responsible for the administration of the Serious Crimes Unit since July 2001. He said the East Timorese were going to have to accept the Jakarta tribunal as the last chance for prosecutions of the Indonesian military. When I asked him about the progress of the indictments, he said, by way of excuse, 'Justice is a very hard area to make real progress in. Especially when you've got courts like you have here – lack of people, lack of resources, lack of interpreters, lack of judges.' He also admitted there was no possibility at the time of an international tribunal for East Timor. 'Certainly this is a much less expensive process than trying to have an international tribunal like in Rwanda, for example. This is trying to do it locally, with the local courts, then eventually handing it over to them with international backing,' said MacNamara. 'The East Timorese realistically have to rely on the Serious Crimes Unit and the tribunal in Jakarta.' MacNamara said the decision was made at the UN security council in New York in early 2000. 'The security council discussed it and decided they would have prosecutors here and ask Indonesia to do prosecutions.'

Xanana Gusmão and José Ramos Horta were both right. It wasn't really their place to try the Indonesian military or to have the power to amnesty the guilty parties. That responsibility should have rested with the international community, but the international community handed that power back to, of all people, the Indonesians themselves. The results were predictable.

⊷━◦━⊶

IN AUGUST 2003, the Ad-Hoc Human Rights Court in Jakarta delivered its final verdict on the man who was in ultimate command of the whole East Timor operation in 1999. Major General Adam Damiri was sentenced to three years in jail for his role in commanding the military and militia violence in East Timor in 1999, but it was unlikely he would ever spend a day in prison – just as none of the other three army officers, one police-man or two East Timorese civilians convicted by the Ad-Hoc Human Rights Court in Jakarta has. All are still free pending appeals. The other 11 people charged were all acquitted.

This result outraged human rights groups and observers. Amnesty International, Human Rights Watch Asia and the European Union dubbed the result 'a joke'.

The charges against Damiri read like a list of the most

horrifying massacres of 1999 in East Timor: the Battalion 745 withdrawal in which Dutch journalist Sander Thoenes was shot and mutilated; the mob murders at the Carrascalaos' house in April; the murder of a group of nuns, church workers and a journalist near Los Palos; the massacres at the churches in Liquiça and Suai; the murder of pro-independence supporters at the Maliana police station (where the UN had told them to seek protection as they evacuated in September); the massacre at Passabe in Oecusse, where the victims were marched into the forest with their hands bound, then killed and left to be discovered by the arriving Australian peacekeepers.

Shortly after the peacekeepers arrived, the human rights workers of the NGO *Yayasan Hak* discovered signed orders from Damiri detailing the supply of weapons and other supplies to military units in East Timor. They were dated September 4, the day the post-ballot destruction of East Timor and the widespread massacres began. Since then Damiri had been assigned the overseeing of troop deployments to the conflict in Aceh and has been unable to attend several court hearings in Jakarta.

There was no shortage of evidence regarding what had happened in East Timor and the command structure was well known. In many cases, the massacre sites were still undisturbed when the peacekeepers arrived and documents were lying everywhere in the destroyed Indonesian military barracks and offices. But the political will to collect evidence and prosecute those responsible was absent from the higher levels of the UN in Dili, and the Serious Crimes Unit – charged with the role of collecting evidence and serving indictments against the accused

– complained of under-funding and political interference in their work. Because of this, a lot of damning evidence was lost and testimonies ignored.

Eventually, in February 2003, after two-and-a-half years of work and 1500 witness interviews, the UN's Serious Crimes Unit issued indictments against the Indonesian military chief who was acting in 1999, General Wiranto, and seven other senior Indonesian military and civilian officials, accusing them of crimes against humanity. According to the indictment, the crimes 'were all undertaken as part of a widespread or systematic attack directed against the civilian population of East Timor and specifically targeted those who were believed to be supporters of independence for East Timor'.

The charges included those for 280 separate murders, mostly in ten individual massacres, and the forcible deportation to West Timor of 200,000 people. The indictment was clear in attributing responsibility to the TNI for the violence: 'The militia groups jointly acted with the Indonesian military in a systematic and planned campaign that resulted in the crimes of humanity taking place. It is also alleged, that given the relationship between Indonesian military officials and the militias, Indonesian commanders who are accused had effective control over militia groups that were operating in East Timor and are responsible for the crimes they committed.'

Among the senior ranking military indicted were Adam Damiri, Zacky Anwar Makarim, Kiki Syahnakri, Suhartono Suratman, Noer Muis and Yayat Sudrajat. Three of these men were later involved in the implementation of martial law in Aceh: Damiri, who was involved in troop deployments; Suratman, who was in charge of handling the Indonesian media; and Syahnakri, who was identified by GAM as being behind the organisation of militia in Aceh and part of the covert policy of burning the schools at the outset of martial law.

The reaction of the Indonesians to the indictments was immediate and blunt. Foreign Minister Hassan Wirajuda told the *Jakarta Post* that Indonesia would 'simply ignore' the indictments. 'Who gave the mandate to indict Indonesians, under what basis, what authority?' he asked. 'This is an East Timorese tribunal, not an international tribunal. This is a national process which has limited jurisdiction, only within the territory of its jurisdiction.'

In April 2000, President Wahid had signed a memorandum of understanding with the UN regarding the exchange of information and suspects related to crimes against humanity in East Timor, but that had never been honoured by Indonesia and clearly was not going to be. The prosecutors' only hope of bringing the Indonesian military to trial was to pass the indictments on to Interpol and hope that some country, one day, might order the arrest and deportation of one the indictees to a court in East Timor.

President Xanana Gusmão initially tried to distance East Timor from the issuing of the indictments, placing the responsibility back in the hands of the UN and the international community.

'I regret [the indictment] but I could not simply ask prosecutors to drop their charges as the General Prosecutors' Office is an independent institution,' he told the *Jakarta Post*. Gusmão was at pains to tell the Indonesian press that he hoped this would not affect relations between Indonesia and East Timor. 'I consider it not to be in the national interest to realise a judicial process of this nature in East Timor,' he said.

In East Timor, the indictments were widely applauded – at last a recognition by the international community of what the East Timorese people had been through and who were responsible.

A FEW DAYS later, the Serious Crimes Unit issued another series of indictments, this time for 48 Indonesians and East Timorese charged with crimes against humanity in 1999, including former East Timor police chief Timbul Silaen and infamous militia leader Eurico Guterres. The list also included Indonesian soldiers and other prominent militia figures, such as Igidio Manek and Cançio Carvalho. The charges included murder, rape, executions, torture, forced disappearances and forced deportation, and covered several attacks carried out on September 6, 1999 that involved police, soldiers and militia.

I remembered those attacks well, having been pinned down by gunfire in the hotel next door while they were taking place. They were carried out by the same police that Silaen was commanding at the time.

I saw them in the process of carrying out these attacks with my own eyes, yet Silaen had been acquitted of any wrongdoing by the Ad-Hoc Human Rights Court in Jakarta and in late 2003 was promoted to inspector general of police and given the job of chief of police in Papua.

At the same time, it was revealed by the Papuan human rights NGO ELSHAM (the Institute for Human Rights Study and Advocacy West Papua), that Eurico Guterres had arrived in the Papuan mining town of Timika and formed a 200-man militia unit made up of refugees from Ambon, Timor and Sulawesi to counter separatist sentiment in the town. He was still free, pending his appeal, despite having been given a ten-year sentence by the Ad-Hoc Human Rights Court in Jakarta for leading attacks in which pro-independence Timorese were murdered.

By the end of 2003, a total of 40 defendants had been convicted in the East Timorese courts for crimes committed during the violence of 1999. They included former East Timorese soldiers in the Indonesian military who had chosen to return to East Timor, East Timorese who had committed crimes while members of the militia, and one ex-Falintil resistance fighter. But of the 367 people indicted, 280 of those were outside the jurisdiction of the East Timor courts, most of them being serving members of the Indonesian military that ordered the killings to take place. And many of them – from the highest ranking officers, who seemed immune to prosecution, to the luckless East Timorese privates of the former East Timor territorial Battalion 744, who would be on trial if they returned home – were by the end of 2003 serving in the operation in Aceh.

⊳⊶⊶○⊶⊷⊲

WEST TIMOR had reverted to its former status as the poorest province in Indonesia now that East Timor was independent. Driving back into Indonesian-controlled West Timor from newly independent East Timor, you were still greeted by the shabby refugee camps constructed in late 1999. Ragged and dirty Indonesian flags still hung outside the wooden huts whose blue UNHCR (United Nations High Commission for Refugees) tarpaulin roofs were now covered in dust and dirt. There were still people around wearing tattered black militia T-shirts or the blue pro-autonomy photographers' vests they had handed out in 1999 with the picture of an Indonesian flag stuck into the heart of East Timor on the back. But the young men no longer seemed threatening, half the huts were empty and the spaces between them were filled with corn planted by the few people who still lived there. There was none of the fist- and machete-waving you used to get from the people when you drove through. The place just looked poor and the people apathetic.

What little tourist industry the West Timor capital of Kupang had sustained by being the cheapest port of entry and exit between Australia and Indonesia via the 50-minute flight to Darwin had finished when the flights stopped late in 1999. The influx of lawless militia and frustrated soldiers from East Timor had led to the closing of the old tourist bars. There were many fights between the local West Timorese and the militia and military, who for a few months after arriving could still be seen with their looted cars from Dili and weapons given to them by the TNI. None of that remained. The bars had closed and the hotels along the sea front catered mainly to travellers and businessmen coming and going from East Timor. Some of the militia were still there but only the poorest among them still wore their tattered T-shirts. The rest, like their leaders, had moved on to other parts of the archipelago or remained in the camps by the border, where they still had some influence over the people who remained there out of fear of retribution for what they had done or been forced to do in 1999.

Ever since three foreign UNHCR workers had been beaten, stabbed and burnt to death in the border town of Atambua in September 2000, a level-five security designation had been in place by the UN. That basically meant that for the two years when millions of dollars in foreign aid was pouring into Dili, no personnel or projects were allowed to go ahead in West Timor for security reasons. The local administration was still trying to get the security rating changed, as it made even non-UN affiliated NGOs wary of establishing projects there. But it was pretty much too late anyway. The world had moved on and West Timor was left to deal with the problems of the 30,000 unwanted East Timorese who wouldn't leave and an economy depressed by its reputation as a dangerous place thanks to the militia.

The only reminder I could see of the old days in Kupang, before East Timor's independence, was an Australian pensioner drinking in a restaurant early in the day. I recognised him as one of the people who used to hang out at Teddy's Bar in the mid-1990s but he didn't recognise me – he was too far gone on beer before noon. I had a conversation about how quiet things were with the man looking after him, who I also knew used to run a backpackers' lodge in Kupang. To be honest, I didn't have much sympathy for the way this place had been passed by. The foreigners who lived there, mostly Australians, had always gone out of their way to deny or belittle what was going on across the border; in much the same way as the Australian government did throughout all those years, the drunken Australians in Kupang would tell you how the East Timorese were a violent, emotional people; they were communists, they said, and the stories of the atrocities were fabricated, or the guerrillas had committed them themselves.

They regurgitated every bit of misinformation fed to the casual listener by the Indonesian state and its media. Much like the foreign governments that supported Indonesia then, and sadly much like the foreign governments that support Indonesia now in its campaign against Aceh and Papua.

In a way, you couldn't blame the Australians living in Kupang for this attitude. They just liked the comfortable life – the cheap beer, the cheap women, the lazy ex-pat lifestyle, only 50 minutes away from Darwin. They didn't want to get involved with politics that might jeopardise their little foreign paradise. The conversations always ended with the assertion that it was impossible to cross the border, and not to bother.

Many West Timorese were the same and didn't seem to mind profiting from the troubles in East Timor at that time, whether it was from trading at the border, making money from the military presence, spying on foreigners or turning in East Timorese.

When East Timor was looted, most of the cars and motor-cycles ended up in Kupang, where the old blue taxis were still in use. Three years later they were disintegrating on the streets of Kupang while Dili was full of new Japanese cars and former UN and aid organisation four-wheel drives.

There was no love lost between East and West Timor, and now the West Timorese grumbled about lack of foreign aid and speculated when the flights to Darwin would start again. They probably never will, they all go directly to Dili now.

I went to have dinner with an old friend from Kupang who had sometimes helped me with translating. I had first got to know him in 1997 when he had sort of attached himself to me as guides used to, in the hope of making more money. Then, over the next few years as I had come back and forth from East Timor to Darwin, I'd see him all the time. He was a good source of information. Eventually he went to Dili and I introduced him to the Reuters news agency where he worked as a translator when things got very dangerous for the East Timorese and trans-lators were in demand. I had always been suspicious of him, but after a while I just kind of accepted that he would pass infor-mation on. Later, when the militia leaders fled to Kupang, he always knew where to find them and how to arrange interviews.

We were drinking beer and he started talking about when he met me in 1997. The Indonesians were trying to kill guerrilla commander David Alex. He recounted how his brother, who was in the army, had told him that I might know something and to watch me and talk to me. We were a bit drunk by that stage and he was laughing, saying his brother had told him that it was worth 7 million rupiah if he could get information from me. That was before inflation and the crash of the rupiah, so it would have been worth three times that, about US$2000. I was amazed, not that he had been spying, but by how much they had offered him. The Indonesian military killed David Alex in 1997 but not through any information he may have passed on from me. To be honest, at the time I had no idea where David Alex was, but this man's casual recollection of the event had thrown me off balance and I spent the rest of the night going over it again and again in my mind. It was one of the ways things were done by the military in Indonesia.

The following night I caught the Pelni passenger ship to Papua, and after a day and a night it reached Ambon City, which looked like something from the Balkan wars. A whole burnt-out city surrounding a beautiful bay. It was full of small, six or seven-storey office blocks, shops, department stores and apartment blocks, all gutted and empty. It was another testament to the violence inspired by the Indonesian military and the intractable problems of holding the false state together. The conflict there between the Muslims and Christians had apparently started over an argument between two men on a bus in January 1999. No-one has ever really established why it spiralled out of control and resulted in the deaths of between 5000 and 10,000 people over the next three years. There were many instances of the military siding with and arming the Muslims but also reports of the police aiding the Christians. As the religious slaughter ran its course, turning the Malukus island group into a war zone of burnt-down communities, frequent bombings and bands of villagers forced to defend themselves with homemade weapons, elements among the Indonesian military supported the movement of 2000 Laskar Jihad Islamic volunteers to be sent to the islands, initiating another round of ethnic slaughter.

The accepted version of events in the Maluka is that the military provoked and prolonged the conflict to further their own interests there and the state of emergency that was announced in 2000 was only rescinded in late 2003. Officially, there are still 300,000 refugees from the conflict but the real figure is much higher, many people having left for other parts of Indonesia.

Local authorities in Ambon were still trying to facilitate the removal of an estimated 200,000 weapons from the communities that now exist in a kind of enforced segregation with strict Muslim and Christian areas. The situation in early 2003 was quiet, with only the occasional outbreak of violence. But the truth is, no-one really knows what is happening there. Since April 2002, all foreigners have been banned from travelling to Ambon and the surrounding island group. The ban was imposed as a part of the revised peace accords now in place. It was insisted upon by the Muslim side, who alleged foreign church representatives and NGO workers were aiding the Christians.

There is also a nascent separatist movement called the RMS, or Republic of South Moluccas, who were accused of receiving assistance from the Netherlands, where many of the members of this group have lived since the Dutch left. Many Ambonese soldiers fought with the Dutch against independence in the late 1940s, and many chose to emigrate to the land of their former colonial masters.

By the end of 2002, it was reported in the Indonesian press that 63 foreigners had been refused entry into the islands since April of that year, most of whom who were tourists unaware of the ban.

Coming through the port in May 2002 on my way from Papua to the East Timor independence celebrations, I had almost been hauled off the boat by soldiers who identified themselves as Kopassus. I'd been on the boat taking pictures of the soldiers on the docks who were dividing Christians and Muslims as they disembarked. They were hitting the Christians with their gun butts and loading them on to trucks and allowing the Muslims to leave. I had no intention of getting off the boat but the soldiers raced up the gangplank looking for me. After I refused to go with them, one grabbed me by the shirt and yelled into my face, 'I am Kopassus. Don't you under-stand, you do what I tell you!' Luckily the commotion had attracted the crew's attention, who convinced the soldiers to search my bag. They eventually agreed to leave if they could take all my exposed film. But if they'd had their way, they would have dragged me off the boat and imprisoned me. They had orders – no foreigners and no photos in Ambon, and no exceptions. Unfortunately, some of the films they took from me had pictures of *Organisasi Papua Merdeka* (OPM), free Papua fighters at attention in the bush with their old rusted shotguns, and I wondered if Kopassus would develop them and what they would make of them at the Ambon headquarters. On this trip back to Papua I didn't take any photos and the ship pulled away without incident.

It was another three days on the Pelni boat to Jayapura, the capital of Papua situated near the Papua New Guinea border that divides the island between Indonesia and Papua New Guinea. I had been talking to an oil worker from Sorong, an oil town on the western tip of Papua, who had been working in Kuwait since 1992 and was going home for the first time. 'Take a look downstairs – what, is there a war going on in this country and no-one fucking told me?' he said. Sure enough, down in the lowest economy deck, the whole floor was occupied by what seemed to be an entire fresh TNI battalion going to Jayapura. It was like a military barracks down there – uniforms, kit bags, guns hanging everywhere. All the equipment was brand new and the soldiers all looked very young and inexperienced, complete with very aggressive attitudes. I passed on the invitation to watch a screening of *Die Another Day* with them and went back to my cabin.

Their officers ate in the first- and second-class dining rooms which had murals of village life in Papua and pictures of smiling Indonesian settlers building houses in the red dirt of the south coast on the walls. The boat was an old one that had been doing the Java–Bali–Timor–Ambon–Papua route for many years and had taken countless thousands of subsidised transmigrant families to their new lives in Indonesia's most promising far-flung colony. Most Indonesians still referred to Papua as Irian Jaya or, if they were older, they still used the Sukarno-era name of Irian Barat.

On the boat it was a contentious issue, as the younger soldiers had their own mental picture of where they were going to fight to save the Indonesian nation from disintegration. They called it Irian Jaya. Some of the older commanders in first class still called it Irian Barat and one told me how he first went there in 1969. The civilians returning home, whether they were Melanesian or not, tended to call it by its new name of Papua.

The transmigration program had finished with the end of Suharto but the local Papuan leaders still accused the Indonesian state and the military of sponsoring migrants to come out. They feared that the Papuan-born ratio of the almost 2.5 million population – currently 60 per cent – would be reduced by more immigrants and they would become a minority in their own country.

There was evidence this was in fact part of the Indonesian policy to counter separatism, and the groups of newcomers were fertile recruiting grounds for the militia groups being set up by the army and Islamic militants like Laskar Jihad who also worked with the military to provoke conflict with the local Papuans.

The head of the pro-independence Papuan Presidium Council, Thom Beanal, told me as much a few days later when I interviewed him at the airport at Sentani, near the capital, Jayapura. 'Laskar Jihad is now in several forms,' he said. 'They can be militia or a kind of military supporting group, with some local Papuans recruited by the military.'

'Laskar Jihad is reconsolidating itself here. When they say they disband in Maluku after the Bali bombing, it doesn't mean that they stop activities here.'

The Islamic militants of Laskar Jihad had been arriving in Papua from the conflict in Ambon for the last two years. The setting up of an office in the town of Sorong in 2002, ostensibly to preach their own brand of Islam, was a front for their activities in that area, which locals say included the establishment of 12 training camps in remote areas, and which were guarded by members of Kopassus. According to Presidium member Willy Mandowen, the office in Sorong was visited by members of Jemaah Islamiah before the bombing in Bali.

Now Laskar Jihad was operating in the border area with Papua New Guinea. 'There are four places – Imunda, Amanat, Green River and Wahlis – all close to the border where they build headquarters,' said Lawrence Mehui, who had recently carried out an investigation of these groups for Presidium. 'They have weapons from the Indonesian military. They are trained in these camps by Kopassus.'

In the transmigrant settlements near the town of Arso, on the Indonesian side close to the border with PNG, the Javanese members of Laskar Jihad had been recruiting and training trans-migrants and local Papuans in conjunction with members of Kopassus. 'We have information from when Kopassus have a meeting with the local people in Arso in November,' said Mehui. 'The local people come and tell us that there is a direct connection with the Kopassus members and the Islamic groups.'

'It is easy for them, they pay people maybe 200,000 rupiah [AU$80].'

As I was talking to Beanal, Mehui and Mandowen, I noticed a man watching us intently. He was West Timorese. I recognised him from when I had interviewed the militia leader Eurico Guterres at his house in Kupang in December 1999. I'd also seen him in Dili before the Indonesians left. And here he was now in Sentani watching Thom Beanal talk to a journalist. He was obviously Indonesian Intelligence involved in surveillance of the Papua leaders. The same people who had failed to derail the East Timorese independence movement were now being deployed to thwart the Papuan movement for independence.

All the leaders of the Presidium were getting regular death threats according to Willy Mandowen. 'We are getting used to the intimidation now. We get SMS messages that we will be killed, our families get intimidated, we are getting used to that, it still continues. We can't go alone, we always have our body-guards wherever we go. In my home I have about four every night, they stay 24 hours.'

The Presidium had emerged after the fall of Suharto and had pursued a policy of nonviolent campaigning for independence and the rights of Papuans. After Theys Eluay was killed by Kopassus in November 2001, Thom Beanal became the leader. Regarding the intimidation and the threats Beanal said simply, 'We are trying to stand with courage before them and not show that we are weak or we are scared of them. And we will continue to fight peacefully in a democratic way to solve the problems.'

It was in that area near the border that the wife and daughter of a prominent Papuan human rights activist and head of human rights monitoring group ELSHAM, Johannes Bonay, were ambushed by unidentified gunmen between the border posts of Papua New Guinea and Indonesia on December 28, 2002. More than 40 bullets were fired at the vehicle they were in and Bonay's wife and child were among the three seriously injured in the attack.

Bonay later told me that he had already been warned by an Indonesian journalist that something might happen. His organ-isation had been one of the first to accuse the military over the ambush in which two American and one Indonesian Freeport mine workers had been killed in August 2002. After his wife and child were shot, Brimob kept coming around to his office, and then he started to get threatening phone calls. Someone left messages on his answering machine that were recordings of someone being tortured. He ripped the phone violently from the wall in his terror.

The situation was getting worse, he said, and the mysterious killings of Papuans becoming more numerous. 'In Jayapura since the end of last year there are incidents of masked men killing during the night hours. People are afraid of travelling during the night. There has been unidentified killings in Arso and here.' He said there had been about 20 deaths recently.

According to ELSHAM, the groups of Laskar Jihad and locally recruited militia on the border were being formed into TBO (*Tenaga Bantuan Operasi*) units – operational support groups for military operations who were trained by Kopassus.

'If we analyse the reports made by the people and the investigations made by the police we can ascertain that Kopassus is behind this,' Bonay said.

The rhetoric of the Laskar Jihad groups fits comfortably with the aims of the Indonesian military in Papua. 'One of their objectives is to protect the unitary state of Indonesia in Papua. They are using Islam to claim they are fighting against the Kaffir here in Papua,' he said.

Bonay also talked of an earlier shooting incident at the border, where the attackers were a TBO group consisting of 20 Papuans, five West Timorese and two Kopassus personnel. It was clear to me that the same network used in Timor and Aceh was being used in Papua to destabilise the situation, using the same methods and the same people. The fact that the international community had never punished these people meant they were free to continue their work.

⊢⊣⬦⬧⬦⬦⊢⊣

I SPENT A few weeks in Jayapura. There were some demonstrations – students protesting against the law that had just been passed by Megawati to divide Papua into three provinces. These demonstrations were relatively orderly considering the move was in direct contravention of the autonomy law that the international community had been supporting. This support, along with that of some of the Papuan elite, was a way of quietening down the separatist movement in Papua. It offered the province more of the massive mining and logging revenue that went to Jakarta. The rallies were small and watched over by many police and intelligence operatives. Not many people came because they were too scared.

The pro-division rallies organised by the government were much larger. People were brought into town in government trucks and given food and water. At one of these rallies, a filmmaker colleague, Carmela Baranowska, was almost arrested. It was one of the few events that you would have presumed the government would be happy to have filmed considering they had staged it, but it brought us to the attention of the police. Which created its own problems.

I got in touch with a translator who I had worked with on a previous trip. He told me that he had recently been kidnapped from the airport by seven Kopassus men. They kept him for two weeks, during which time he was beaten and slashed with knives and given nothing but salt water to drink. He said a guard had been paid money to help him escape.

At first I didn't fully believe him – he could have been working with Kopassus. I was a little suspicious about his story until he showed me his back, which was a mess of deep knife marks that had been inflicted while he was held to the ground at Kopassus headquarters. He said they had told him they were planning to kill all the Papuan leaders as they tortured him for information. The slash marks were only just beginning to heal and he had been in hiding since he had escaped. A friend of his who had gone to the Kopassus headquarters to inquire after him was still missing.

>—·—·—·—<

MERAUKE IS at the southern extremity of the Indonesian–Papua New Guinea border, only 400 kilometres across the Torres Strait to mainland Australia. The only way to get there is by flying across the whole province of Papua from the capital, Jayapura, on the north coast or by boat around the south coast. The only roads from Merauke go north into logging country, but they don't really lead you anywhere, they just kind of peter out as the swamps turn into jungle and then into mountains. It was on one of these roads heading north from Merauke that they killed the local OPM leader, Willem Onde, and his assistant John Tumin, in September 2001.

Onde's is a sad story. He had become involved with Kopassus in 1997 after he started peace talks with them as the local OPM leader. He had facilitated a weapons hand-over to the Indonesians and they in turn had given him money and a new weapon which was really just a status symbol for Onde; he never used it to fight the Indonesians. He hung around with the Kopassus men, drinking, spending the money they gave him and enjoying Merauke's many military-run brothels, which were responsible for giving this remote town the highest HIV rate in Indonesia.

Then it was payback time, and Onde carried out a high-profile kidnapping of 13 employees of the Korean logging company Korindo. Of course the hostages, which included three South Koreans, were released in January 2001 after negotiations with the military – and no doubt a review of the security costs to the logging company for protection against the OPM provided by the local military. This was how business was conducted in Papua, which is why the military like it there so much.

The next thing the military asked Onde to do was to publicly support the autonomy proposal for Papua and to get the other OPM leader in the south, Bernard Mawen, to do so as well. Willem Onde refused. There were a few meetings with the local authorities and then a message was sent to Onde from the Kopassus commander in Jayapura, Colonel Hartomo, who was later charged for the killing of OPM leader Theys Eluay. It basically said, 'Your demand for freedom is openly against the law of Indonesia. If you will surrender and come back again with Indonesia we will not disturb you and your men any more. We wait your reply.'

Another message was then sent to Onde by fax to the office of the logging company in the remote area to the north of Merauke at a place called Asiki, near where Onde was living in the bush. It said, 'From now on the military command in Jayapura will not assure your safety.'

It was basically a threat. The military had been cultivating Onde with gifts but he was refusing to publicly support the autonomy proposal. He had played the game of allowing them to blame the OPM for the kidnapping of the timber workers so the military could then extort more money from the logging company, but on the matter of supporting autonomy and publicly denouncing the goal of independence for Papua he wouldn't go along with the military who had been paying him.

Onde was last seen riding his motorcycle with his assistant on the back. Four days later his body and the body of his assistant, John Tumin, were found. A logging truck had passed the area where they had disappeared and had been moved along by two Kopassus soldiers at the estimated time of their deaths. Their presence in this remote part of the bush at the same time as Onde's disappearance meant only one thing to the local people. They had ambushed and killed him and his assistant. In that part of the world when the Indonesian military tell you they cannot guarantee your security it usually means you are targeted.

Onde had been partially scalped and his body was decomposed. Even his sister refused to say it was him as she was terrified of the military, and if she publicly identified her brother the same military would then kill her. By then, everyone in the small, isolated community of Merauke was scared and Bernard Mawen and the other OPM members in the area had melted back into the jungles of Papua New Guinea on the other side of the border.

There have not been any reports of OPM activity in Merauke since Onde's death. The grisly manner of his murder had made the point to the local people that if they oppose the military in this remote, far-flung corner of Indonesia they will be next and the perpetrators can get away with whatever they want. It is the same impunity that the military has in Aceh and had in East Timor. If they were called to account for their actions they would lose control of these places, as the fear that keeps the population under control would vanish, just as it did briefly after the fall of Suharto.

DOWN IN Merauke I got hold of a document from the Department of Internal Affairs, dated June 9, 2000, which listed Theys Eluay and Willem Onde as leaders who had to be dealt with and made to support autonomy. The document came from a meeting that had been held at the Hotel Nirmala in Jakarta on May 28, 2000, where military leaders and officials from the interior ministry discussed ways to deal with the problem of separatism in Papua. It was a formalisation of the policy of killing leaders in Papua that is still continuing today. But the fact that the program was initiated in a meeting in Jakarta with members of the civilian interior ministry meant that it was government policy and not just the actions of some overzealous officers in the field – which is how it was portrayed in the trial of the killers of Theys Eluay.

There has never been an investigation into the death of Willem Onde and in all likelihood there never will be.

There had been some killings by Brimob in the village of Kimaan on the island of Yos Sudarso which lies to the west of Merauke in one of the most undeveloped parts of the world.

A group of villagers had attacked some fishing boats from other parts of Indonesia that docked there. The people there on the island of Yos Sudarso still lead a mostly subsistence life, living in huts, hunting and growing food. They still go naked or wear only grass skirts and speak their local dialect. When the Indonesian fishermen came they attacked the boats with spears and bows and arrows as they do not have much contact with the outside world. After the attack, Brimob headed off to Kimaan, like a punitive expedition in colonial Africa, and shot some people and burned down their huts. I was shown photos of dead bodies wearing grass skirts.

The small coastal communities in the swampy mangroves of the island were dealt with harshly by the Indonesians, who treated them like animals and just shot them without further ado. It was an unreported atrocity by a police force used to dealing with the local Papuan people as though they were less than human. There was no attempt at arresting anyone or any legal procedure. Because it is such a remote place, Brimob knew no-one would find out and didn't think it was important to follow any regulations. I thought about going down there to speak to the people. But there was no way to get there other than hiring a team of canoeists or a boat and loading up with supplies for a week-long expedition like a nineteenth-century explorer.

<hr />

THERE WASN'T a lot to do in Merauke. I wrote a story about how the military-run prostitution industry and the military-run sandalwood trade in the area had given this remote place the highest officially declared rate of HIV in Indonesia, which had started to spread even more rapidly. Basically, the military would trade their prostitutes with local tribal leaders in exchange for sandalwood, which they would sell back in Jakarta for as much as 5 million rupiah ($995) a kilogram. 'The military gets the money. It is very good business,' said Leo Mehaye, a local health worker I spoke to.

There is also large-scale prostitution run by the military to service workers in the logging and fishing industries in Merauke. Many of the prostitutes employed by the military are also sent to the coastal towns of Sorong and Timika, where large mining and oil operations provide customers.

Since the trade began five years ago, the HIV rate has soared. Official statistics from January show 537 cases of people with HIV/AIDS living in Merauke. Mehaye said a further 200 have already died in the town. 'The testing happens only if people come to the hospital when they are sick,' he said.

He compares the official statistics with those of Jakarta, a city of 11 million, where 1200 HIV cases are recorded. In Merauke, which has a population of only 38,000 in the town and 320,000 in the district, the reported number is almost half the Jakarta figure.

The local people believed it was just another way the Indonesians were trying to wipe them out. A Médecins sans Frontières (MSF) doctor was working with the HIV patients there, but her position with the authorities was precarious and there was not much she could tell me. There was a silence in the town that suggested it was firmly under control of the military. When the police shot seven people when they had tried to raise the symbol of Papuan independence, the blue and white striped flag with the morning star in the corner, on Papuan independence day, December 1, 2001, there had been no further trouble in town. Then the police burnt down the pro-independence *Satgas Papua* posts almost as soon as they had been put up, and there were no repercussions following that, either.

┝╾◇╼◊┥

WITH ANOTHER day to wait for a flight out of Merauke, I hired a small minivan at the marketplace. The driver had insisted on bringing his friend along when I told him to drive to the border. They had never been that far out of Merauke and they seemed nervous about leaving the Indonesian town to drive into the wilderness that surrounded it on all sides. We drove the 60 or so kilometres to the border with Papua New Guinea. The old Dutch priest who had been in Merauke since the 1950s had told me there was a marker at the border. He recounted how the Indonesians had lost one man in the river as he parachuted into the town when they took it over in 1962, and how the Dutch had lost one man while fighting the Indonesians at the airport. Some Pakistani peacekeepers had been based in Merauke during the UN administration when the country was handed over to Indonesia in 1963, and after that all the Dutch had left, except for him.

The road ran straight as an arrow to the border, which was built on a levee above the surrounding swamps. In some parts the red dirt showed through and there was scrub and some gum trees so it looked like northern Australia, which geographically it is very close to.

There were a few military bases set off from the road and a small village at a crossroads. Close to the border there were rows of small Javanese-looking houses for the families of the soldiers at the bases, which looked out of place in the open ground with the long grass and clusters of gum trees.

At the border there was nothing except a broken picnic chair and a concrete cairn put there by the joint Australian–Indonesian army survey team in 1983. The sealed road stopped abruptly and was joined by a narrow, muddy track that led off into the trees. I walked along it for maybe two kilometers, with the nervous Javanese driver and his friend chattering behind me.

We came across an old man and two women sitting under a tree and I asked them how far it was to the PNG post on the other side. They looked at me seriously and said it was three days and three nights of walking. That was it, I thought and headed back to the vehicle. That was the end of Indonesia – a muddy track through the wilderness in some swamp that had been arbitrarily divided in Europe in the nineteenth century, and where now no-one even bothered to make a road. And now, here in Papua, as in Aceh, the only way Indonesia could keep alive Sukarno's dream of a nation that spread from 'Sabang to Merauke' was by killing those people who, after all these years, continued to oppose this artificial creation.

As we drove back towards Merauke we passed the monument at the crossroads with 'Sabang to Merauke' proudly written across it, and the eagle seal of the republic of Indonesia beneath. We didn't stop. I was bored and a bit annoyed about wasting the time to go out there.

An Indonesian soldier with a small Papuan boy stepped onto the road and flagged us down. He got into the back seat and told the two now silent Javanese men in the front to keep driving.

Intentionally or not, the soldier had the barrel of his M-16 pointed at my head as he started speaking in English.

'I am from Kostrad. You know Kostrad. They send us to where it is danger,' he said.

I went to light a cigarette and he grabbed the pack from me. He wanted to know what I was doing – and what I was doing there in particular. The driver answered quickly that I was a tourist.

The soldier laughed and said he thought I was CIA, 'You know like James Bond. Ha.' He then started telling me how he had been in East Timor, in 1994 in Los Palos and in 1995 in Suai. 'Maybe I see you there,' he said, grinning. Then he went on to say he had been in Ambon in 2000 and then in Kalimantan. 'They send us to all the hot spots,' he said.

He would die for Indonesia, he said. He would kill for Indonesia. 'I would do anything to defend Indonesia. I love Indonesia.'

He was laughing but there was an element of threat in the laughter and as we drove, the only car on the road through this swampy area as it was starting to get dark, I had a real feeling of dread. It felt like I had somehow been set up, that the military was going to take the opportunity to issue yet another warning to the foreign press to stay out of their affairs.

I was getting angry with myself for being out there for no real purpose as the soldier went on about how the Papuan people loved Indonesia, and shook the small boy beside him, who was also smoking my cigarettes. The boy grinned and laughed, showing betel-stained teeth.

The driver and his friend in the front were falling over themselves to agree with the soldier and laughed nervously as he kept talking about Indonesia and how he would kill to defend it. Being there in the back of the car with the soldier, and his gun in my face every time I turned around, talking about how he would kill for Indonesia, I really had resigned myself to having my head blown off at any moment.

Out there in the scrub at the end of Indonesia, the two Javanese in the front were obviously scared for themselves and afraid of what the soldier might do. The Papuan child was grinning and obviously enjoying watching the soldier bully the strange foreigner while the soldier was working himself into a rage. I was becoming increasingly paranoid about his continued vague references to places and times when I had been reporting on conflicts in his country. Although the conflicts in Indonesia had been running long before the soldier and I were born, our similar ages had meant we had been in the same places at the same time. It was probably just coincidence, but to me it was menacing. I thought he was going to kill me.

The only way the military can control the country is by killing people, and the less information recorded about the killings, the longer they can continue to do it. In East Timor and Papua, and currently in Aceh, they have kept the outside world out and suppressed the information about what they are really doing to maintain the country of Indonesia. They have therefore managed to avoid prosecution from an international community that doesn't really want to know anyway.

Then, just as suddenly as the soldier had arrived, he banged on the roof of the minibus and yelled for the driver to stop. I saw a red flag in the scrub that must have been the marker for his post and he left, still talking about what he would do to maintain the integrity of his country. I knew what that involved, having seen the countless bodies of the victims of the Indonesian military as it fought to maintain its own wealth and power under the myth of a country that runs from 'Sabang to Merauke'.

Postscript

On May 13, 2004, a week before the first anniversary of martial law in Aceh, the Indonesian government announced that the operation was officially over. It was to be replaced with what was called 'civil emergency status'. Power in Aceh would now be shared by the civilian governor and the military. The numbers of military personnel stationed in Aceh were to remain the same. The military announced that of an estimated 5251 GAM fighters when the campaign began on May 19, 2003, 1963 had been killed, 2100 had been arrested and 1276 had surrendered. By the military's figures, 88 more GAM fighters had been accounted for than had existed at the start of martial law. But no one really believed the military – it was quite well understood in the press and among NGO groups that most of the victims were simply Acehnese civilians. The figures were impossible to verify as no-one was allowed access to Aceh. The operation had cost Jakarta $US229.8 million.

None of the senior commanders of GAM had been captured and fighting still continued in areas of Aceh. The press was still banned. The international media watchdog, Reporters Without Borders, noted in its 2004 annual report that, 'The Indonesian army did everything possible to keep the news media away from Aceh province where it resumed the war against the separatists.'

Human rights workers and foreign aid workers were also still banned. Amnesty International issued a statement that week noting, 'Nearly all aspects of the lives of ordinary citizens are adversely affected by the military emergency . . . People are terror- ized by the numerous killings and the ever-present threat of arrest, torture and ill-treatment. At the same time economic and social life has been severely disrupted by the intense military operations.'

The statement went on to add the details from testimonies of people who had been tortured by the military and the police and, in the case of a 12-year-old girl, raped by the military. Amnesty also said there was strong evidence that of the 2100 people impris- oned by the authorities under martial law, there was strong evidence to suggest that most of them had been tortured. The Indonesian commission on human rights, Komnas Ham, released a similar statement at the same time detailing the abuses of the military under martial law. They stated that after the first six months of martial law there had been an increase in the number of civilian victims of violence, including arbitrary arrests, torture, kidnapping, sexual abuse and extra judicial killing. In December 2003 Human Rights Watch released a fifty-page report detailing a similar pattern of abuse from testimonies of refugees from Aceh, mostly illegally sheltering in Malaysia, where the government had pledged to deport them back to Indonesia. That report was dismissed out of hand by the Indonesian government with one official calling it 'complete rubbish'.

Malik Mahmood, the exiled GAM Prime Minister in Sweden, responded to the change of status in Aceh: 'The change is merely a window dressing exercise to hide the dismal failure of the military to perform its duty, other than carrying out indiscriminate killing of thousands of civilians, kidnapping, rapes and other gross violations of human rights as have been well documented by international NGOs, including the reports released by the US Department of State.' (February 25, 2004).

He was one of the few GAM leaders still able to comment on the process. On May 17, a further 171 Acehnese were transferred from jails in Aceh to prisons in Java. It was the third such transfer and included the head of SIRA, Muhammad Nazar, who had received a five-year sentence in May of 2003 for charges of 'spreading public enmity against the government'. His crime was addressing the free speech rally. Earlier transfers to prisons in Java had included the GAM negotiators who had been in custody since they were arrested on the way to peace talks in Tokyo in May. On October 22, a court in Banda Aceh sentenced Teuku Kamaruzzaman to 13 years imprisonment for engaging in a diplomatic offensive representing the Free Aceh Movement and motivating others to 'revolt against the government of Indonesia'. The other members of the team – Sofyan Ibrahim Tiba, Muhammad Usman and Amni bin Ahmad Marzuki – received 15, 13 and 12 years respectively and have since also been transferred to prisons in Java.

Amri bin Abdul Wahab, the other member of the negotiating team from the Kuala Tripa, escaped the same fate by changing sides during the days before martial law was declared. Initially GAM said Amri had been kidnapped by Indonesian Special Forces and it is still not known whether he defected voluntarily. He was flown to Jakarta and appeared at a press conference at the office of Susilo Bambang Yudhoyono, where he made a statement stiffly calling on GAM to surrender. A laptop he gave to foreign affairs was later used as evidence by Indonesian foreign affairs to try and convince the Swedish Government to cancel the exiled leadership's visas on account of their apparent involvement with terrorism.

The female activist, Cut Nur Asikin, was also convicted of treason and spreading hatred and jailed for 11 years on October 22. The speech she gave in November 1999 at a rally calling for an independence vote for Aceh was given as the reason for her conviction. She reportedly shouted, 'Long live Aceh. Allah destroy Indonesia' when the verdict was announced.

The GAM leadership in the field in Aceh seems to have escaped martial law. Sofyan Dawood taunted the Indonesians by claiming he had escaped in late July 2003 and was in Malaysia. Commander Darwis is reportedly still operating in the Bireuen area.

In June 2004, International Crisis Group Indonesia coordinator Sidney Jones was expelled from Indonesia. The head of Indonesia Intelligence Services, Hendropriyono, was responsible. Neither President Megawati nor the leading presidential candidates, retired generals Susilo Bambang Yudhoyono and Wiranto, raised any objection to her expulsion. Jones believed her reports on Aceh, Papua and Jemaah Islamiah had been to blame.

Acknowledgments

I could not have finished this book without the love and support of my partner Meredyth Tamsyn over the three years it took to gather material. Thank you.

Index

INDEX